THE LUNACY OF MODERN FINANCE THEORY AND REGULATION

This provocative book provides insight into a finance industry that is run for the benefit of banks and service providers who rely on Beatles-era theories and regulation which are totally unsuited to the modern world. The author has a near-unique perspective based on over 30 years of working – literally around the globe – for corporates, fund managers and as a finance academic. In his most recent role his research has focused on investment decisions, and during 2012 he interviewed 34 fund managers in Istanbul, London, New York and Melbourne. He blends rich understanding of finance theory and practice to unravel the investment industry's structure and show how banks and other finance institutions privilege themselves at investors' expense.

The book highlights that the finance industry's self-regulation is weak. Risks from inexpertise, theft, bad data and other sources are high. Regulation of the industry appears to be ineffectual with the setting of such a high bar that it is virtually impossible to successfully prosecute even the most blatant and egregious offenders.

The book closes with the simple suggestion that corporations' regulations be altered to introduce the strict liability offence of being a director or officer of a large bank that becomes bankrupt. This follows the strategy of legislation that has been effective in cleaning up the environment, making workplaces safer and reducing crime by punishing those responsible for an offence.

Les Coleman is a Senior Lecturer in Finance at the University of Melbourne. His main research interest is financial decision making by firms and funds, and he has published two research monographs (by Gower and Springer), four book chapters and nearly 30 journal articles. Les trained originally as an engineer, and spent over 20 years in senior management positions with Anglo American and ExxonMobil Corporations in Australia and overseas.

More recently Les completed a PhD in Management at the University of Melbourne where his thesis was published as *Why Managers and Companies Take Risks* (Springer, 2006).

Outside the University, Les has part-time appointments with two investment managers. He has been a trustee of two superannuation funds, and a director of ten companies involved in finance, retail and distribution. He has written and spoken widely on finance and investment strategies, and for four years was a weekly columnist with *The Australian* newspaper.

THE LUNACY OF MODERN FINANCE THEORY AND REGULATION

Les Coleman

Routledge
Taylor & Francis Group

LONDON AND NEW YORK

First published 2015
by Routledge
2 Park Square, Milton Park, Abingdon, Oxon OX14 4RN

and by Routledge
711 Third Avenue, New York, NY 10017

Routledge is an imprint of the Taylor & Francis Group, an informa business

British Library Cataloguing in Publication Data
A catalogue record for this book is available from the British Library

Library of Congress Cataloging in Publication Data
Coleman, Les.
The lunacy of modern finance theory and regulation / Les Coleman.
pages cm
Includes bibliographical references and index.
1. Banks and banking. 2. Financial institutions—Law and legislation. 3.
Finance—Corrupt practices. I. Title.
HG1601.C65 2014
332.101—dc23
2014018212

ISBN: 978-1-138-77899-3 (hbk)
ISBN: 978-1-138-77900-6 (pbk)
ISBN: 978-1-315-76696-6 (ebk)

Typeset in Bembo
by Book Now Ltd, London

MIX
Paper from
responsible sources
FSC
www.fsc.org   FSC® C013056

Printed and bound in Great Britain by
TJ International Ltd, Padstow, Cornwall

Lloyds Coffee Shop, London 1798. By William Holland.

CONTENTS

FIGURES

TABLES

PREFACE

The pure and simple truth is rarely pure and never simple.
Oscar Wilde (1854–1900)

My principal job is in academia where I teach students at one of Australia's best universities about theories that underpin the finance industry. I am also fortunate to hold part-time appointments with two investment funds, and regularly sit through presentations by fund managers while they showcase their skill and performance. Most readers will share parts of this experience, and also my exposure to financial planners' advice on investment strategy and asset allocation. With financial institutions, these groups – academics, investment professionals and financial advisers – constitute the modern finance industry: most times they interface seamlessly, and the industry's structure appears robust.

The core thesis of this book, however, takes a quite different perspective. The reality is that the finance industry is split into two totally opposed camps that stoically ignore each other. Advocates of modern finance theory – which is most academics – see their discipline as magickal: although its key premises are at least three decades old and some will soon pass their 50th birthdays, it is an article of faith amongst academics that the Beatles-era finance giants got theory so right that – virtually alone of all disciplines – finance sees no need to change its central tenets. This holds true in the face of crisis after crisis, forests of contradictory data and research, and transformation of the investor community from individuals to institutions. Belief in traditional theories also ignores the inability of even elite academics to successfully apply finance theory, which was most obvious when Nobel finance laureates Myron Scholes and Robert C. Merton helped found Long Term Capital Management in 1994 only to see it collapse five years later with losses of $5 billion. Despite mountains of evidence refuting the practical value of ageing finance theory, devotees provide tenacious support for its logic and tractability.

The inability of finance theory to survive contact with the real world is obvious to residents of the latter. They are mainly investors, especially money managers, and are derided by academics as 'practitioners'. Rather than basing their financial decisions on theoretically driven calculus, real-world investors use intuition and qualitative information or make all but reflexive responses to external drivers using heuristics gained from experience or handed down during their apprentice-style training. Academics depict this atheoretical behaviour as biased or irrational, and apply unworldly tests to prove that practitioners' financial decisions destroy value.

The truth – as it usually does – lies somewhere in the middle. Finance theory may not be applicable to the real world, but it does provide a useful framework to explain what is going on in an important and complex industry, so that practitioners find it a logical framework that is effective in attracting and convincing investors. And finance practitioners do not evidence stellar performance: finance experts rarely are, and many financial institutions are badly run. The finance industry is riven by hubris, mistrust and venality. Above all, it adds little value for investors.

Even worse, the industry has become corrupted in recent years after financial institutions adopted short-term profit objectives, ratcheted up their debt, introduced exotic techniques to squeeze more returns out of thin margins, and compensated themselves with much of the economic rent provided by normal market operations. Fraud became routine. During the last decade, finance has distinguished itself as the only industry where leading players – including (as discussed in Chapter 5) Citibank, JP Morgan Chase, Morgan Stanley, UBS and others – have received eight to ten figure fines for criminally deceptive practices that defrauded their customers.

As leverage and institutional control increased in tandem, so did risk. The information asymmetry between financial institutions that control markets and the investors and entrepreneurs who provide the money and opportunities meant that the former systematically ripped off the latter. Investment returns stagnated and finance became increasingly identified with scams and crashes. Regulation, however, failed to keep pace, and investors bore all the costs of failure.

The core commodity of finance – money – promotes undesirable behaviours, particularly greed, hubris and theft. Regulators are supposed to remedy such defects, but their salaries and career opportunities are much less attractive than those offered by finance houses, and those recruited to regulators' ranks prove unwilling or unable to change their chronically ineffective strategy.

The current finance industry displays attributes that would be expected if it had been designed and run by insiders for their benefit. These include hefty profits for financial firms, additional income from manipulation of markets and insider trading, generous salaries, and virtual immunity from prosecution for individuals even in the case of gross failures. Regulation is benign and tolerates scams ranging from soft commissions to front running. Investor protection is weak. And, although legislators huff and puff for the cameras, they do little to rein in the excesses that are now associated with finance. Financial institutions' activities are so inimical to the interests of investors that conspiracy theories can survive.

One of the worst aspects of the industry is that even badly judged decisions by incompetent advisers and bankers are rarely punished because it is almost impossible to convict them of breaching the web of tangled regulations that govern the finance industry. In short, the whole finance industry is arranged so that nobody bears any financial (and few personal) risks, except investors who bear all the costs. Self-regulation of the finance industry does not work.

The consequences of this situation are truly appalling. The most significant is that international equities – which are the foundation of savers' portfolios – grew in value by just 1 per cent per year during the 12 years to the end of 2013.[1] Low returns mean that industrious baby boomers – the workers of 1970–2010 who more than doubled living standards[2] – face uncertain income in their retirement. There are other important consequences, too, particularly for companies and governments that are key to economic growth but face difficulty in efficiently funding their expansion and investments.

As one hard-bitten observer of the industry told me in an interview: 'Banks accepted investors' money and gave them the finger.' When you link this to crashes that occur like clockwork every seven to ten years and disappear a third of investors' savings, finance begins to look like some meso-American religion that regularly consumes its followers.

In short, the conduct of modern finance theory and regulation appears close to lunacy.

The sad situation of finance research, practice and regulation motivates this book. It takes a high-level approach to examine the context and major drivers by looking at the industry situation and firm strategies, rather than the detail of who did what, which is well recorded in books such as *All the Devils are Here* (McLean and Nocera, 2010).

There are three themes to this book. The first is that finance research does not address key questions in practice, and so our understanding of markets and firms is still primitive. The second theme is that excess liquidity and financialisation of markets have promoted development of enormous over-the-counter derivatives markets and contributed to repeated asset bubbles and resulting crashes in equity, housing and commodity markets. And the third theme is the inability of regulators to keep up.

My interpretation of the cause of this situation is that the finance industry has structured itself so that savers and investors bear *all* the risks. Executives of companies – especially banks – have generous base salaries, and receive additional benefits by sharing in profits (including those due to factors beyond their control such as rising commodity or security prices). Investment advisers receive fees based on the value of funds under management, and regulators face no risk because they are salaried. Each of these groups enjoys generous compensation, even when returns are negative, because investors and taxpayers have all the downside exposure.

The cure? This comes in three parts. The first recognises that the shortcomings of finance theory have been on display for decades, and proposes that an urgent objective of academics and practitioners should be to develop a paradigm that is more robust to real-world influences. This book is intended to help that effort. The second is to dramatically improve the transparency of the industry and hold it to higher performance standards.

A third proposal directly tackles the problem of banks and other firms that have become too big to fail and would ban them from high-risk activities such as off-balance sheet investment, use of over-the-counter derivatives, and high leverage. In addition, regulation would be more punitive towards those who drive the largest firms and banks into bankruptcy by making this a crime with strict liability. This is based on two key intuitions. The first is that the existing approach to securities and corporations regulation has repeatedly failed over three decades. Thus we need to radically change the process-based system that outlaws specific actions and places high bars on convictions. The second is that the environment, workplaces and streets have been made cleaner and safer by outcome-based bans on damaging actions that pay little heed to how or why the offence occurred. My proposal is to clean up finance using the duty of care approach that has proven so successful with cleaning up the environment and workplaces.

These proposals bring finance industry regulation into line with best practice in other areas.

Despite the risk that my ideas may be dismissed as impractical, I hope to dream with my eyes open. My thoughts are founded in experience, particularly two decades involved in investment and financial decisions inside ExxonMobil Corporation and another decade as a finance academic and researcher, during which time I also held part-time roles with two fund managers. Throughout, I have steadily developed my ideas, and validated them through papers published in peer-reviewed journals and presented at international conferences.

To ensure rigour in my conclusions, I tested them in more than 30 face-to-face interviews with fund managers in Istanbul, London, Melbourne and New York during 2012. These interviews had four core questions: What finance theory is useful to investors? How do money managers select individual investments? What determines security prices? and How can investors manage their risks?

Many readers will know that finance texts make these questions appear silly by giving clear answers: most, using discounted cash flow analysis, rational valuation of information, and through portfolio diversification. My intuition, though, was correct because large investors responded quite differently: very little, using judgement and qualitative data, supply and demand, and with great difficulty.

Is this book just another rehashing of the financial crises of 2007–12? Definitely No! Certainly I wrote most of the material during 2012 when the nature and fall out of the global financial crisis (GFC) or great recession were clear. So I took them into account. But to me the GFC was just another in the rolling cycle of financial crises that come every seven or so years, and the scams and frauds leading up to it are typical of those going on all the time in finance. So the GFC informed my thinking, but is only part of the analysis.

Even though truth is a frequent casualty of many studies, few myths can withstand the facts and so I have supported key contentions by embedding evidence in the text as graphs and tables. My discussion tries to cover all important points, but – for those who wish to delve further – notes at the end of chapters point to references and sources. Many examples are from the United States, and this rationale is clear: the US is home to nearly half the world's securities and investments. Many of these are held by non-American investors, and US financial innovation is aped around the world. Time and again, collapse of the US market leads world markets down (and vice versa), and every decade or so takes them into recession. We all have an interest in finance, and so in the US markets.

This book has had a long gestation, as it combines learnings from my industry and academic careers along with many people's insights. Thus I owe numerous debts for assistance received over decades. First to Rob Brown, Professor of Finance at the University of Melbourne, who employed me to conduct my hobby of research, and encouraged me to apply my industry experience to puzzles in applied finance. Many academic colleagues since then have provided support for this study and encouraged its development. Prominent amongst them are Kevin Davis, André Gygax, Carsten Murawski and Sean Pinder. Over decades, I have been fortunate in gaining the right industry experience and insights to form and shape my ideas. I acknowledge the input of a great number of colleagues at Mobil and Anglo American Corporations and other companies, and recent interviewees literally around the world who generously provided their time and thoughts.

Finally, much of this book was written whilst I was on sabbatical at Koç University, Istanbul, and I gratefully acknowledge the hospitality of Professor Baris Tan (Dean of College of Administrative Sciences and Economics), Finance Professor Oguzhan Ozbas and their colleagues.

Whilst warmly thanking my many advisers and informants, I affirm they bear no responsibility for this work and any errors and omissions are mine.

Les Coleman
University of Melbourne
November 2013

Notes

1 As measured by the Morgan Stanley Capital Index for World stocks in US dollars: available at www.mscibarra.com/#
2 Average GDP per head across OECD countries expressed in constant USD rose from $US14,132 in 1970 to $30,104 in 2010: OECD (2012).

THE AUTHOR

Les Coleman lectures in finance at the University of Melbourne. He completed a bachelor's degree in mining engineering at the University of Melbourne (1974), a bachelor of science in economics from the University of London (1978), a master of economics at the University of Sydney (1984) with a thesis entitled 'Australian Mining Policy', and a PhD in the Department of Management at the University of Melbourne (2004). His doctoral thesis was published by Springer as *Why Managers and Companies Take Risks* (Springer, 2006).

Prior to returning to study in 2002 and then moving into academia, Les worked for almost 30 years in senior management positions with resources, manufacturing and finance companies in Australia and overseas. He started as a mining engineer with Anglo American Corporation in Zambia, and the highlights of his subsequent career include four years in Mobil Corporation's international planning group at its global headquarters near Washington, DC, and six years as regional treasurer for ExxonMobil Australia. He has been a trustee of two superannuation funds, and a director of ten companies involved in finance, retail and distribution. Les has written and spoken widely on finance and investment strategies, and for four years was a weekly columnist with *The Australian* newspaper.

Les has published three books, four book chapters and over 25 journal articles. His main research interest is applied finance, especially financial decision making by firms and investment funds. This has involved extensive field research, most recently through interviews during 2012 with 34 fund managers in Istanbul, London, Melbourne and New York. He also has an interest in sustainability and risk as decision stimuli, and his book entitled *Risk Strategies: Dialling up Optimum Firm Risk* (Gower, 2009) foreshadowed a body of theory on risk so that it can be managed strategically (in much the same way as human physiology and physical sciences support modern medical and engineering techniques, respectively). Les is a member of the editorial board of two academic journals, and is a joint recipient of an Australian Research Council grant. He delivers executive education programmes in Australia and overseas, and has received research and teaching awards.

Les has three adult children and lives in the coastal hinterland near Melbourne.

1

INTRODUCTION

These footprints in the stone? They don't belong to me!

Blues group, New York, 2012

The finance industry has a simple mission, which is to link entrepreneurs and investors so that funds flow between them at an equitable price. Put simply: the industry should arrange for monies saved by individuals for future expenses including retirement to be successfully invested with governments and growing firms to benefit all parties. Unfortunately, nobody with better than Coke-bottle vision could have missed evidence that the finance industry in virtually every country fails to meet this core mission.

Consider, for example, the US equity market which is the world's largest. As shown in Figure 1.1, its value as measured by the S&P 500 Index was at the same level in late 2013 as it had been in mid-2000: capital gain from US equities in 13 years was zip! All that investors saw from holding funds through this time was volatility (and meagre dividends) as the market cycled several times in the band between 800 and 1500.

This book is motivated by failure of the finance industry to fulfil its core mission. It sets out to explain the reasons why, and then proposes practical remedies.

There is no doubt that finance is an intimidating topic. Each of us has different and changing financial needs as we age, achieve varying employment success and shift the mix of our expenditures. Thus we move in and out of debt and investments, and rub up against a variety of financial advisers and counterparties. The volume of investment information is large and rarely consistent for long. The media breathlessly report scams and incompetence and highlight the inability of finance industry regulators to contain white-collar crooks. The good intentions of governments in many countries to encourage savings to support their ageing population's security

FIGURE 1.1 S&P 500 Index since 1970

in retirement compound uncertainty through complex tax arrangements that regularly change. Worry is chronic, and doubts and uncertainty are rife.

But no matter how complex the language and structure of the finance industry, investors should bear in mind three immutable features. Finance theory rarely survives contact with the real world. Finance experts earn millions, but cannot best amateurs. And, despite expensive and intrusive regulation of the finance industry, it suffers a near-fatal crisis every seven years or so. These repeated crises are like the nocturnal visits of Shakespearean ghosts, indicting theory and regulation by their presence. Finance, though, dismisses them as short-term embarrassments, which should be papered over expeditiously and then forgotten lest they question its culture and risk damage to the industry's brittle structure.

This record does not suggest a discipline that is well founded. In fact, the limited science behind finance renders it one of the weaker fields of learning. Thus questions – especially about markets such as the basis of share prices or investor decisions – attract answers that sound more like religious dogma, rather than evidence-based depictions. To paraphrase H. L. Mencken (1917), there is always an easy depiction of every finance tenet: neat, plausible and wrong.

It is trite to observe that humans constantly seek to make sense of an unknowable future (and – ofttimes – present!), but that seems to be driving many in finance. For example, analysts – who are specialist advisers in broking and investment houses – spend time and intellectual capital in preparing highly impressive models which they use to deliver authoritative forecasts of company profits, commodity prices and economic parameters. Then, as everyone expects, the forecasts are quickly overtaken by events and become irrelevant. Despite the almost inevitable inaccuracy of forecasts, their preparation remains important because the industry is dominated by processes and inputs, not results.

Many analysts and other experts resemble the economists described in a book by M. A. G. van Meerhaeghe (1971: xxvi) which influenced my thinking about markets.

He described them as living in a dream world with their own cabalistic language where they engaged in impressive mental gymnastics that ignored the evidence and so are of little relevance to the real world. A like-minded critic loudly hissed a similar sentiment at a university seminar I attended: 'Beautiful math – stupid idea.' Finance academics seem to be poor students of their own economics, and their discipline mimics religion in a belief system based on a blancmange of fact, fiction, mystery and hope.

Despite seemingly fatal shortcomings, finance theorists and practitioners survive because they are adept in operationalising the Orwellian idea that if you can successfully frame the language used to describe a mysterious phenomenon and set it within a comfortable analytical frame, then you can bluff investors about its true nature. A good example involves the simple question: based on history, what return can be expected from investing in equities over the medium term (say: three years)? There cannot be a definitive answer even to such explicit questions because financial markets do not have an endpoint where results can be tabulated. This is in marked contrast to (say) betting on sporting events where the returns of any strategy can be readily assessed. Financial markets require choice of an endpoint (as well as a starting point), and return varies accordingly. In the last 20 years, the annual return on international equities, for instance, ranges from -19 to $+21$ per cent depending on the three-year period chosen.

A standard rhetorical device when the occasional sceptic points to theory's ineffectiveness is to counter that gaps arise because managers and investors are irrational, or do not cleave to the normative objective of utility maximisation. Thus Nobel laureate Bob Merton (2003) said that making investment practices more effective is 'a tough engineering problem, not one of new science'.

It is troubling that an industry which is critical to meeting a major life goal of most people (that is, to generate enough savings to have a secure retirement) has weak theoretical foundations and is so badly managed.

Whilst structural features of the finance industry contribute to shortcomings in its theory and practice, the most important cause of them is that finance's subject matter is all about the future: how best to use evidence available today to invest funds that successfully capture a benefit that may not be realised until many years down the track. Fundamental to success in such endeavours is being able to recognise the drivers of financial phenomena ranging from the prices of shares and gold to levels of interest rates and consumer demand. This boils down to understanding cause and effect. A second fundamental requirement is being able to collect data to quantify the causal factors and predict the financial effects.

An important premise of this book is that neither of these fundamental requirements can be met. Thus any finance theory that relies on predictability (which is most of them) cannot be successfully applied, and it is not practicable to make meaningful forecasts of markets or other financial parameters.

There are three reasons why predicting financial changes is so hard. The first is that cause and effect are ill understood. The most obvious evidence comes from expert unpacking of financial effects. Consider headlines in London's *Financial Times*[1] which explain the interaction of oil and US stock prices over one seven-month period: 'Bourses Brush Off Oil Fears as Wall Street Rises' (3 March 2005) and 'Oil Fears Take Toll on Wall St' (23 June 2005): clearly higher oil prices can be associated with a rise or fall on Wall Street. Consider also: 'Wall St Rallies as Crude Tumbles' (4 November 2004) and 'Wall Street Lower as Falling Oil Hits Energy Sector' (12 May 2005): this time it is equally clear that Wall Street can rise or fall on *lower* oil prices. So we have an authoritative financial medium variously concluding that stock markets can either rise or fall when crude oil prices rise or fall. Not much understanding of cause and effect here! Nor in numerous similar examples.

Consider an obvious cause and effect relationship: when two billiard balls collide, we do not see the *exact* process whereby the white ball accelerates the red ball, but are reasonably confident of the cause. This is quite a different level of understanding to that of Pavlov's dog that sees dinner come just after a bell rings, and (presumably) believes that a ringing bell causes dinner. Following philosopher David Hume (1777), we should recognise that simultaneous, or conjoined, events do not prove cause and effect, and so causality requires not only an intuitively logical explanation but also evidence that whenever one event occurs another inevitably occurs, too. Dinner following the ring of just one laboratory bell or stocks inconsistently responding to movements in oil prices is not cause and effect. In the case of finance, our understanding of causality has far more in common with Pavlov's dog than the skilled eye of Walter Lindrum.[2]

A second, related barrier to prediction is that finance experts – whether in academia or any of the world's financial districts – are quite unable to observe the most important financial phenomena. On a typical day, the world's stock markets alone see 500 million transactions involving 46,000 companies (WFE, 2011). These transactions result from myriad individual decisions, which are made in private, and their motivations cannot be known, merely guessed at.

The third factor complicating prediction is the absence of data about the future. This is essential because of the core intuition held by many in finance (and a foundation of 'rational pricing') which is that the price of a share or other security equals the present value of its expected future cash flows discounted at a risk-adjusted rate of return. This sounds perfectly logical, but it proves very hard to estimate future cash flows with any precision. Even firms – which should know most about their future cash flows – cannot estimate them very far ahead as shown by regular revision to market guidance on their profit outlooks.

A good example is given by BHP Billiton, the world's largest mining company, which in 2000 spent a good deal of time studying its financial exposures. To help better understand and communicate risks, BHP (2000) settled on a measure termed cash flow at risk (CFaR), which is 'the worst expected loss relative to projected business plan cash flows (earnings after interest, but before taxes, depreciation and amortisation) over a one year horizon under normal market conditions at a confidence level of 95 per cent'. In 2000, BHP's cash flow was $US2.5 billion and CFaR was estimated at about $US0.8 billion, so – in 95 years out of 100 – cash flow should lie in the range between $US1.7 and 3.3 billion. Just two years later, though, cash flow was $US4.4 billion, and it reached $US16.5 billion in 2006. This was due to booming commodity prices, and showed how easily BHP's risk outlook could be swamped by unexpected market changes.[3]

A moment's thought shows that financial prediction is a mug's game and little more than guesswork. If it were possible to accurately predict (say) the return from a stock, then its future price would be known (today's price plus expected return) and the current price should adjust so that holding the share provides a return similar to that from secure bonds. But that does not happen because returns are not predictable, and so prices move in something close to a random walk. Holding shares, then, is either a gamble, or a leap of faith that they will provide a reasonable return.

To set the scene for subsequent discussion, let me describe how I see finance in practice.

The starting point is with large financial institutions (hereafter FIs or banks) as just eight of them dominate global finance, control access to markets through their role as intermediaries, and often set security prices. Banks maximise rent from their monopoly control in two ways: trading with investors and other banks to make a profit, and facilitating transactions between investors whilst levying fees for their services. The former requires superior investment skill and taking market risk because such trades are speculative and involve both winners and losers. The latter business model involves no market risk, although it does bring operational risk in the event of failure to generate and accurately execute sufficient profitable transactions.

Thus the total value to be obtained from the finance sector is the sum of banks' investment surplus and transaction profit. The former is driven by skill in security selection and equals capital appreciation plus income less the cost of funds invested. Transaction profit is driven by scale and operational efficiency.

You can infer volumes about finance from the fact that only a minority of firms (most of them boutiques) take the former, risky route to profits. The largest and most profitable banks concentrate on providing services and do not seek significant profit from trading using their own advice and skill.

Table 1.1 shows revenue sources from the annual reports of Citigroup and Goldman Sachs, which are typically seen as leading US banks. This shows that

Table 1.1 Sources of bank revenue, 2011 (US$ billion)

	Citigroup	Goldman Sachs
Net interest revenue	48.5	
Commissions and fees	12.9	
Principal transactions	7.2	
Administrative and other fees	4.0	
Realised gains on investments	(0.3)	
Insurance premiums	2.6	
Financial advisory		2.0
Underwriting		2.4
Execution of clients' equity transactions		9.0
Execution of clients' transactions in other markets		8.3
Investing and lending		2.1
Investment management		5.0
Other	3.5	
Total revenue	**78.4**	**28.8**

close to 90 per cent of Citigroup's revenue comes from low-risk lending and transactional activities; and the proportion is not a lot less for Goldman, despite its more entrepreneurial image.

This is reminiscent of profit sources on the gold fields almost two centuries ago when discoveries on new frontiers brought fortunes to those selling tools, tents, liquor and prostitutes to the '49ers (who rushed to make their fortunes in California in 1849) and their counterparts on the Yukon and Rand, in outback Australia and elsewhere. By contrast, hardworking miners disappeared into anonymity despite their geological skill and hard work. Finance mimics this split of profitable service providers and poorly rewarded entrepreneurs. Even though banks appear to be the players with the most insight and experience in finance, they separate out execution of others' transactions from investment on their own account and focus on capturing rent from the former. Citi, Goldman and the rest manufacture and sell the tools of investment, and leave most financial risks to clients and – increasingly – to hedge funds.

One intriguing corollary of this argument is that the commercial (and even some investment) banks do not affect skill in investing. This inexpertise is surprising as banks have extensive resources, employ specialists across a wide range of investment topics, and – because they manage customers' transactions – can observe private capital flows: each should underpin economically useful forecasts. The doubt over banks' expertise is consistent with one of the very few accepted facts in finance which is that investment managers do not add value. That is, the average returns generated in funds managed by professional investors cannot outperform the market index, even before fees.

One is tempted to wonder, then, that if even the best-resourced banks are not confident of their skill in investing, can investment be anything more than gambling for the average investor? This in turn leads to another question in this book: who in finance does have any expertise?

Lack of investment skill is obscured by day-to-day practice in the finance industry that puts great store in the normative notion that the future can be predicted and managed. Banks promote products and deals; investors are provided with detailed analyses and outlooks for securities' performance; financial advisers spend considerable time understanding their client so they can provide a purpose-built portfolio. Reality, of course, is that exogenous factors – such as changes in macroeconomic variables and firm performance – cannot be forecast; and endogenous variables – investor preferences and future needs – are also hard to determine. Most financial plans turn out to be aspirations; many are fantasies. Even though much of the finance industry's analysis is depicted as application of sound theory, it is really just sophisticated window dressing. It is hard to find anybody who takes money from the public that can demonstrate skill in forecasting or investing.

Thus it becomes logical for banks to adopt a profit-generating business model that pays lip service to the myth of finance theory but in reality relies on fees for transactions. What is less logical is the refusal by independent observers such as academic financial economists – who would be expected to impartially examine and report the facts – to accept how little finance theory can be employed in practice. To be fair, a number do suggest exactly that, and have built a literature that concludes fund managers, hedgers and the like do not add much, if any, value. For them, finance experts are not. Even so, virtually all mainstream research relies on traditional theory and blames performance shortcomings on poor execution of theory (usually termed agency problems or behavioural biases) rather than acknowledging its limited value.

Thus the banks, which have greatest insights into markets and the most resources to analyse them, show by their conduct that they do not claim skill in investment; but academics, who have the best perspective to observe markets, support the contention that expertise should exist in finance. Both groups have a vested interest in obscuring the facts: banks because they want to attract investors to use their services, and academics who want to preserve careers built on normative finance theory. The collective of finance insiders hides shortcomings of their discipline's theory, and assures investors of its successful application. Nobody has any incentive to point out the emperor's scanty attire.

Why don't investors pick this up? Again some do, and this is the reason why passive or index investing has become more popular in recent years (although it still only represents about 15 per cent of equity investments even in the US where investors are most sophisticated). Most investors are deterred from forming their own opinions by a lack of financial education, information asymmetry and high search costs. It takes time, skill and hard work to conduct investment research. Just as few investors develop the skill to service their car or maintain their health, so they contract out management of their savings to experts, hoping the chosen agent will get it right.

More than any other discipline with claim to a scientific basis, the underpinnings of finance are what people hope for rather than having support in solid evidence. Bertrand Russell saw most clearly why investors believe in the myth of finance theory when he wrote in *Proposed Roads to Freedom* (1919) that the strength of people's beliefs is related to their desires. Thus they will be reluctant to believe something unpalatable despite overwhelming evidence, but accept an attractive postulate on scant evidence. For him 'the origin of myths is explained in this way'. Thus myths of financial expertise survive in the face of consistent evidence of their improbability because people *want* to believe in them. As a New York lawyer who specialises in finance told me: 'most human beings engage in magical thinking and have an unlimited capacity to convince themselves of truths'.

Even if investors' self-delusion props up banks' unfounded claim to expertise, why cannot investors secure protection from regulators of the finance industry (whose miserable performance is another target of this book)?

Markets are run by those who issue securities (such as listed companies for equities) or trade them (brokers, investment banks and funds). Investors buy the securities, and – even though they know far less about what will happen to their money than the banks and firms who take it, and bear all the costs of poor investment decisions and market failure – find that regulation is designed so that they have no control over the structure and operation of markets. This can be seen in the two approaches that regulation employs to limit risks: managing the problem of information asymmetry between investors and entrepreneurs, and minimising losses in the event of bank failure.

Managing information asymmetry is the higher-profile regulatory activity, and typically seeks to preserve a level playing field so that investors who buy securities have the same information about their future prospects as issuers of securities and banks that manage transactions. This is the doctrine of continuous disclosure, whereby listed firms must immediately report price-sensitive developments to the market.

To see how well disclosure operates, take the classic situation of when two companies agree to a friendly acquisition, and consider the example of the Exxon-Mobil merger which is one of the world's largest and occurred between two oil giants which could expect tight scrutiny of their decision. According to a joint proxy statement issued by the two companies (ExxonMobil, 1999), their chief executive officers began formal talks about a merger in June 1998, informed their boards a few weeks later, finalised the deal over Thanksgiving weekend in late November 1998, and announced details before the market re-opened. As shown in Figure 1.2, although Mobil shares rose a few dollars immediately after the announcement, there had been an $11, or 15 per cent, jump in price during the previous week indicating that details had leaked about the immensely valuable deal. Regulators did not take any action. We return to insider trading in Chapter 7.

The second approach to finance industry regulation is to ensure that banks make adequate provision to cover deposits in the event of failure. Banks are liability

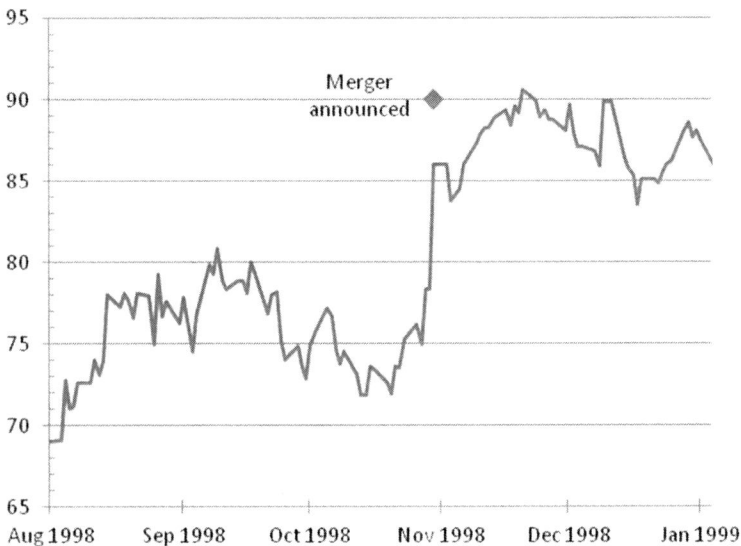

FIGURE 1.2 Mobil share price around its merger with Exxon

funders in that they accept deposits and arrange other borrowings (which collectively form their liabilities) and use them to make loans to other parties (which are
their assets). This is very different to most other borrowers whose debts (that is,
liabilities) are covered by their own hard assets such as plant and equipment. The
ability of a bank to repay its depositors depends not on the market value of its own
assets, but on the quality of loans the bank makes and the performance of borrowers' assets: if these turn bad, borrowings cannot be repaid in full.

To protect depositors, regulation requires banks to hold capital on their balance sheets to cover any shortfall in repayments of loans and hence in the
realisable value of their assets. The quantum of this reserve capital is proportional
to the risk of the loans and so banks typically have shareholder funds of a little
above 5 per cent of liabilities. This strategy, though, is primitive, akin to end-of-
pipe control of motor vehicle pollution. The regulation assumes that some
portion of loans will default and simply sets aside a reserve to cover losses, much
as early emission controls allowed inefficient engines to produce pollutants and
required catalytic converters to combust them. It seems obvious that finance
industry regulation should mimic modern vehicle engineers and redesign the
banking system to eliminate failure.

In summary, the book develops a set of themes built around the nature and
causes of crippling deficiencies in finance research and practice. The first is that
theory does not address key questions in finance practice and gives at best a sim-
plistic depiction of markets and firm finances. The second is that financial
innovation and debt of bankers have contributed to repeated asset bubbles and
resulting crashes in equity, housing and commodity markets. Third is the inability
of regulators to keep up with changes and eliminate the finance industry's worst
practices. Sadly the whole finance industry is arranged so that nobody bears any
financial (and few personal) risks for its obvious deficiencies, except investors who
bear all the costs of every badly judged decision.

The second set of themes in the book provides responses to these problems and
proposes shifting regulation to make it an offence to be a director of a large bank
or corporation that goes bankrupt or accepts government bailout funding, and
promotes greater transparency by firms and investment funds to more closely align
the interests of investors with those of the firms they finance.

Looking ahead, the first part of this book amplifies the poor record of financial
experts and regulators and discusses evidence of their inexpertise. However, taking
cheap shots at those facing complex tasks is easy, and Monday morning quarter-
backs are a dime-a-dozen in the corridors of university finance departments. Thus
the second part of the book sets out a model of finance theory that better matches
the real world, and extends this to propose an intuitively more successful regulatory
framework.

The book is structured as a tour of contemporary investment theory and practice. It draws on research and publications by leaders in finance, and is designed to
challenge and inform readers with an interest in the decisions of investors and
finance managers.

Notes

1 All taken from www.ft.com
2 Walter Lindrum (1898–1960) held the World Professional Billiards Championship from 1933 until 1950, and established 57 world records.
3 BHP's share price rose from under $A10 in late 2003 to peak around $49 in 2008.

2

CHRONIC FAILURE OF FINANCE THEORY TO SURVIVE CONTACT WITH THE REAL WORLD

These heroes of finance are like beads on a string: when one slips off the others follow.

Henrik Ibsen (1828–1906)

One of the most challenging aspects of modern finance is that its core theories give only a poor depiction of actual processes, and thus see limited use by finance professionals in banks and investment funds. A consequence of theory's weak applicability is to limit interaction between finance academics who research the field, and those who make their living in the finance industry. This has led many academics to consider finance practitioners as incompetent, and destroy value every time they go near markets. As a result they teach a concept called agency theory which assumes that corporate managers are lazy or venal and will only deliver value for shareholders if closely supervised or strongly incentivised.

I have strong opinions on this lack of theoretical and practical engagement between academics and practitioners after spending the last 20 years in finance roles, divided into roughly equal periods as a corporate treasurer and then as a finance academic holding part-time roles with two fund managers. In the companies I saw well-trained, hardworking people making good decisions. So, too, in fund managers where few were incompetent. And it was similar in academia: smart people with ten years' university education who teach well and diligently research their topics of interest.

This dichotomy between qualified and experienced finance academics and practitioners has puzzled me for a number of years, and led to my research focus on applied finance, in particular the way that firms and investors make decisions. Thus a starting question during interviews that I conducted during 2012 with fund managers was: did they use finance theory and – if not – why not? A lot of managers expressed frustration at the poor applicability of finance theory, and the result was published as an article entitled 'Why Finance Theory Fails to Survive Contact with the Real World: A Fund Manager Perspective' (Coleman, in press), which I use as background to this chapter.

The centrepiece of finance theory is a practical failure

The capital asset pricing model (CAPM) of William Sharpe (1964) and John Lintner won the former a Nobel Prize. Even five decades after its publication, CAPM remains the core of investment courses, and is probably the most commonly taught finance theory. For example, Chenghu Ma (2010) assured readers of his text *Advanced Asset Pricing Theory*: 'CAPM forms the cornerstone of modern finance theory.'

CAPM is used to determine the return expected from a portfolio or security, and is built on the assumption that there is a linear relationship between expected return and risk,[1] so that investors are compensated for accepting higher risk. This depiction is intuitively elegant and well suited to analysis using available markets data. Thus it is widely attractive to finance teachers, and is a staple in academic studies. CAPM is also routinely incorporated in presentations by fund managers and other practitioners. In particular, it supports the truism that investor returns come from bearing market risk: that is, markets go up and provide a return to investors which compensates them for uncertainty in returns and accepting the risk that markets also go down.

In fact, much of finance relies on the concept that bearing risk brings return, and some investors go so far as to argue that managing statistical risk can optimise returns. Thus the Victorian Funds Management Corporation – one of the largest public sector funds in Australia – proclaimed on its website that 'risk is our scarce resource: we manage it for best incremental return'.

In practice, though, CAPM proves completely useless. Understanding why a finance centrepiece is invalid will help illuminate my criticism of finance theory generally.

A pithy dismissal of CAPM came from Fama and French (2004) – American professors who are giants in the world of finance – who concluded that CAPM's poor empirical record in the real world means that 'most applications of the model are invalid'. In particular, it performs poorly in comparison to ratios such as price-to-earnings and price-to-book. Moreover, it is known that stock returns are related to variables other than market return such as scale and momentum, and are also subject to environmental effects such as industry. Putting this together means that CAPM can tell only a slice of the story of any security's value, perhaps managing to explain a few per cent of future prices and hence is of no commercial value.

Apart from CAPM's narrow focus, it is impractical to apply because investors cannot form meaningful expectations about the variables required to use it. Consider Figure 2.1 which shows betas for three large US stocks – ExxonMobil, General Electric and IBM – that have been calculated since the 1960s using daily

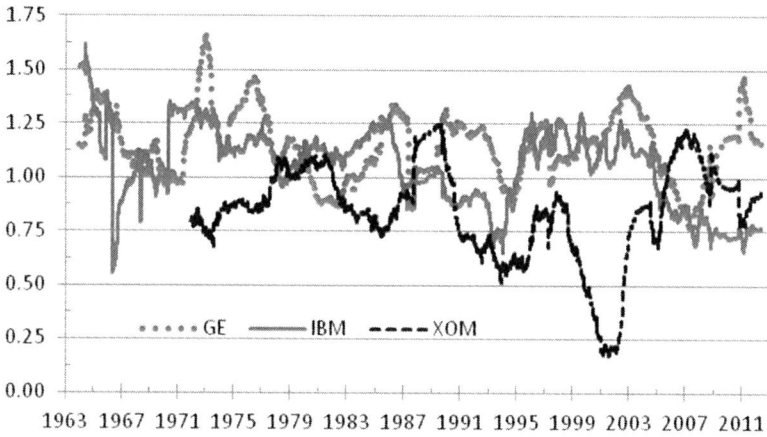

FIGURE 2.1 Betas of large US companies

returns over the previous 500 days. Values range between 0.5 and 1.5, which means that the share prices variously move by between half and one-and-a-half times the change in the S&P 500. The chart also shows that values of beta often shift significantly in a relatively short period of time.

This points to two facts that are well recognised, if usually ignored. The first is that beta is not stable: even if good estimates are available for future beta and market moves, they would give fluctuating forecasts of security returns. Second, past beta is not a good predictor of future beta, and – in the absence of reliable data on the future – it is impossible to forecast beta. Thus historical data will not give a good estimate of future beta, and its actual value fluctuates so much that practical application is questionable. This is not a very efficient basis for portfolio construction.

In one of my interviews, a London equity manager spent some time explaining why his team found that application of CAPM is 'fraught with difficulty'. The first reason is that the risk-free interest rate (which is the basis of market return) is not stable and – as shown by the LIBOR scandal where leading UK banks lied about the interest rates they charged – can be artificially influenced. He expressed even less conviction in the risk premium which has such a wide range that you can come up with any answer. The second input is beta, which is also questionable in terms of calculation because the time period chosen makes a difference; it, too, is unstable. In this investor's experience, each CAPM variable fluctuates significantly, even over short periods. The reality for him is that using the theory is dangerous.

Perhaps the greatest defect of CAPM is its fundamental premise that risk and return move together, which is false because return does not seem to bear a direct relationship to risk. For instance, studies of the link between security risk and return variously conclude that it is positive, negative or insignificant.[2] In many respects it seems that the relationship between return and risk is not linear, but concave (or ∩-shaped), which is put neatly in an early edition of *Palgrave's Dictionary of Political Economy* (Higgs, 1926): 'The classes of investments which on the average return most to the investor are neither the very safest of all nor the very riskiest, but the intermediate classes which do not appeal either to timidity or to the gambling instinct.'

Despite theory, risk and return have a complex relationship: almost certainly one does not bring the other, and so mathematical finance falls apart.

Diversification is of no use when it matters

The second most important theoretical plank in finance and one of the most commonly followed financial strategies is diversification. For investors, this means allocating funds across a range of assets, or adopting a passive strategy by buying the Index so that returns equal the market average. Spreading out investments in this way smoothens fluctuations in returns. Similarly, banks avoid concentration risk and spread their sources of funding so they do not all dry up at the same time; and they spread loan books to ensure not all go bad at once.

Apart from smoothing returns, diversification is a prudent strategy given the high failure rate of firms and funds. For instance, the proportion of entities that survives more than a decade is two-thirds for mutual funds (Bu and Lacey, 2009) and firms (Fama and French, 2003); and one-third for hedge funds (Grecu *et al.*, 2007). For those investors who cannot predict these failures (and that is most of us) but rely on survival of most of the stocks or funds in their portfolio, diversification makes good sense.

Diversification makes such strong intuitive sense that it led to development of the Markowitz (1952) modern portfolio theory. The idea is that investors quantify the correlation between alternative investments or the extent that their prices move together, and then build portfolios with a mix of assets that have low correlation, so that their prices will tend to move in different directions. The basic objective is encapsulated in plots of the risk (that is, standard deviation) of a portfolio against its number of stocks, which show that building a portfolio of about 15 minimally related stocks reduces diversifiable risk towards zero. The optimum portfolio combines investments that give the sweet-spot combination of high return at lowest risk, and lies along the familiar efficient frontier. This concept is seductive, and forms an important part of any investment advice. But portfolio theory, too, is defective. According to President of the American Finance Association Michael Jensen (1972: 371): 'the evidence seems to indicate fairly strongly that the [Markowitz mean-variance portfolio model] does not provide an adequate description of the process determining common stock returns'.

Even though diversification sounds prudent and seems simple, it requires accurate forecasting of investments' risk, return and correlations. Sadly, this has proven impossible like much else in finance: the future is unknowable, and so modern portfolio theory is reduced to guesswork.

Further, if you think about the effects of diversification, it doesn't just dilute risk but also returns. That is, returns from the best-performing stocks in a portfolio will be averaged down by worse-performing stocks. If you can pick good stocks, the most successful strategy is probably to put them in a single, high-performing port-folio. With all your eggs in one basket, you naturally need – as Mark Twain (1894) had Pudd'nhead Wilson say – to guard that basket carefully.

Another shortcoming of diversification is that it does not give any protection against operational risk, or the possibility of failure of the people, products or processes that underpin securities and funds. This type of risk is only to the downside, so it is hard to diversify. We will cover the nature and magnitude of these risks in Chapter 4.

Perhaps the most important weakness of diversification is that it does nothing to reduce non-diversifiable or market-based risks. This means that it only avoids losses relative to a benchmark. Just as a falling tide drops all boats – although the sell-side marketers prefer the version that 'a rising tide lifts all boats' – so a falling market drops the value of all portfolios, whether diversified or not. Thus a well-diversified portfolio will – somewhat perversely – closely match the market's fall, and the benefits of diversification evaporate just when they are most needed.

To see how this can happen, consider a situation where equities in developing country markets suffer a sharp fall. Diversification says that other stock markets, commodities and so on should hold their prices and balance out any loss in developing markets. But a leveraged investor or trader who is long in the developing markets will face margin calls and must raise money, which tends to come from selling part of their holdings. Because the most favourable prices tend to be found in markets that have not fallen, these latter positions will be liquidated and so the forced selling pressure quickly spreads. Suddenly previously quite independent markets start to move in the same direction, and a wide range of markets can fall together. In the jargon, correlations tighten during downturns.

A good example of this is shown in Figure 2.2 which plots the value of the CRB Index (which is the best-known measure of commodity prices) and an exchange traded fund for financial stocks. One would expect that holding commodities would

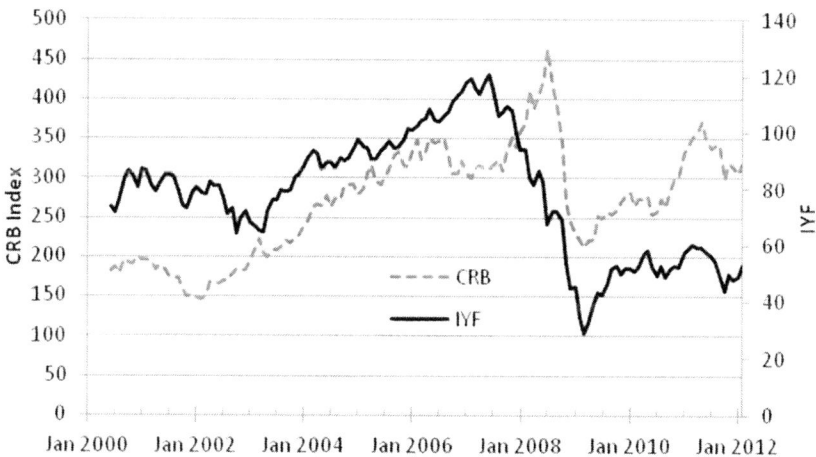

FIGURE 2.2 CRB Index and finance sector ETF

be a hedge against bank stocks. Perhaps at times it is. But in this plot of the last decade or so, the two have moved together. In particular, after bank stocks collapsed during the global financial crisis (GFC), so did commodity prices.

The effect of diversification is to concentrate market risk in the tails of return distributions: investment risk is low during good times that lie in the middle of the bell curve of returns, but becomes high during the occasional bad times in the left tail. When liquidity tightens or investment risk rises, asset prices drop across the board and diversification proves of no value.

A cynic like me concludes that CAPM and diversification fail to add value because they have so little inherent substance. In fact, modern finance theory does not seem to show much advance in the five centuries since Shakespeare had Antonio succinctly describe portfolios, diversification and the role of covariance:

> My ventures are not in one bottom trusted,
> Nor to one place; nor is my whole estate
> Upon the fortune of this present year.
> Therefore my merchandise makes me not sad.[3]

Markowitz and his ilk made little advance on centuries-old conventional wisdom other than to give its heuristics some empiricism.

Weaknesses in other finance theory

Apart from CAPM and portfolio theory, the other core investment paradigms are efficient markets, agency theory and the relationship between prices of different security prices (such as in the Black Scholes option pricing model). Together these comprise what Jensen and Smith (1984) termed the 'fundamental building blocks' of finance theory in an overview of the discipline's history. Each of these, too, is defective.

Consider the efficient markets hypothesis (EMH) of which Professor Michael Jensen (1978) said: 'there is no other proposition in economics which has more solid empirical evidence supporting it'. In efficient markets, rational investors use publicly available information to project securities' cash flows and discount them at a risk-adjusted rate to their present, fundamental value. A critical corollary is the rational expectations hypothesis which holds that forecasts by individual investors will collectively form an unbiased estimate of securities' value, and so their prices should quickly converge to equilibrium (Fama, 1970).

The rational expectations hypothesis took hold almost as soon as it was developed in the 1970s at the University of Chicago by Lucas and Sargent (1981). It is attractive to researchers because it relies upon information and financial principles, if not strict laws. Thus it is easy to work with. A more ominous advantage of rational pricing is its ideology, because expectations have libertarian overtones that directly challenge Keynesian orthodoxy that sees a dominant role for policymakers and regulators in setting prices and controlling markets. Advocates of rational markets dismiss intervention because market participants can see through government monetary and fiscal policy, project its endpoint and adjust prices immediately when a policy is announced and so destroy its effects. In any event, rational expectations became the ruling paradigm for security valuations.

Whilst rational pricing and efficient markets sound logical, markets actually take little account of information. An excellent piece of supporting evidence was reported by Roy Fair (2002) who examined the United States, S&P 500 futures contract between 1982 and 1999 to identify moves of greater than 0.75 per cent within any five minutes, which is about seven standard deviations above average. He found 1,159 moves, and then searched newswires at that hour for a trigger. But – even well after the fact – he was not able to discern the causes of 90 per cent of the largest moves in stock prices. A similar situation applies with individual stocks where Bouchaud *et al.* (2009) show that large price jumps (a one-minute return exceeding three standard deviations) typically occur in the absence of new public information. In other words, the largest change in value of stocks and the major stock index during any week are almost always caused by factors other than new information.

The most common explanations for why security prices change in the absence of price-sensitive news include some combination of irrational, or at least non-economically rational, behaviour by investors and managers (e.g. Barberis and Thaler, 2003); orders placed by investors based on private information that are large enough to move prices (e.g. Biais *et al.*, 2005); and the tendency for security prices to move together. All too rarely do researchers reach the obvious conclusion and question the validity of rational security valuation.

More broadly, there is no justification to support efficiency of markets because it is not testable. This is expounded by Fama (2010) who pointed out that testing market efficiency requires accurate assessment of expected returns which are not available. Put differently, if markets are efficient they should accurately price securities, and to validate this you need a measure of proper value. This is what finance academics coyly term the joint test problem: you have to make one unprovable assumption (say, that CAPM predicts future stock prices) to prove an untested theory (such as market efficiency). A corollary is that most asset pricing models are not testable because they assume market efficiency. This, of course, flies in the face of centuries of scientific philosophy best encapsulated in Karl Popper's contention that all theories must be falsifiable. Finance researchers, though, do not seem to care that most theories cannot be tested.

A second building block of finance is agency theory which was set out by Professors Jensen and Meckling (1976), and points out that modern firms are so large that they need to be run by professional managers. Managers have relative freedom in their decision making, and – because they cannot be monitored by shareholders – are assumed to act in their own interests. The solution to this agency problem is the introduction of appropriate governance and contracting mechanisms, particularly performance-based pay which aligns the interests of managers and shareholders. Like the EMH, agency theory has been seen as contributing to the GFC and corporate demises. This was because agency theory promoted performance-based compensation for managers through shares and stock options to encourage them to initiate strategies that lift share prices. The defect was that it also encourages managers to increase risk because success increases the value of their holdings (Dobbin and Jung, 2010), and too many risks proved disastrous.

What is the alternative? It depends on your starting point. The agency problem arises from opinions of how managers behave and reflects Theory X of McGregor (1960) where they are assumed to be naturally lazy, selfish and unmotivated. Finance always seems to see the worst in managers. An alternative perspective (which I find much closer to the real-world behaviour of most, but certainly not all, managers) is based on the stewardship theory of Tosi et al. (2003) where managers primarily act in the interest of shareholders. This is because of a natural sense of duty overlain by the wish to protect their reputation (which is often termed human capital). Agency and stewardship theories are very different worldviews of how managers behave, and they point to differences in the nature and strength of optimum governance mechanisms, including compensation, to secure managers' performance. Lazy managers need dangerous incentives; honest, hard-working managers need fair pay and modest bonuses tied to clear performance objectives.

Moving on to other finance building blocks, these tend to be empirical relationships with little or no theory. An example is the four-factor asset pricing model of Fama and French (1993) and Carhart (1997)[4] which projects security returns on the basis of market returns and three factors related to the firm, namely its size and value, and recent price change. This, however, is little more than a fitted equation where the authors use fancy math to develop relationships between historical returns and characteristics of shares. It is free of theory, and Fama and French merely make the circular conclusion 'that if assets are priced rationally, variables that are related to average returns, such as size and book-to-market equity, must proxy for sensitivity to common (shared and thus undiversifiable) risk factors in returns'. That is, they adopt the core finance assumption that returns are related to risk, which makes it axiomatic that factors influencing returns must reflect risk. Unfortunately the relationships between returns and the factors are not stable, and so anybody wishing to apply the model needs to recalculate them (or else consult values that Ken French publishes on his website). Such pricing models change their predictions so regularly that they are useless beyond the very short term.

Another finance building block – and one of the weaker arguments in finance – are the irrelevance propositions of Nobel Prize winners Miller and Modigliani (Miller, 1988). The first proposition argues that a company's value comes from its earnings stream, and therefore its capital structure – how much of the firm is funded by equity, debt or retained earnings – is irrelevant. The second, similarly justified proposition is that a company's value is unaffected by what it does with earnings in terms of dividends, share buybacks, reinvestment and so on. These propositions follow the early nineteenth-century argument by David Ricardo that the source of government funding – taxes or debt – was irrelevant because spending would be the same and all of it would eventually be paid from taxes, with debt merely affecting the timing of tax receipts.

According to what became known as the M&M propositions, capital structure and payout policy are irrelevant to company value because it is set by expected cash flows and not by how they are financed or distributed. To be fair, the authors acknowledged numerous simplifying assumptions and couched their propositions with many caveats. But this only highlights their lack of real-world credibility. Thus it should not be a surprise to see the extent to which firm managers rebut the irrelevance propositions and pay considerable attention to capital structure for its effect on risk to the firm, and to payout policy for its importance to shareholders. As a result the irrelevance propositions are irrelevant, which seems extraordinary for a Nobel-Prize-winning, commonly accepted theory.

This leaves open what Barclay and Smith (1999) termed 'a perennial debate in corporate finance' which is the optimum capital structure for a firm. In other words, what is the best mix of debt, equity and other funding sources to finance a firm's assets? Despite more than a century of corporate finance research and teaching, there is no clear answer to this question, and hence no firm guidance for company executives. Again we see the sober conclusion that core finance theory has no real-world application. It can only be lunacy that such demonstrably ineffectual theories retain currency and continue to feature prominently in textbooks and research.

Unfortunately the M&M propositions also set an important pathway for future finance research as the first, trenchant assertions that finance theory should be based on normative notions rather than investor and manager objectives and practices. Subsequent research has treated finance as some kind of ideal system in which humans are relevant only as elements to be controlled. That is, instead of looking at the behaviour of investors and managers as guided by the invisible hand of Adam Smith to make informed responses that optimise the system's performance, researchers see them only as abusing it for their own interests. That is why managers are subject to the agency problem and investors are irrational. M&M set the pattern for academics to define an ideal of how managers should act, and criticise those managers who did not pass normative tests. This approach fell on fallow ground because by then Harry Markowitz had cemented the centrality in finance theory of complex modelling and statistical analysis.

Thus Markowitz, Miller, Modigliani and their contemporaries prop⸍
opment of finance theory along a pathway that dislocated it from the re.
and set its structure as a numbers-based discipline. Quantitative finance became a tautology with arrival of the personal computer which has been prominent on every researcher's desk since the 1980s. This has suited several generations of researchers because there is so much data around about key finance products: prices of securities are continuously available, every second for liquid securities; companies and fund managers provide information about their financial products and performance; and there are myriad databases making all this and more readily available. Fortunately for many, it meant that research could be done well away from

the messy real world in comfort and security behind a desk. Unfortunately this built a tradition of dismissing qualitative research such as surveys and interviews (at least in part because they only collected practitioner opinions that were worthless). As Michael Jensen (1993) concluded: 'The finance profession has concentrated on how capital investment decisions should be made, with little systematic study of how they actually are made in practice.'

Economists' hubris

Shahin Shojai is head of research at fund manager Capco and has written a series of articles under the heading 'Economists' Hubris'.[5] His objective is to 'look at the practical benefits of economics/finance literature to the world of business and policymakers and critically examine whether there is any relationship between academic thought and business or policy application'. This objective resonates with my own, so it is interesting to briefly paraphrase his thoughts, especially as it is uncommon to see such ideas in print.

Dr Shojai starts by reviewing mergers and acquisitions and points out that few academic studies address business-critical questions looking at: what type of firms make good acquirers; how acquirers should choose a target; and how much premium above current share price they should pay. To the contrary, academics wait until the merger is complete and then critique it using market or accounting data, with little consideration for managerial issues. Even when they address a salient issue – such as whether or not it is advisable to make diversifying acquisitions of firms in other business sectors – the conclusions are conflicting.

A second paper examines asset pricing theory, particularly CAPM. He points to its well-known weaknesses, and wonders rhetorically why developing a more robust asset pricing model is not seen as the central challenge of finance research.

His third paper is on risk management and points out two factors which were major contributors to the collapse of the derivatives markets that ushered in the GFC. First was the inability of credit ratings agencies to determine the risk associated with highly complex derivatives whose price eventually melted away as counterparties defaulted. The second arose from the fact that there was no true public market for these assets, which meant there was only limited sharing of information about them and no reliable price. Investors (along with the auditors and regulators who should have protected them) were simply unable to value the products and so bought them based on hope and/or guesses.

This highlights the practical weakness of risk management in finance, which is that it takes statistical techniques that prove useful in analysing large datasets over long periods and applies them to much narrower targets. To compound this shortcoming, risk management relies on use of historical data, even though risk is continually changing because unexpected events occur that quickly render historical data irrelevant.

Shojai observes that many market observers believe major shocks are becoming more common, and describe them as black swans or outlier events that are rare, but have high impact. Like Europeans' shock discovery of black swans in the Antipodes, they can only be identified in hindsight (Taleb, 2007). One contributor to more frequent financial shocks is the disappearance of natural circuit breakers in markets, such as exchange controls on international capital flows and manual processing of security trades. This is amplified when investors herd and drive markets in one direction; or central bankers jointly increase liquidity and create global, credit-fuelled bubbles. The ever-strengthening linkages between once-discrete activities weaken natural variation between markets and offset the best risk management tool of all – diversification.

The capstone defect of risk management is the hosepipe of data which no system can effectively capture, analyse and monitor. Despite these deficiencies, there is immense hubris over financial risk management, which is displayed by academics who cannot build theories that can price assets or model risks, and also by practitioners who maintain faith – in spite of the evidence – that their risk management tools can work. We return to this issue in Chapter 4.

The fourth article examines asset management and portfolio theory. Here, too, finance research has failed to answer questions that are important to practitioners such as how to choose a security or managed fund. A particular shortcoming in portfolio theory is its insistence on the need to consider both the risk and return from an asset. Each involves *expected* values which are impractical to determine, and there is no agreement about which of several risk measures should be used.

In the fifth article, Shojai examines the practical implications of articles that won best-paper awards in leading finance research journals. His conclusion: 'none provides anything that can be of practical use to market participants'. Quite simply, the best finance research has no practical application.

Through these papers, Shojai (sometimes writing with a colleague or two) points to structural weaknesses in finance research such as a preference to study questions that can be quantified rather than ones that matter to practitioners. This in turn reflects a lack of understanding of business by most academics, which means they are frequently playing catch up with what is really happening. He argues that the failure of finance researchers to engage with the real world means that their research papers – no matter how numerical or impressive – are seen by practitioners as little more than irrelevant conjecture.

As an aside, it is interesting that Shojai's ideas have not reached the research mainstream: Google Scholar, for instance, gives a citation count for his five papers of just 37, and only one is in a good journal. This is not to say, however, that he has been ignored, as Shojai's papers on the Social Science Research Network (SSRN) have been downloaded 85,000 times and this criterion ranks interest in his work at a highly credible 42 out of over 30,000 authors who have papers on the network. The conclusion from this? Many finance researchers and academics understand Shojai's criticisms and are interested in their implications, but few are willing to embrace the consequences in their own work.

Finance theory has a long way to go before it can bear to face the facts.

Finance is full of dark matter

Astronomers believe that gravitational forces shape much of the universe's behaviour, but cannot identify sufficient mass to explain what they see. Their solutions to this missing mass are creative. One involves the existence of dark matter that cannot be observed but is still exerting gravitational pull. A second proposal is the existence of parallel universes which similarly have mass that cannot be observed. Think about it for a moment: sober, analytical physicists opine that our world only makes sense if it has an invisible component, not God but either undetectable massive objects or *doppelgängers*!

Modern finance has a similar problem. In particular, it sets the standard for financial decisions that they are economically rational, which means that investors use available data to make the choice that has the highest expected return. Thus a recent paper in the pre-eminent *Journal of Finance* begins: 'the classic paradigm of financial theory assumes that investors operating in frictionless markets make rational decisions' (Elton *et al.*, 2004: 261). Unfortunately, the authors of this paper confirm the finding of many others which is that there is clear and pervasive evidence that investors and finance managers do not always make rational decisions because they fail to use available data or to follow finance theory.

These shortcomings in financial decisions should hardly be a surprise because non-financial decisions made by these same investors and managers do not employ purely economically rational criteria. Most decisions are made in response to need: for food, a car, school or vacation. Decisions are then narrowed according to price, hedonics (Porsche or Ford), availability, and personal preferences (new car or holiday). Certainly some economic factors are considered. But even when the decision occurs in a setting with many characteristics of financial markets (such as eBay or consumer markets like petrol retailing, which both give a range of bid and offer prices and have interactive supply and demand channels), far more is involved than just economic rationality.

The fact that rational pricing is uncommon makes it interesting to see how rarely it is questioned as the proper basis of security valuation. Sometimes researchers express tentative doubt; Elton *et al.* (2004), for instance, wondered after their analysis: 'we as a profession [may] have overestimated the rationality of investors'. But, like most other researchers, they do not take the next, logical step and consider whether or not it is appropriate to continue to apply the yardstick that investors *should* be rational.

This is where the dark matter comes in, because the solution advanced by finance researchers to explain investors' irrationality has been to invent a whole new sub-discipline (which seems as dubious as the solution proposed by astrophysicists to solve their puzzles). This new sub-discipline is called behavioural finance, and reports the influence on decision makers of psychological and other non-economic factors ranging from practical limitations on their decision capacity to emotion and cognitive illusions. There is now a lengthy catalogue of anomalies, biases and other irrationalities which are traced to psychological or behavioural misperceptions in financial decision makers. For a concise introduction try *Behavioral Finance* by Hersh Shefrin (2001).

The field has become so important that a Nobel Prize went to one of its pioneers Daniel Kahneman, who set out his ideas when accepting the Prize in an address entitled 'Maps of Bounded Rationality' (Kahneman, 2003). This discusses three areas where he studied divergences from the rational agent model and they form a pretty good basis of behavioural finance. The first area of Professor Kahneman's research is that – where the evidence is uncertain – people use heuristics or mental shortcuts in making decisions. The second is that people's attitudes towards risk (and other aspects of a decision) are situational, and so they will take greater risk when they find themselves in a poor position. The third is that the way material is presented or framed affects decisions.

Have I missed something? Isn't a person who buys from a farmer's market, a Japanese car manufacturer or a friend using heuristics to manage uncertainty? Haven't we all seen a football coach whose team is losing rush an untried player out onto the field in a final high-risk throw? And surely the whole advertising industry is predicated on presenting products in the most favourable fashion? Do Nobels now come from stating the bleeding obvious?

People generally make good, rational decisions within their context. That is, they review a reasonable amount of the available data, interpret it within the framework they believe applies to the decision, and choose the course that maximises benefit to them. What economists depict as irrationality is what most of us do when making any decision, which is to take into account non-economic factors. This highlights deep tension between theory and behaviour that should force reconsideration of the former.

The tension between academics' theory and practitioners' behaviour

The relationship between finance academics and practitioners is unusual to say the least. When I graduated first as an engineer, my degree was a toolkit that had direct relevance in the workplace. So, too, with doctors, lawyers, dentists, veterinarians and so on: they leave university and hit the ground running. Finance practitioners, by contrast, use little of the theory taught to them.

A significant contributor to practitioners' neglect of finance research is that the discipline's theory is driven by academics who display little interest in questions that are important to practitioners. Consider, for instance, the gales of creative destruction that are at the heart of capitalism's purported strength and play out as mergers and acquisitions. These major transactions are not only critical to corporations involved, but are also important income sources for financial institutions who advise them. Academics, though, are totally uninterested in the practical issues involved. The net is that finance theory and research have little impact on important topics, and it is no wonder that practitioners feel short changed and ignore theory.

Practitioners' disregard for research is reciprocated by academics who take the perspective that managers pose an agency problem, and typically conclude they destroy value every time they go near markets. For instance, the corporate finance literature across time and countries finds that initial public offerings (IPOs) are under-priced and leave 15 per cent or more of founding owners' value on the table; hedging is usually loss making; and myriad capital decisions prove poorly judged. This is a surprising set of conclusions because experts in most other fields can best amateurs. Again a bit of digging is illuminating.

A good way to explore the basis on which academics criticise practitioners is to use the example of mergers and acquisitions (M&As), which are the highest-profile decision in finance. The research literature conclusively finds these have poor outcomes for bidders: invariably the acquirer loses money, although target company shareholders usually do well (Andrade *et al.*, 2001).

Despite academics' confidence in this conclusion, their evaluation of merger outcomes follows the standard finance criterion that decision makers should unconditionally seek to maximise financial returns. This dates to Adam Smith (1776) who determined that utility maximisation was *the* goal of economics. Academics' criterion for success in M&As is value generated for the acquiring company's shareholders immediately following the announcement, and acquisitions typically fail this test.

But a very different conclusion emerges when you examine the typical reasons *managers* give when announcing an acquisition. Consider a couple of recent, large examples.

On 20 March 2011, AT&T announced it would acquire T-Mobile USA from Deutsche Telekom for $39 billion.[6] Its press release justified the acquisition in terms of diversifying its customer and asset base, and provided a long list of plans to expand customers and benefits by obtaining access to additional infrastructure. Whilst the merger would bring 'substantial value for shareholders through large, straightforward synergies' they would only reach $3 billion after three years and looked modest in the face of the acquisition cost.

On 10 January 2011, Duke Energy announced it would acquire Progress Energy shares for $14 billion in its own stock and assume $12 billion debt.[7] It explained that the $26 billion transaction 'creates a utility with greater financial strength and enhanced ability to meet our challenges head-on ... This combination of two outstanding companies is a natural fit ... Together, we can leverage our best practices to achieve even higher levels of safety, operational excellence and customer satisfaction, and save money for customers...' The only financial comment was a one-liner: 'The combination is anticipated to be accretive to Duke Energy's adjusted earnings in the first year after closing.'

These and many other statements suggest that a major objective of acquisitions is to give more stability to the company and its earnings. This perspective is actually not new to academics, as Jack Treynor and Fisher Black (1976: 311) suggested it decades ago. The idea is that an acquisition is not just intended to increase absolute return through economies of scale or scope, but is also designed to enhance a firm's competitiveness or secure diversification of shareholder income. By generating similar returns at lower risk, acquisitions add shareholder value because discounting them at a lower risk-adjusted rate yields a higher present value. Thus a review of recent literature by DeYoung *et al.* (2009) confirms that diversifying mergers do reduce firm risk.

Despite the benefit of risk reduction, it is generally seen as an agency problem arising in managers' desire to build empires or protect their human capital by reducing bankruptcy risk. Risk reduction is so rarely considered as a merger performance metric that it is not mentioned in the recent comprehensive study of M&A literature which was published in the prestigious *Journal of Management* (Haleblian *et al.*, 2009).

A second trait of academics' evaluation of M&As is to examine returns during a narrow window following announcement of the merger. That is, they look at changes in share prices in the few days after the deal is made public. This ignores the fact that abnormal returns can accrue to acquiring companies for years as merger benefits unfold. Also, because M&A announcements rarely provide much more than brief details of the deal, market reactions can only be crude guesses at the long-run financial effects. Researchers fail to see that watching a few days of market response tells them little about the outcome of a multi-year decision.

This is a good example of horizon mismatch, where the period during which the analysis is conducted is too short to reveal the effect being measured, so it is not detected. In fact a study of UK takeovers using short-term and long-term windows around the announcement (–five days/+five days and –six months/+two years, respectively) found that short-term abnormal returns to acquirers are 0.03 per cent (which matches results of most studies), whilst long-term returns are an attractive 53.5 per cent (Hodgkinson and Partington, 2008). The deals are highly profitable by the end of two years, but this is not seen in the brief timeframe used by most researchers.

Examples such as this highlight the rationale for academics' criticism of practitioners which is an insistence on normative – often idealised – processes; these, though, can develop theory that has limited practical attraction. A good illustration is given by portfolio theory – which is one of the discipline's most elegant – that was developed by Harry Markowitz (1952) at the age of 25 whilst writing his PhD. In his autobiography on the Nobel Prize website, Markowitz explains that the theory revealed itself to him whilst reading in the library one afternoon. He deduced that the value of a stock should equal the present value of its expected future dividends. Further, because investors held a portfolio rather than the single, expected best performer, this indicates a concern with risk as well as return. And he followed the lead of Irving Fisher (1906) in choosing portfolio variance as the measure of risk. 'Since there were two criteria, risk and return, it was natural to assume that investors selected from the set of Pareto optimal risk-return combinations' and so they choose portfolios with the highest return for a given risk. This was the way that investors should act. To this day, finance theory is normative, and – despite the elegance and intuitive attractions of many of its core principles – is rarely informed by practice. Thank heavens this is not how engineers design bridges or physicians plan medical interventions!

In summary, academics test managers' acquisition decisions using the criterion of value added, whereas managers frequently have quite unrelated objectives such as enhancing competitive position or diversifying returns. Even if value added were a fair criterion, academics measure it using share price reaction over a few days around the announcement, whereas the real benefits take much longer to become clear. Finally they test everything against an ideal structure which may not be worldly. Finance conclusions inevitably depend on the questions asked, and all too often these are badly framed by researchers.

The post-GFC fallout

The rolling financial crises after late 2007 were described by Reuters (2009) as 'the worst since the Great Depression', and led many to echo the question posed by Queen Elizabeth during a visit to the London School of Economics (LSE): 'why did no one see the crisis coming?' (Besley and Hennessy, 2009). The British Academy responded by holding a seminar that explained the cause was 'principally a failure of the collective imagination of many bright people, both in this country and internationally, to understand the risks to the system as a whole'.

This is code for the fact that financial economists not only missed the approach of the GFC, but many had actively promoted contributing factors such as deregulation, incentive-based compensation and excessive liquidity. Few had any understanding of what was happening during its lead up, which admittedly was complex and was best illustrated by Mark Jickling (2009) of the Congressional Research Service, who has prepared a table that sets out 26 causes of the GFC! Even though most financial economists missed the onset of the GFC and were mute about solutions as its worst excesses unrolled, once calm set in many popped out of the woodwork to rubbish their discipline and colleagues. They put on display the great strength of financial economics: its ability to logically and clearly explain what has already happened.

For example, the working paper by David Colander and colleagues entitled 'The Financial Crisis and the Systemic Failure of Academic Economics'[8] is scathing about financial and macroeconomic models which rely on steady-state markets and the assumption that economies operate efficiently and rationally with no prospect of recurring crises. Nobel economics laureate Paul Krugman held nothing back in his regular *New York Times* column (2 September 2009):[9] 'The central cause of the profession's failure [to foresee the GFC] was the desire for an all-encompassing, intellectually elegant approach that also gave economists a chance to show off their mathematical prowess.'

Barry Eichengreen, Professor of Economics and Political Science at the University of California, Berkeley, wrote in *The National Interest* (May 2009): 'The great credit crisis has cast doubt over much of what we thought we knew about economics.' An article by Professor Amin Rajan is subtitled 'How elegant theories contributed to the 2008 market collapse',[10] and concludes that financial theories which reigned supreme for half a century despite a lack of empirical support contribute to financial crises. This theme was echoed by Paul Woolley in a thoughtful chapter of the LSE's *Future of Finance* report (Turner *et al.*, 2010): 'The evidence of the past decade has served to discredit the basic tenets of finance theory.' Two of these were incentive compensation which was designed to align manager and shareholder interests, but just fuelled excessive risk-taking; and efficient markets which were assumed to be able to value securities, but failed dismally to identify toxicity in so many.

Financial economists are remarkably skilled: their knowledge of mathematical techniques is staggering and their use of them impressive. But it's the old GIGO maxim: if you put garbage into any receptacle, no matter how scientific and impressive, you get garbage out. Virtually the only benefit of the GFC has been to once and for all nail the total inability of financial economists to see ahead and the weakness of their theories and models. For me the GFC (and its numerous predecessors) should have made it clear that the most pressing research objective in finance is to develop an explanation of markets' behaviour that is robust to real-world evidence. Unfortunately the discipline is all but mute on what constitutes better theory.

Let me move on from explaining how fatal the real world is to finance theory and advance some reasons why academic finance has got it so wrong.

The economics discipline is caught in a time warp

The *American Economic Review* (*AER*) is the discipline's premier journal and celebrated its hundredth anniversary in 2011 by commissioning a distinguished panel of researchers to choose the top 20 'admirable and important articles' that the journal had published (Arrow *et al.*, 2011). This presumably would list researchers' most innovative, important and influential thinking. So it seems nothing short of staggering that the most recent of these articles dates to 1981: the leading economists of our day think that it is 30 years since the pre-eminent *AER* published any idea that ranks amongst the discipline's most important! Of the other articles, three were published in 1980, seven during the 1970s, five in the 1960s, and four even earlier.

It is hard to believe that a discipline that pretends to any credibility has not seen a thinking breakthrough published in its leading journal in over three decades. The *AER* seems to celebrate the cognitive slowing of economics. It suggests that researchers show little curiosity about new theories, almost as if all economics questions have long since been answered and everything can now be interpreted through a Beatles-era prism.

From my perspective, finance – which one author quipped is 'the business school version of economics' (Fox, 2009) – seems to be equally mired in an increasingly ancient past. It, too, is little changed in 40 years, and even then it was seen as narrow in that it assumed perfect foresight (to develop forecasts of security cash flows and hence expected returns), and ignored non-economic objectives (which theoreticians decided were irrational) and frictions (which is the generic term for real-world complications such as taxes, transaction costs, illiquidity, operational risk and so on). How, though, can one objectively make such an assessment of a major discipline, much less identify the nature and causes of shortcomings in its research?

Rigidity of thought is clearly seen in finance teaching. Consider the two most commonly used textbooks in the core finance courses of corporate finance and investments which have those names and are authored, respectively, by Brealey *et al.* (2012) and Bodie *et al.* (2011). The staggering aspect of these texts is the extent to which they rely on decades-old theory, and the total absence from their pages of descriptions of core practitioner tools such as fundamental analysis of asset prices.

What, though, is the cause of this? Why have finance researchers done such a poor job in developing robust theory for their discipline? In medicine and engineering – which are two other knowledge-based disciplines with a focus on the future – academics and practitioners work closely together. The best medical practitioners compete avidly for university appointments and teach students what they practise. Engineers, too, take their craft seriously, and apply their university learning from the first day on the job. Why do finance graduates need total retraining? Why is finance theory so unworldly? Why is it so slow to evolve?

The custodians of finance theory

Perhaps more than academics in any other discipline, those in finance jealously guard their exclusive right to develop and succour theory. This preserves a yawning gulf between their knowledge base and what goes on in the real world.

Ruminations along these lines brought an amusing contribution from John Percival (1993) who was then (as he is now) an adjunct faculty member at Wharton. He wrote a piece which described a frog pond in an enchanted land where turtles taught tadpoles how to be frogs using a normative theory of what fish should do in a pond. Frogs who did not follow the theory were deemed to be irrational. Even though the reason for frogs behaving like fish was a puzzle, the instructing turtles could not explain it nor could the irrational frogs. He closed by observing that 'the moral for tadpoles to learn was that we should not let what appear to be facts cause us to deviate from our commitment to sound theory'. As other economists have quipped over the years: introducing more realistic assumptions into theory would only make it unworkable.

There have been just seven articles that reference Percival's parable: academia was not amused. But one of them was by Director of Corporate Planning at Hershey Foods Corporation Samuel Weaver, who makes an excellent case to support surveys that probe managers' decision making. These are used in many other fields as a particularly effective tool that can elucidate the how and why of behaviour. The best examples apply the extended case method, which involves sequentially surveying relevant literature to identify core concepts and theories; compiling empirical data to test these concepts and theories; and then filling in gaps and resolving puzzles by detailed investigation typically through interviews. The last, interview stage involves multiple iterations as actual practice is identified, tested for conformance to theory, and – as necessary – examined further in subsequent interviews to ensure its validity. The approach has proven useful for theory development across the social sciences.

In financial economics, though, surveys and interviews are marginalised as 'qualitative research' that rarely appears in leading journals. It is true that these techniques have weaknesses. I know from my own survey and interview research that as soon as respondents find an academic is involved they instantly start thinking back to their lectures for the answers. Moreover, responses to survey questions cost nothing and are usually anonymous, so respondents are free to report anything other than what they actually do, including what they would like to do. Like a camera, surveys and interviews can only record superficially, or what the subject wishes to reveal.

The intensely analytical approach of mainstream finance research contrasts sharply with the methodology of security analysts in brokers, consultants and investment funds who overlay their models of firm performance with judgements formed from meetings with company managers and other qualitative examination of their subjects. Similarly, management studies tend to be far more qualitative, and interrogate managers about their motives, usually through surveys or interviews. It is a surprise that this seemingly important data rarely transitions in any scale to finance research given that firms and markets appear equally complex, with common roots, because the main topic of finance – asset pricing – involves putting a value on managers' skills.

I am not proposing absolute reliance on surveys and interviews. But we need to recognise that hard data has defects, too: my friend Sean is fond of observing that even a stopped clock is right twice a day. Although using more qualitative data inevitably involves the analysts' values in selection and matching of data, all research techniques involve subjectivity. No data – whether accurate numbers compiled by Compustat or Reuters, or more qualitative material from newspapers or interviews – speaks for itself. To become knowledge and hence of use, all data needs to be codified, analysed and interpreted. Along the way many subjective decisions need to be made: What period and mix of observations will the data span? How will outliers be treated? What explanatory variables will be used? How will endogeneity and auto-correlation of variables be handled? And so on. Thus qualitative data and descriptive models are not uniquely soft, or inherently inferior to qualitative approaches. To me a true understanding of the decisions underlying the financial behaviour of managers and investors comes from observation, discussion and measurement: the three need to be combined to understand what is going on so that a robust theoretical explanation can be developed.

As an aside, there is one area where finance academics do a good job as custodians and that is in ensuring professionalism in research. A plus for researchers, for instance, is that plagiarism – although often talked about – is not commonly seen. A survey asked editors of economics journals how many cases of plagiarism they would see in a typical year. Over 70 per cent said zero, and the balance reported an average of just 1.5 (Enders and Hoover, 2004). Research is also amazingly free of howlers. We see them all the time in small newspapers or tabloids as man-bites-dog stories or breathless reports of alien sightings. But I have not seen too many in finance journals.

Narrow conceptualising of finance processes

Finance has grown up as a mathematically based, analytical discipline that has not imposed a real-world nexus. Decades ago Nobel laureate Wassily Leontief (1982) pointed this out in an interesting letter to *Science* where he argued that too much economics research had come to consist of arbitrary, if plausible, assumptions that produce clear, but totally irrelevant, conclusions. Thus 'econometricians fit algebraic functions of all possible shapes to essentially the same sets of data without being able to advance in any perceptible way a systematic understanding of the structure and the operations of a real economic system'.

Little seems to have changed in the 30 years since this letter was published. In a commentary on the 2008 financial markets crash, University of Hertfordshire Professor Geoffrey Hodgson (2009) wrote: 'To get published in leading journals in economics today it is unnecessary to read or cite any economist beyond the recent past. Most economists are interested in mathematical models.' As a result issues of importance to taxpayers and shareholders – such as the nature and causes of the wealth and poverty of nations and firms – are of limited interest.

Another confining aspect of finance research is that it is biased towards questions that have data. Because it is natural to rely on datasets that are easy to obtain, the answers to finance research questions tend to be sought in public databases that contain security prices, accounting records, and material that can be gleaned from tables in annual reports such as executive compensation. In common with the drunk who has lost his keys and looks for them under the street light where it is easier to see, finance researchers analyse readily available material *ad nauseam*, and this inevitably narrows their conceptualising.

This reliance on hard data to examine what financial decision makers have done leaves researchers unable to tell us anything about *why* individual decisions were taken, nor how data emerged and are evaluated. The inability to observe decisions requires researchers to infer their reasons. Thus, when a stock price changes, analysts give a single explanation drawn from remote observation of aggregated data even though many motives were probably involved. Analysis is rarely informed by real-world practices.

Thus anecdotes abound that poke fun at economics research, with leading academics cheerfully leading the pack. The best example is Professor William Vickrey who won the 1996 Economics Nobel Prize. He was reported by the *New York Times* (12 October 1996) as telling one of its reporters that the main paper leading to the Prize was 'one of my digressions into abstract economics. At best, it's of minor significance in terms of human welfare.' This was echoed in my interviews with fund managers who see academic finance research as having a low standard and little relevance. And, as noted earlier, even the most awarded finance research often has no practical implication.

The data-centricity of finance leaves researchers blind to many non-quantified or difficult-to-quantify variables that are intuitively significant for firm performance such as organisation structure, safety, insurance, manager traits, board effectiveness, company ethos and ethics, training and performance monitoring. So, too, with strategies that go beyond the few for which data are reported such as capital expenditure.

Consider, for example, the mental and emotional capacity of a firm's chief executive and other senior managers. Most organisational behaviour literature concludes that the best measure of predicting performance in any occupation is cognitive ability (Ones *et al.*, 2005). Other studies conclude that 'the CEO is the single most important factor in a company's stock price' (Jackofsky *et al.*, 1988). It almost seems silly to analyse firm financial performance without controlling for its most important driver (that is, CEO brain power), but that is what finance researchers routinely do.

Further narrowing the perspective of finance research is that most powerful constraint in academia – the publish or perish imperative. Academics need to publish to meet hiring conditions and secure tenure; and publication in the best journals is a requirement for promotion to senior ranks. Demography compounds the constraint because researchers tend to be most productive in the early stages of their careers. Whether correct or not, younger academics see the top journals as very conservative and unwilling to take risks with new ideas: they accept a standard presentation style, and conform to the discipline's core tenets. In addition, they have limited resources to undertake research, and time is against them. Thus even the best researchers rarely dare to attempt anything more than incremental adjustments to accepted paradigms. Most obviously, such a limited objective can be completed expeditiously. In addition, conventional results are acceptable to rusted-on traditional academics who are the 'peer reviewers' at top journals. So a conservative strategy offers lower risk of rejection and a brighter career path. Sadly it perpetuates flat-earth theories.

Unfortunately, this aversion to career risk slows progress in the discipline, and leads to what economists term cognitive capture where psychic costs of dissenting from the ruling paradigm are too high. This means that all but marginalised researchers ignore contradictory evidence and other challenges to financial orthodoxy. This depressing attitude led the author of a Business Council of Australia report into higher education (BCA, 2011) to quip that 'suede patch tenured academics are more interested in the status quo than working to produce graduates with the skills necessary to succeed in business'.[11]

Such risk-averse behaviour is understandable for ambitious researchers, but it makes scant progress in their discipline's knowledge and never supports the helicopter view that is essential to build a new paradigm. It also echoes the unkind comment – attributed to Max Planck and common in many disciplines as well as finance – that progress is made one funeral at a time.

Academics' lack of industry contact

One of the most striking features of finance academia is its almost complete lack of meaningful dialogue with the finance practitioners who they educate and whose performance they study. This, too, is entrenched. A major contributor is that academics and investors have different objectives from research. Academics seek to add knowledge by identifying new information that is statistically reliable. Unlike investors, they are not forward looking, nor even greatly concerned about the economic significance of their new knowledge. Thus anomalies, tools and heuristics identified by academics are frequently of no practical use (Hudson *et al.*, 2002).

This was brought home to me in discussion over coffee with an academic colleague. He had previously been head of research at a large European investment manager, and told me of his experiences there after making the seemingly logical assumption that recent findings from papers in top journals should be of use in developing new trading and investment techniques. His group found that a large number of the findings could not be replicated using their databases. 'So what did you do?' I asked. 'We contacted the authors to clarify their techniques – most simply didn't reply.' He filled the silence that stemmed from my bemusement by observing that 'the data must have changed'. There are myriad explanations for the inability to replicate published results. The important conclusion, though, is that much academic research does not transition to the market.

Another important reason why academics do not interface more closely with industry is that there is no market for finance research. For academics, authorship of articles brings promotion, research grants and further opportunities in proportion to the prestige of the journal: this is a barter system where no money is received even for the most valuable intellectual property (Sutter, 2009). Thus the return to research for academics – who author most of the articles in research journals – comes from publication. For finance practitioners, though, there is quite a different return to research as it comes from investor acceptance. The lack of a market for research can mean that academics site themselves in a self-regulated intellectual bubble and remain isolated from the real world to the detriment of their analysis and conclusions.

A Norwegian fund manager expressed frustration to me at the weak involvement of most academics in his business:

> I despair about my academic colleagues. They provide no assistance in making critical decisions, and the limited advice they do give is naive. Take diversification – what do they actually mean? In 1880s USA it meant buying a range of railroad stocks; and a century later it meant TMT stocks. Both look pretty undiversified today. So reweighting is required. But to what? The Index – you just leverage into momentum. Share of GDP – this has a poor correlate to equity prices. Invested funds such as total assets – this means you can become mired in decaying industries.

Certainly there are attempts to make academics' products – such as journal articles – more market oriented. For instance, AQR Capital Management offers a $100,000 prize each year for the academic finance paper that offers the 'most significant practical implications toward improved investment performance'. Otherwise, not much links academics and the finance industry beyond the mundane fact that universities educate the talent that goes into financial institutions, which are the classic knowledge-worker industry.

Is financial economics a science?

An important element of developing better theory within financial economics is to determine whether or not it is a science with the meaning attributed by Kuhn (1970), Popper (1959) and others. Their work is based on the scientific method of enquiry in which observation of reality is integral to building knowledge, and they proposed that a true science has a paradigm which sets out its core concepts and provides a framework to support accepted facts and theories. Thus scientists sequentially conduct systematic observation, measurement and experiment, and on this basis form, test and modify hypotheses. They also require that propositions should be testable along the lines that 'all swans are white' or 'the moon will set at 6.27 am tomorrow'. For theory to be any good it must make useable predictions.

On this basis, financial economics is not a science. It follows a technique that is commonly employed in the social sciences which is to build theories intuitively in the absence of data. It does not have much of a paradigm because – as discussed earlier in this chapter – virtually all its theories and concepts are either disproven, the result of data mining, or untestable. The inability of managers to add value in acquisitions, hedging and other corporate finance decisions shows that finance teachings cannot succeed in the real world. The catalogue of biases in behavioural finance shows that failure to maximise utility is statistically observable.

In summary, financial economics as currently practised lacks the traits of a true science. Moreover, as finance is all about the future for which reliable data are largely non-existent, it seems impractical to develop mathematical expressions of the $E = mc^2$ type. Whilst researchers should not abandon all attempts to develop quantitative models, it would appear appropriate to make a lot more use of theories that have a descriptive or qualitative basis.

What practitioners have to say about finance theory

A major purpose behind my fund manager interviews during 2012 was to understand how much finance theory they use ('very little' was the consensus), and if not, why? I found that their answers had several clear rationales.

The principal reason why fund managers make so little use of finance theory is that it is data-intensive, and the required data are not available. Moreover, theory fails to use information that managers believe is important to their investment selections.

A tops-down investment strategy is very common amongst large investors. The fund's investment managers, perhaps meeting regularly as an investment committee or similar, establish the outlook for global and national economic indicators, and then evaluate the implications for different asset classes and portfolio sectors. This leads to tilts towards or against various sectors and stocks and ignores theoretical rules of portfolio construction.

Thus an Istanbul fund manager told me that financial theory breaks down in practice because of the flow of information, much of which is very difficult to quantify. In addition his investment process relies on predominantly tops-down judgement and strategizing, and so has too many non-quantifiable inputs that cannot fit into quantitative theory such as portfolio construction. Another fund manager in New York told me:

> I don't believe in academic theory, all the curves and lines and equations. We cannot look far ahead: particularly with volatility of returns, I have no idea what they will be. And theory doesn't fit much of our outlook because it has a qualitative foundation. Quantitative assessments are useful for monitoring, but they have no relevance to my investment decisions.

A New York equity manager told me: 'We have dispensed with theory. This took me a long time, but theory is a complete distraction.' A London equity manager summed up many of his colleagues' thoughts: 'Finance students are being given a knowledge framework that is not useful in the real world. We'd be in trouble if that's the way universities trained doctors or engineers!'

A London private equity investor dismissed the value of theory and quantitative analysis and said he didn't believe anyone had the ability to calculate the most important variables over a meaningful time frame. Their biggest uncertainty, in fact, arises from information asymmetry which depends on the quality of existing management. Other important factors such as the market outlook depend on competitors and customers and are unknowable. Last, but not least, comes exit price, which reflects state of the industry at some point in the future. For him, none of this sits within the standard framework and so his thinking is almost alien to that taught in business schools.

Several managers employ quantitative techniques using what they term a pragmatic or a theoretical approach. This is not much more than data mining: identifying price relationships – such as which stock is leading prices in its sector – and trading them until the links break down.

Other managers are bottoms-up stock pickers. They take pride in choosing best-in-class stocks and roughly equally weight them in a portfolio. At best, quantitative portfolio construction becomes important only at the margin when (say) choosing which of two stocks to include in the portfolio. A New York equity manager told me that 'portfolio construction is a consideration, but not a limit'. They shift capital to capture the best risk-return trade-offs, where risk includes liquidity and concentration of interest by other funds.

All the managers seemed to think that they add value through qualitative judgements. A South African global manager told me that his firm's edge is in research, looking at companies and management and using in-house knowledge to identify out-performing investments. Another manager described his investment process as something spiritual.

Many fund managers seem to doubt that stocks have a fundamental value, at least one that lasts for very long. Information does impact stock prices, but is continually arriving, and so the time to trade it is short, maybe days or even hours. After that something else has happened and the original price impact has disappeared. Investors see so much noise in the market that fundamentals make little sense. Several managers had latched onto the idea of Black Swans or high-consequence market shocks with uniquely rare causes that cannot be predicted from historical data, and felt they were so significant and frequent as to undercut the value of compliance, risk management and conventional analysis.

Older fund managers felt that supply and demand dominate markets, and set the price of a stock. These order flows are speculative about what will happen, so that prices rarely reflect fundamentals based on historical data. Most managers noted the importance of behavioural and psychological factors, and were alert to biases in their own decision making. They also pointed out that many buy–sell decisions are involuntary with individuals' investments controlled by mandated retirement saving, thus rendering them forced buyers and sellers, and funds subject to investor cash flows and other factors beyond their control such as ratings changes that mean they cannot hold a security.

Investment managers see risks in the tails of return distributions, and their major worry is a significant fall in the value of an investment, especially soon after buying it. Because correlations between stocks and asset classes tighten during a market fall, even a properly diversified portfolio will lose heavily during a crash.

By contrast the best stocks in any sector outperform no matter what the conditions, because the market does distinguish between quality, largely based on the firm's management. Thus managers look at relative valuations and pick undervalued stocks. In many cases they spend limited time on attempting to forecast future returns, and prefer to use valuation yardsticks such as the price-to-earnings ratio.

An important influence on use of finance theory was the culture of the firm and the investment paradigm of its senior management. Almost invariably, firms where evaluations about non-quantifiable factors like management skill dominated decisions had a qualitative framework. These firms used committees and macro-research to emphasise the importance of human judgements, provided few resources to apply quantitative investment techniques, and employed staff with generalist backgrounds. All of this served to discourage use of finance theory, even by portfolio managers with strong training in the field such as Chartered Financial Analyst (CFA) accreditation or a finance MBA.

One of the more quantitative managers I spoke to is a London private equity investor and he laughed: 'All the investment cases are wrong: things never happen exactly the way you think they will.' So, even though they spend a lot of time building models, these were to structure debate about the future, particularly the sensitivity of returns to the market, the business, the management team and opportunities. For him, the biggest driver of returns is not what they pay but the business that they buy. Even if you buy cheaply, if it is the wrong business that can be a disaster.

Most of the equity fund managers agreed that their business models involve buying good companies with good prospects and management, but at a discount to their true value. One grinned: 'Nobody would tell an investor they are paying over the odds.' A New York value manager said that all his competitors claim to be investing in companies with a strong franchise, good management and top business model. But these never sell cheaply, and so their intent is not realistic. This forces funds to move away from reliance on public information and standard techniques in favour of proprietary approaches that provide a competitive edge. Invariably these are qualitative.

There were two elephants in the room during these discussions. The first was that most managers seem to adopt a variant on the simple strategy of buying good companies on the cheap, which they cannot all be doing. The second was deciding which investment technique *does* work. Most of the fund managers agreed that neoclassical finance theory is not applicable. Several also acknowledged that returns using their proprietary techniques had not been good either. One New York manager encapsulated this with the observation that 'we are much more humble than a few years ago'. The word humble came up in a similar context in three other interviews.

How, then, can a professional manager successfully choose securities for his or her portfolio? To be honest, I did not get a satisfactory answer to this question!

Conclusion

Finance has long faced probing questions that are important to individuals and firms: What sets stock prices? How can I invest? How can I identify a good takeover target? In response, finance academics have developed explanations which find support amongst analysts, financial planners and others who make a living by providing financial advice. Those who do not fund the investments seem to have settled on shared responses to tough questions from those who provide the investment funds.

Despite seemingly broad acceptance of financial theory by academics, researchers and investment industry professionals, it proves impractical to use as a basis for generating superior investment performance. In fact, professional investors – even presumed experts such as fund managers – have difficulty besting amateurs. This is demonstrated by study after study that shows the average fund manager can barely match the return of the Index, and performance does not persist so that this year's winners do not do well next year (Busse *et al.*, 2010).

Researchers respond by criticising practitioners' failure to follow their normative proscriptions, and attribute this to a lack of rationality. A similar schism divides researchers from practitioners, as the former tend to rely on independent, quantifiable data while the latter place importance on less-quantifiable factors. Much of the gap between researchers and practitioners can be traced to use of different data and analytical frameworks. Reality is that finance theory has crippling shortcomings in its development and validation and such weak foundations that it sees little real-world application. Theory rarely survives contact with the real world.

Well before the mid-2000s, it was clear that finance theory had shaky foundations and lacked real-world applicability. Then came the GFC which was a once-in-fifty-year flood that rocked the discipline's foundations. With longstanding doubts about the robustness of theories and recent evidence of their inadequacy, one would expect to see a vigorous debate amongst finance researchers over new theories. We should see new finance theory being generated on an industrial scale. I sought for this effort in vain, finding only a few contributions (discussed above) which were generally insightful but focused on shortcomings of existing theory rather than a new finance paradigm. At this stage, the leading candidate for new theory is behavioural finance, which – despite its growing popularity – is still no more than loosely linked anecdotes.

Does it really matter that finance theory cannot survive contact with the real world? Yes, for two reasons.

The first reason why better finance theory matters is that virtually all of us face retirement funded at least in part from investments: our standard of post-employment living is directly related to the return on our savings. We are each poorer if finance does not deliver the highest-achievable return. Second, these savings are usually invested through finance experts and we rely on sound practice and regulation to keep them honest and effective.

Even though there remains little empirical support for key tenets of finance theory, the profession shows no urgency in developing replacements. Too many look only at what they want to see. It sometimes seems that finance researchers and their schemata would be more at home in a Harry Potter novel.

Notes

1 The best-known depiction of CAPM relates to expected return of individual securities: $R_i = \alpha_i + \beta_i.R_M + \varepsilon_i$; where R_i, α_i, β_i, R_M and ε_i are, respectively, the expected return from security i, its expected excess return (which is known as alpha and should be zero for a fairly priced security), the co-variance of security i with the market (which is known as beta and reflects systematic risk), the expected return from the market (which equals the risk-free interest rate plus a premium related to the risk of investing in the market), and an error term. Under the assumptions of CAPM, investors only receive compensation for non-diversifiable or systematic risks, which are those associated with the market as a whole. The systematic risk associated with individual securities is given by beta, which is the security's return as a proportion of change in the market Securities with a beta of one move in line with the market, while securities with a beta above one have a greater expected return which implies higher risk. Diversifiable or idiosyncratic risks of individual assets can be reduced or averaged out by investing through a portfolio, and so offer investors no reward for taking them. Put differently, diversifiable risks are defined by statistical probabilities and can be reduced to zero by insurance or diversification.

2 For surveys of these findings, see Anderson *et al.* (2009), Bali (2008) and Scruggs (1998).

3 William Shakespeare. *The Merchant of Venice.* Act 1, scene 1. 'Bottom' refers to a ship.

4 This is best expressed in the CAPM-style formulation of expected return: $R_i = \alpha_i + \beta_i.R_M + s_i.SMB + h_i.HML + p_i.PRIYR + \varepsilon_i$ where R_i, α_i, β_i, R_M and ε_i are, respectively, the expected return from security i, its expected excess return or alpha, the co-variance of security i with the market or beta, the expected market return, and an error term;

SMB, HML and PRIYR are returns on stock size, book-to-market ratio and prior year return; and s_i, h_i and p_i are co-movements of security i.

5 Published during 2009–11 in the *Journal of Financial Transformation* and available from his SSRN site http://papers.ssrn.com/sol3/cf_dev/AbsByAuth.cfm?per_id=342721

6 www.att.com/gen/press-room?pid=19358&cdvn=news&newsarticleid=31703&mapcode= corporate/financial

7 www.duke-energy.com/news/releases/2011011001.asp

8 www.ifw-members.ifw-kiel.de/publications/the-financial-crisis-and-the-systemic-failure-of-academic-economics/KWP_1489_ColanderetalFinancial%20Crisis.pdf

9 www.nytimes.com/2009/09/06/magazine/06Economic-t.html

10 www.the300club.org/Portals/0/The_300_Club_Death_of_Common_Sense_300412.pdf

11 Julie Hare, 'Business Takes Dim View of Academe'. *The Australian*, 30 March 2011, page 29.

3

FINANCE INDUSTRY'S INABILITY TO MANAGE WALLS OF MONEY

> A financial expert knows the price of everything and the value of nothing.
>
> With apologies to Oscar Wilde (1854–1900)

A common occurrence in finance is the emergence of an unusually large, sustained cash flow that seeks suitable investments. Some of these are natural such as increased savings when wealth grows. But more often the walls of money are artificial and emerge relatively quickly, either as a result of policy such as tax-promoted retirement savings or from price distortions including speculation. Sadly, these walls of money are rarely handled well: most lead to a run up in asset prices, collapse of the resulting bubble, and local or even global recession. Most offer a wonderful, infrequent opportunity to generate wealth for investors that is usually squandered.

What are these 'walls of money'?

An early wall of money accrued to members of the Organization of the Petroleum Exporting Countries (OPEC) after they doubled oil prices in the early 1970s and then tripled them a few years later. The flow was termed 'petrodollars' and saw motorists in the United States, Japan and Europe transfer massive sums to Middle East oil producers. Some other countries benefited, too, amongst them the Netherlands, whose North Sea oil exports rose so high that they caused the 'Dutch Disease'. This afflicts a previously diverse economy that experiences a sharp rise in export earnings which leads to a strengthening of its currency, decline in traditional exports such as manufacturing and tourism because prices are too high in other currencies, and consequent narrowing of the country's economic base.

It was an interesting coincidence that just as the second 1970s oil crisis collapsed the most important of all walls of money started flowing when governments began to sponsor retirement savings programmes. The first emerged in the United States with the Revenue Act of 1978 which introduced tax incentives that encouraged Americans to save for retirement, and made 401K plans commonplace by the early 1980s. The trend soon became global. In Australia, for instance, a minimum of 9 per cent of all employees' wages is now compulsorily directed to superannuation (retirement savings). The amounts involved are huge. By the end of 2010, Americans' retirement assets totalled $17.5 trillion, with 27 per cent in mutual funds and about another 20 per cent in direct equities. Retirement savings already represent close to half the value of US-listed equities, and another $1 trillion is saved each year, with much of that going to buy more equities.[1]

There have been two other important walls of money in the last decade. The first is the growth of Sovereign Wealth Funds (SWFs), which are government-owned institutions set up to manage revenues from balance of payments surpluses driven by high commodity prices or export volumes, proceeds from privatisation of government entities and similar large fiscal inflows. According to their association, the Sovereign Wealth Fund Institute, there were 68 SWFs at the end of 2012 with a total of $5.4 trillion in funds that is growing by about $400 billion each year. Assets are concentrated, with 80 per cent in the 11-largest SWFs, and – thanks to high oil prices since 2002 – some 60 per cent of SWF assets are sourced from oil and gas revenues.[2] The largest SWFs are government funds in Abu Dhabi, China, Norway and Saudi Arabia, each of which has over $500 billion in assets.

A second wall of money has been driven by central banks in most countries through their policy of easy liquidity. They flooded the world with cash by increasing lending at low interest rates to banks and by buying bonds and other debt securities from investors at ever higher prices (this is termed quantitative easing, QE). It became easier for everyone to borrow at low interest rates. The official line is that this encourages business and consumers to support economic growth. But because uses of borrowings are not controlled, a lot flows straight into speculation.

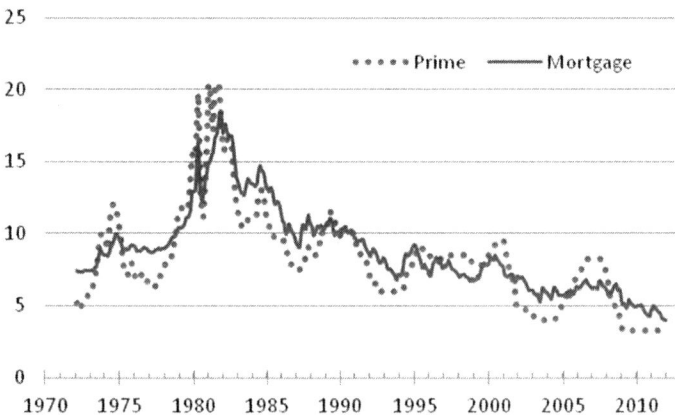

FIGURE 3.1   US prime and mortgage interest rates

The history of this liquidity splurge is most pronounced in the world's largest economy, and Figure 3.1 plots the two main US borrowing rates: prime, which is the rate on short-term lending to businesses, and the rate on a 30-year conventional home mortgage.[3] Interest rates have fallen in a virtual straight line since the inflation-driven spike following the 1970s oil crises.

Loose monetary policy made it easier to borrow money, which as shown in Table 3.1 dramatically increased the level of US debt.

Since 1980, the US economy as measured in dollars of the day has grown about five-fold to $16 trillion, but debt has risen ten-fold. Importantly, growth in debt was not uniform: business debt rose a bit above GDP, and household debt a little faster, whilst federal government debt rose to be 15 times higher.

Far more significant in both relative and absolute terms has been growth in financial sector debt, which surged a whopping 23-fold, or half as fast again as that of the much-criticised government. Through the last 30 years, the financial sector went from being a smaller debtor than any of households, business and government to the largest debtor sector of the economy. In truth, nobody should have been surprised that this led to another classic bubble, which followed the well-known script by collapsing and ushering in a global recession in 2008–9.[4]

A number of fund managers were adamant in their interviews with me that the strategy of lax monetary policy led by the US Federal Reserve caused the boom–bust cycles that have characterised markets since interest rates began falling in the 1980s. Interestingly the strength of this view was proportional to distance from Washington DC, and was especially strong in Istanbul where the manager of a global fund told me forcefully:

> The policies that [US Federal Reserve Chairman] Greenspan created have had a great influence on the direction of asset prices, not just in the US but globally. The basic cause for misevaluation of major markets – and the cause of major financial risks – is excessive liquidity, especially after the late 1990s.

As we will see, a consistent result of walls of money such as easy liquidity is asset price inflation, often of bubble proportions, which few could see as benign. But there are other dangers in these walls of money that merit examination.

Table 3.1 US GDP and debt[5]

	US nominal GDP ($ trillion)	US debt outstanding by sector: $ billion (year end)				
		Home mortgages	Consumer credit and other household	Business	Financial sector	Federal government
1980	2.9	927	470	1,468	585	735
1990	6.0	2,489	1,082	3,768	2,614	2,498
2000	10.3	4,814	2,449	6,679	8,168	3,385
2012	16.2	9,436	3,533	12,727	13,912	11,594

Innovation in credit markets

One of the most striking consequences of the wall of money from higher liquidity and banks' debt has been the creation of new markets and securities for investment. On reflection this should not be a surprise for two reasons. The first is that retirement savings had already begun to swamp existing asset markets such as equities and property, and so any additional investments needed to find a new home. The second is that much of the growth in credit stayed within the finance industry, and went to what it terms financial innovation that created a whole new range of assets to invest in.

Most of these new assets took the form of derivatives sold over the counter by financial institutions, which as private contracts with investors were virtually exempt from regulation. Banks dominate this sector, and the face value of over-the-counter (OTC) derivatives owned by US banks rose slowly from $17 trillion in 1995 to $45 trillion in 2001 and then surged to $223 trillion in 2012.

Table 3.2 uses US data to show how the wall of money impacted on different securities by comparing the face value of all derivatives against that of their underlying asset, which in each case is the physical market. Futures markets are organized, regulated exchanges that trade standardised derivative contracts. OTC derivatives are individualised contracts that trade privately in partially regulated markets.

What can we glean from the table? Mainly confirmation of popular suspicions that increased liquidity fuelled speculative activity that spilled into explosive growth of OTC interest rate derivatives.

What is speculation? The traditional definition is that it involves purchase of a derivative when you do not have an exposure to the underlying security. A firm with most of its debt arranged through bonds that swaps half the bond debt for bills is a hedger, not a speculator. So, too, are farmers who sell corn forward. A hedge fund with no physical exposures that takes the other leg of the swap or buys the corn is the speculator.

Is speculation wise? When stockbrokers were major players in markets, an old stockbroker friend of mine used to call his professional colleagues 'bookmakers to the rich'. The world has changed how we invest, but I suspect his view is still not far wrong! Speculation in the absence of some skill in forecasting is little different

Table 3.2 Face value of US security types, December 2012 (US$ trillion)[6]

Asset class	Underlying		Futures markets	OTC derivatives
	Description	Physical market		
Debt	Debt outstanding	40.3	22.6*	192.1
Equities	Market capitalisation	18.7	2.7*	2.0
Commodities	Ex gate production	Approx 0.6	Approx 0.7**	1.4

Notes: *Covers North America. **Author's estimate from Datastream data. Table excludes $28 trillion in foreign exchange derivatives.

to gambling. And derivatives that offer massive leverage are no different to the high-roller rooms of a casino.

Back to the table, looking first at equities, the face value of OTC derivatives is comparable to that in regulated futures markets, and each is only a fraction of the value of the underlying physical market. Not much speculation going on here. The ratios are somewhat higher with commodities (reflecting speculation discussed below), but the dollar values are small relative to other asset classes.

The real explosion in new assets has been with interest rate derivatives, especially those traded over the counter. The table shows that even five years after the onset of the global credit crisis, the OTC interest rate derivatives market in the United States is nearly five times larger than the physical. This follows a massive surge in the quantum of credit derivatives which grew eight-fold in a decade.

One could understand a derivatives market whose size is up to about that of the physical: that would allow every borrower and lender to hedge or otherwise adjust the risk of their loan. But beyond that level, it is speculators and gamblers who are driving the trades. Because interest rate markets attract a disproportionate number of speculators, they are said to have been financialised. This is code for the fact that paper-based derivative transactions now dominate trading: the volume of derivatives transactions swamps those in the physical markets. There has been similarly large growth in the foreign exchange market, which went from roughly the same size as global exports in the 1980s to a hundred times as much (Turner *et al.*, 2010).

Surely, though, financial innovation adds value? Maybe, but more likely not. Consider innovation after the 1990s in loans for US housing, particularly expansion of the market to those who had not previously qualified (the sub-prime borrowers). According to McLean and Nocera (2010: 362), the home ownership rate was the same in 2010 as it was in 1998: despite trillions of dollars that were squandered through the great recession and collapse of several venerable banks, literally nothing practical was achieved. This supports Paul Volker's comment to the *Wall Street Journal* in 2009 that the vast amounts spent in financial markets rarely bring tangible economic benefit.

The key takeaway from this section is that easy liquidity of the past three decades has stimulated heavy borrowing by the financial sector which has done little more than promote growth in derivatives markets that are used for speculation. Importantly, too, the excesses tabulated above represent the post (not pre) GFC position. This last is significant because it has been notionally low-risk debt securities (and not high-risk equities) that have been central to systemic financial crises such as sovereign debt defaults, the sub-prime crisis, LTCM's collapse and so on.

The extensive volume of debt derivatives that is still outstanding holds the seeds for further crises.

The unanticipated consequences of more working women

An unexpected wall of money can be seen in one of the most basic of human needs, namely shelter, where an increase in the number of working women lifted house prices.

According to a survey in *The Economist* entitled 'Closing the Gap' (26 November 2011), the proportion of women of working age in OECD countries with paying jobs rose from 48 per cent in 1970 to 64 per cent in 2010, which lifted GDP by a quarter (in mute evidence of the inability of official data to capture the value of non-market goods and services such as household work by women).

Although this increase in workforce participation represents great achievements for many women that are both personally satisfying and socially beneficial, it has had a financial dark side. In particular, much of the increase in household disposable income that came from women's wages has simply flowed to funding higher house prices. Many women now find that they have to work in order for their family to buy a suitable house. It seems that instead of generating seamless economic growth the increase in working women has merely precipitated a housing price boom.

To examine the link between more working women and higher house prices let me draw on unpublished work with a colleague. Figure 3.2 uses several decades of data from Australia, and plots the female workforce participation (FWP) rate (which is the proportion of women of working age who are in paid employment or look-ing for work) and the house price ratio (which is the ratio of the median house price to average weekly earnings). The house price ratio is analogous to equities' price:earnings ratio, and is commonly used as a measure of house affordability.

The two variables are strongly linked: as more women entered the workforce, there was a lag and then house prices surged relative to wages.[7] The fact that FWP leads house prices suggests women's income set up a wall of money that washed into spending on houses and pushed their prices higher. This is an intuitively attractive model, and we have identified similar relationships in the Netherlands, New Zealand, the UK and the USA.

It seems that as more women entered the workforce household disposable incomes swelled into a classic wall of money whose potential was (sadly) not properly harnessed and the money disproportionately flowed to bidding up house prices. All the hard work by more working women simply led to asset price inflation.

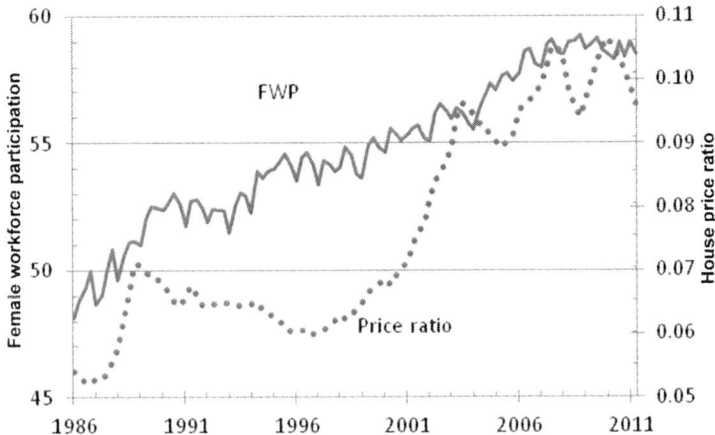

FIGURE 3.2 Australian female workforce participation rate and house price ratio

Financialisation of commodity markets

Another market that has suffered from a wall of money is commodities. The effect here can be traced to collapse of the equity market in 2000 after the dot.com bubble imploded. Then a number of investors decided that commodities could be an attractive investment because their returns are not linked to those of equities and other traditional asset classes. This led to a stampede into commodities, so that a study by the IMF (2011) reported that their share of global pension fund assets rose from 0.4 per cent in 2006 to 1.0 per cent in 2010, an increase worth roughly $100 billion.

What was the impact? A colleague and I answered this question by looking at open interest (OI) in commodity futures markets, which is the number of contracts that are outstanding. If contracts are merely bought and sold between traders there is no net flow and OI is unchanged. But every net new order to buy a commodity future requires an additional contract, so OI rises by one. Thus OI rises and falls according to the total number of contracts that are owned at any time by investors.

Analysis of 22 commodity futures markets looked at prices as a function of the ratio of OI to global production. Our intuition is that consumers and producers should hedge a roughly constant proportion of global production (i.e. total ex mine or farm gate production). Thus OI should move with the total market and keep a constant OI-to-production ratio (or scaled OI), and an increase in the ratio is indicative of increased holdings by speculators (that is, investors who are not hedgers with a matching physical position).

We found strong evidence of speculative activity, particularly in the larger commodity markets such as gold and oil where one would expect it to be concentrated. Figure 3.3 is a typical example and shows results for the gold market and the existence of a strong link between price and OI-to-production.

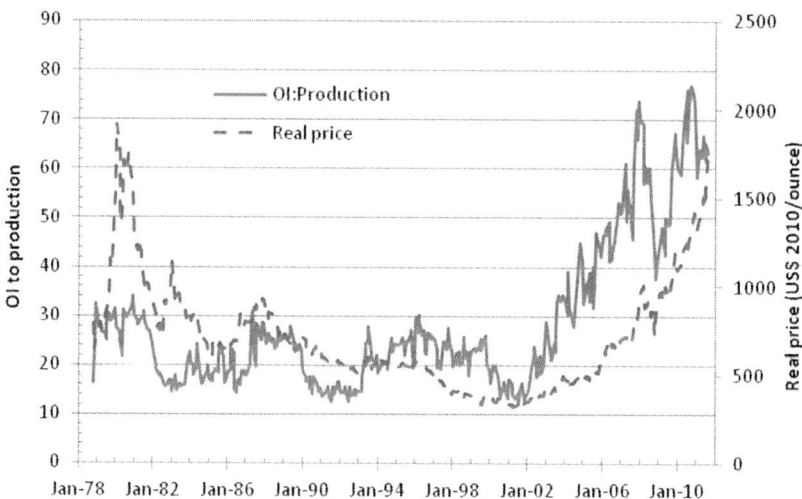

FIGURE 3.3 Real gold price and scaled open interest

Similar relationships apply in other large commodity markets where prices tend to be driven by the level of open interest. That is, as futures market open interest changed relative to the commodity's production, so did the price. Again we have the situation where money has flowed into commodity investments and all it did was contribute to asset price inflation.

The big increase in pension fund commodity investment was matched by other institutions which now dominate futures markets with over a third of OI, and because they tend to hold their positions their strategy is equivalent to hoarding in order to reap speculative profits. The move into long commodity positions led George Soros to tell a European conference in 2008: 'You have a generalized commodity bubble due to commodities having become an asset class that institutions use to an increasing extent.'[8] This view was echoed by hedge fund manager Michael W. Masters in his testimony that year to the US Congress.[9] He argued that commodity prices were being driven up by conventional institutional investors that were allocating a portion of their portfolios to commodities with little concern about fundamental valuations.

Always alert to opportunities, hedge funds and other traders sought to capture the price momentum. The result was a surge of speculative investment in commodity markets whose total value according to a US Senate Inquiry 'increased tenfold in five years, from an estimated $15 billion in 2003, to around $200 billion by mid-2008' (Levin and Coburn, 2009: 5). Although the amounts involved are not large relative to the funds' total portfolios, they are significant in the relatively small commodity markets and constituted another wall of money.

Even worse, traditional hedgers in commodity markets have lost out because the markets' changing composition means that prices are set by investor asset allocations rather than the fundamentals of supply and demand. Thus futures markets no longer provide efficient hedging mechanisms for commodity producers and consumers. This means that everyone from Kansas corn growers to South African gold miners has lost a valuable tool to manage their price risk.

Mutual funds pressure corporates for performance

As noted above, tax-driven retirement savings have flowed into the equities market, but in this case the effect has been positive for investors.

A good idea of the power of tax-promoted savings is given by the US Census Bureau's *Statistical Abstract*[10] which sets out details of the nation's retirement assets held in 401Ks and IRAs. At the end of 2010 they totalled $17.5 trillion, with 27 per cent in mutual funds and another 20 per cent in direct securities, which represents around half the value of US-listed equities.[11] A net of about $1 trillion is added to retirement savings each year, with half going to buy equities. Much of this money is placed in the hands of professional investment managers in mutual funds, which means that these institutions have grown massively and brought considerable change in the ownership of listed companies.

In the 1970s, companies were mostly owned by individual shareholders who were atomised: they had minimal clout, and company managers could ignore them with impunity. Since then, mutual funds and other institutions emerged as fewer, much more powerful investors. Because only the most successful investment firms can prosper, they placed pressure on companies to lift their returns.

The result is shown in Figure 3.4, which for me is one of the most telling charts in finance. The solid line shows the proportion of listed US stocks that is held by institutions and the dashed line shows corporate profits.[12] As savers lifted their ownership of equities after the late 1960s and boosted the clout of institutions, companies responded with a lag by dragging up their profits. To appreciate the scale of this transformation, think of all the restructuring, downsizing and innovation over recent decades: most of this was in response to rising profit expectations of powerful investors.

This wall of money seems to have been beneficial to equities by forcing profit-generating restructuring by corporates. So why did we see a different, more favourable outcome here for investors, whereas higher liquidity did not benefit commodities and debt markets? The principal reason is scale. US equity markets are capitalised at around $19 trillion and net inflows each year are about $500 billion, or 2 per cent. Proportionately this inflow is about a tenth as large as that to commodity markets. Not surprisingly the price impact on equities has been small (many would point to equities' poor performance since 1999 and say it has been negative!).

Second, equity markets have an efficient pipeline to increase their asset base whereby companies issue shares either as initial public offerings (new listings) or seasoned equity offerings by already listed firms. In fact the volume of IPOs during the last decade has been roughly equal to the increase in equity investment through institutions. Thus there has been muted price reaction by equities to net inflows that are modest relative to existing assets and in line with new asset creation. A

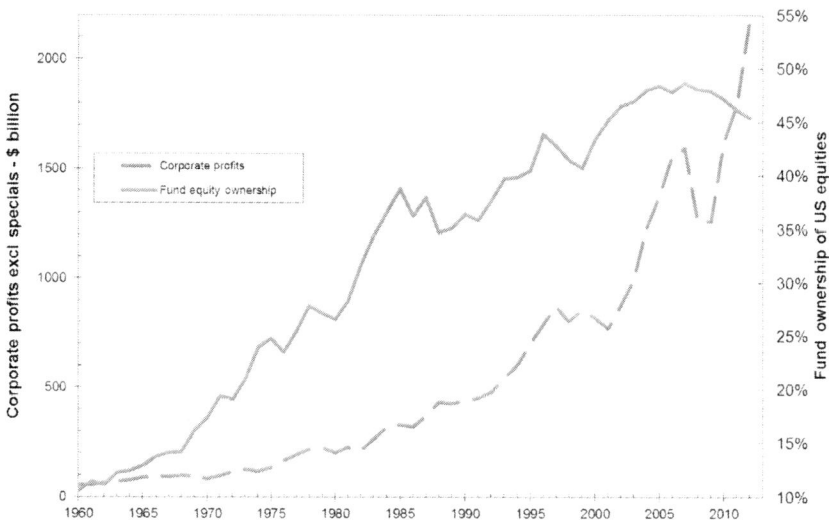

FIGURE 3.4 US mutual fund equity holdings and corporate profits

little more speculatively, equity markets have well-established mechanisms for handling investments so there is good information, reliable counterparty arrangements and reasonable transparency.

In summary, we experience walls of money in many markets – housing, credit, commodities – that unfortunately tend to simply translate into asset price inflation: that is, bubbles. The sequence has been pretty consistent: money surges into the market and drives prices higher. Bubbles then burst, markets move violently down and investors are hurt.

So far we have considered walls of money at the macro level. They have various drivers such as commodity-based sovereign wealth funds, retirement savings, working women and greater liquidity. They typically just lead to asset price inflation, bubbles and tears for investors.

But how do these poor outcomes happen? Why is it that finance experts cannot harness the hosepipes of cash to benefit investors? Let us pursue these questions in the balance of the chapter.

The 'drag' from financial institutions

The principal economic (and social) role of financial institutions is to act as intermediaries and advisers to investors, borrowers and security issuers. They take deposits and make loans and so cut out the search costs if depositors and borrowers had to find each other and arrange transactions. A second role is to provide advice to clients who wish to buy and sell securities and so improve the efficiency of markets (which should benefit investors as well as investees). Over and above that, financial institutions provide services such as transactional banking, insurance and the like, and operate on their own account through trading. Again these latter activities should improve efficiency of markets.

Despite the important roles played by financial institutions, they do not create any wealth. All they do is to grease the wheels between investors who have the funds and the companies and governments which put the money to productive use; it is only the last group – entrepreneurial firms and prudent governments – that create wealth. Certainly services provided by financial institutions represent an economic benefit equal to search costs that they save. Significantly, though, this is largely without risk to banks, and any additional revenue represents income foregone by investors and a drag on their return.

Thus one barrier to investors obtaining reasonable returns from the walls of money has been the size of the take by finance the sector. As we will see, banks that organise new investment opportunities receive around half the potential return. The disproportionate share of banks has been demonstrated in my own unpicking of numerous transactions and is well recognised. McLean and Nocera (2010: 120), for instance, report that 40–50 per cent of the $2 trillion in assets raised by CDO issuance during the 2000s went on fees to banks, CDO managers, ratings agencies and others. Much of this is received up front as fees and commissions, which means that investors' share of the returns is not just cut but is delayed and put at risk.

Banks' take is summarised at a high level in Figure 3.5 using data from the US Bureau of Economic Analysis.[13] Since 1950, the share of GDP contributed by all finance sectors almost doubled to just over 20 per cent; during the same period the share of profits taken by the industry more than trebled to over a third of the total profit of US companies. That is, an industry whose only function is to intermediate and generates 20 per cent of GDP consumes a third of the profits made by all domestic companies!

The growth of the financial services sector and its high level of profitability have imposed a drag on investor income that contributed to poor returns. In short, profits of the finance industry constitute an unacceptably large leakage of monies that would otherwise flow to investors. The drag is most obvious in specialist investment managers (private equity, hedge funds and the like) that typically charge their clients all the expenses associated with investing plus at least 2 per cent in management fees, and then still take a quarter or more of the returns. Even though the drag from other financial institutions may not be as egregious, it is still high.

As an example, Figure 3.6 uses data from Australia to give an indication of the cost imposed by banks for the fairly mundane and low-risk task of arranging housing loans.[14] The solid line shows the difference between the average interest rate charged on standard variable home loans and the interest rate paid on $50,000 cash management accounts. Certainly not all banks' lending is for housing loans (although most is for Australian banks) and banks do not just rely on deposits to source funds. But what this gives is a consistent picture of the amount that banks take for organising a loan. In the 1990s, Australian banking was horribly uncompetitive and banks were able to get a 5 per cent spread between their cost of funds and loan revenue. Deregulation brought competition from foreign banks and mortgage brokers which slashed the margin to about 3 per cent, although the GFC allowed banks to claw back profits and their margin surged.

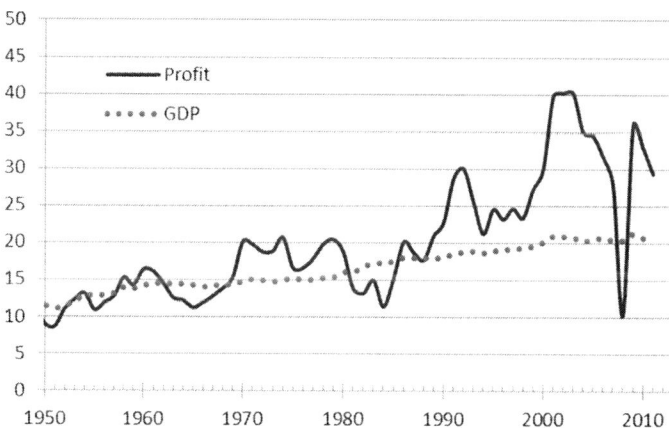

FIGURE 3.5 US finance sector's share of profits and GDP

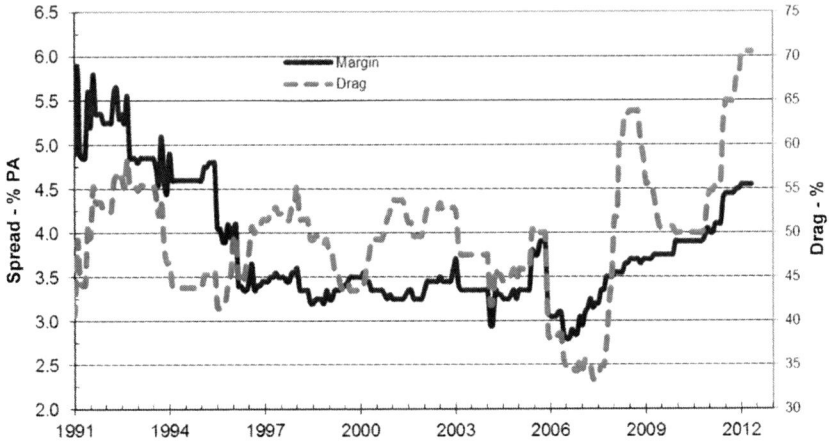

FIGURE 3.6   Australian banks' spread and share of margin

The really interesting aspect of this chart, though, is the dashed line which shows the banks' margin as a proportion of the housing loan interest rate: this represents how the total loan cost is shared between banks (which receive the margin) and investors (who receive the deposit rate). The banks are obviously enti-tled to be compensated for costs of organising the loan, with an allowance for any risks involved, which, of course, is limited as the banks choose who to lend to. But the chart shows that, almost as if it were anchored, through two decades of dra-matically changing industry conditions the banks have consistently taken half or more of the available return.

In simple terms, no matter the state of the lending environment or competi-tive conditions, banks took a roughly constant slice of the interest paid by borrowers. But it is not just in Australia that banks take half the return, as the roughly equal split of interest income between lender and bank is apparent in the United States, too.

Table 3.3 takes information from the *Annual Report* of Citigroup (the most profitable US bank) during 2006, which was the last year before the turmoil of the global financial crisis that led to high write-downs. Citi received interest revenue of $96 billion, paid $57 billion to its lenders and so retained 41 per cent of the interest it received on loans. This is close to the average 48 per cent retained by Australian banks since 1995.

Table 3.3 Summarised Citigroup 2006 annual report

Interest revenue: $ billion	96.4
Interest expense: $ billion	56.9
Interest expense as % revenue	59.0
Compensation and benefits: $ billion	30.3
Other operating expenses: $ billion	21.7
Net profit: $ billion	21.5
Stockholders' equity: $ billion	119.8

Table 3.4 Expenses of listed US financial institutions in 2006

	$ billion	Per cent of bond and equity markets
Wages and salaries	450	0.80
Other expenses (estimated*)	320	0.55
Net income	370	0.65
Total	1,140	2.00
Breakdown of expenses + profit[15]		
Banks	710	1.2
Investment banks	160	0.3
Funds	260	0.5
Other	10	
Total	1,140	2.0

Note: *Other expenses are not reported in Compustat but I estimated them using a ratio of 0.7 times wages which was the cost for Citibank (as per the previous table).

Another perspective comes from the statutory accounts of US financial institutions (FIs), which are collected along with those of other listed firms by an organisation called Compustat and made available to researchers like me. This is the source of the middle column in Table 3.4 which shows costs of doing business for 1,050 US financial institutions (these include banks, mutual funds and other core financial institutions, but exclude insurance companies and real estate investment trusts, REITs). FIs paid wages of about $450 billion, had other expenses estimated at $320 billion, and reported net profits of about $370 billion. The right column of the table shows these expenses as a proportion of the value at the time of physical markets for equities and bonds which was around $57 trillion.[16]

The services provided by financial institutions brought them expenses and profit equal to 2 per cent of market values. That is, the activities of financial institutions took an equivalent of 2 per cent return every year, irrespective of investor earnings. Banks' services impose a significant drag on investors' income.

As an aside, it would be nice to similarly examine operations of mutual funds, but granular data are in short supply, especially for the two largest US funds which are Fidelity Investments and Vanguard Group. Each is privately owned by their founder, his family and employees, and neither publishes an Annual Report for the fund family as a whole, so expenses and profits are secret.

Concentration of finance power

Not only is finance a profitable global industry that takes a significant slice of investors' potential return, but it is also concentrated.

The first feature of the finance industry's concentration is geography: the world's major finance markets, investment managers and finance academics are huddled in and around New York City, with just a few important outposts in the satellite cities of Boston, Chicago and perhaps Raleigh. The explanation is that US markets dominate: US stock exchanges represent over 30 per cent of the c~ tion of all stock markets around the world, and the next largest are To. London at only about a quarter the size of the US (WFE, 2011).

Compounding the industry's geographical concentration is a similarly narrow base of the top finance research journals, namely *Journal of Finance, Journal of Financial Economics* and *Review of Financial Studies*. Using the pre-eminent *Journal of Finance* as a yardstick, the editor's report for 2010 showed that although authors of the 68 articles published came from 85 different institutions, 80 per cent of them were based in the United States, and almost half of all authors came from universities in Illinois, Massachusetts, New York and Pennsylvania. Despite globalisation of communications and internationalisation of finance, it seems that editors of the leading finance research journals draw their material from a limited pool.

Apart from geography, trading is concentrated in a few hands. In the United States, the five largest mutual fund companies own 40 per cent of all funds' assets, up from 34 per cent in 1990 (IC, 2012). On a similar scale, just four banks (namely JP Morgan Chase, Citibank, Bank of America and Goldman Sachs) hold around a third of the market value of derivatives in the United States (OCC, 2012) and across all global markets.[17] Nor is it only stocks that are tightly held because just four swap dealers hold half of the NYMEX oil contracts (Cifarelli and Paladino, 2010).

Concentration of finance is true in many other countries. In Australia the four largest banks made 79 per cent of all loans in 2011, up from 71 per cent in 2002.[18] Large financial institutions now have such market power and concentration that it has become a truism everywhere that they are too big to fail.

There are some natural reasons for bank consolidation, particularly because of their reliance on technology (both IT systems and infrastructure such as ATMs) which benefits from economies of scale, and also capital adequacy where diversification can improve efficiency. But there is no evidence that customers benefit. In fact a study led by Federal Reserve economist Allen Berger found that a major reason for bank consolidation was market power where a more concentrated market allows banks to charge higher fees (Berger *et al.*, 1999).

Apart from parochialism, it is natural for concentration of an important industry such as finance to conjure up suspicions of monopoly power and market manipulation. A hint to banks' possible rationale can be seen in Figure 3.7 which is a plot since 1980 of annual values of the standard deviation of the S&P 500 returns and the US investment banks' share of GDP. The dashed line shows that stock market volatility rose sharply during three periods: 1986–7 around the 1987 market crash; 1998–2002 around the 2000 market crash; and after 2007 and the GFC-induced crash. Each time volatility surged, so, too, did the investment banks' share of GDP. Value added by banks reached a peak leading into each crash.

Uncertainty in equity prices appears to be good for the banks because their profit share grew with each spike in price volatility: even a short-lived surge in equity market volatility provides long-term benefits for investment banks. It is as if a new generation of investors emerges every decade or so that is ripe for plucking, and volatility surges to form a price bubble that sucks money out of their pockets.

It is not a big leap to conclude that banks find advantage in converting walls of money to asset price inflation that lifts volatility of security prices rather than putting funds to productive, less inflationary uses. This leads to thoughts that banks may be

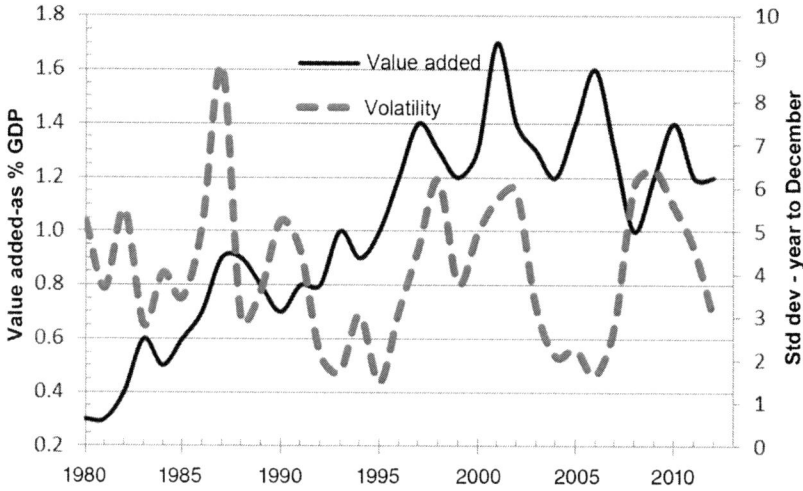

FIGURE 3.7   US banks' share of GDP and volatility of equity prices

running money pumps. Finance, of course, is a zero sum game, with transactions requiring a smart (at least in hindsight) party and a dumb party, along with the lubricant of perceived mispricing of securities. As a result, investors who are dumb, gullible or under-informed run the risk of being taken advantage of by people who create mis-pricing of securities and encourage the less-informed to buy high and sell low.

There is evidence that some people may see retail investors as money pumps. For instance, the letter of resignation by Goldman Sachs employee Greg Smith that was published in the *New York Times* in early 2012[19] described the firm's environment as 'toxic and destructive' and suggested that 'the interests of the client continue to be sidelined in the way the firm operates and thinks about making money'. According to Smith: 'If you were an alien from Mars and sat in on one of these [derivatives sales] meetings, you would believe that a client's success or progress was not part of the thought process at all.' He went on: 'It makes me ill how callously people talk about ripping their clients off. Over the last 12 months I have seen five different managing directors refer to their own clients as muppets, sometimes over internal e-mail.'

Two weeks after the letter was published, I arrived in New York to conduct a series of interviews with fund managers, and tentatively probed their reactions to Smith's sentiments. Those at Goldman and elsewhere expressed shock, and assured me that nobody ever spoke that way about clients. A few others, though, were willing to agree that at least some executives in financial institutions had limited regard or respect for retail clients.

Incentives in investment banking

We saw above that salaries are the largest component of the drag on investor earnings by financial institutions. Even though everybody knows about the high salaries

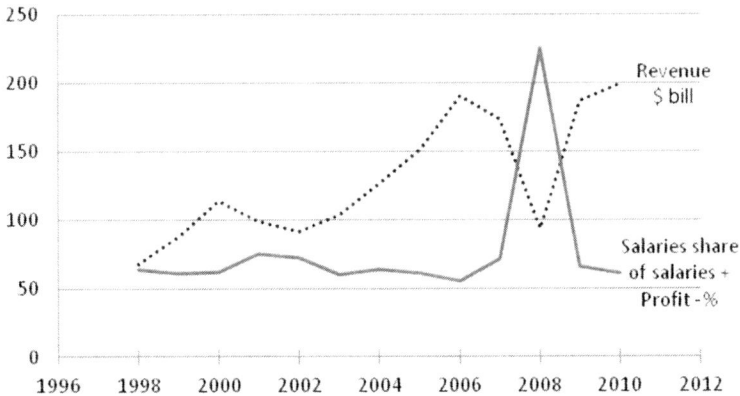

FIGURE 3.8 Investment bank revenues and employee income share

on Wall Street and additional incentives in employee compensation schemes, it is instructive to view them from an investor's perspective.

Figure 3.8 draws on data published by Osiris to show the breakdown of revenue for America's largest investment banks: Bear Sterns, Goldman Sachs, JP Morgan Chase, Lehman Brothers, Merrill Lynch and Morgan Stanley. The upper dashed line shows the banks' total revenue; and the solid bottom line shows salaries as a proportion of salaries plus profits.

The banks have to meet a range of non-salary expenses ranging from travel and rent to interest expense. What is left over is then available to meet employees' regular wages, be paid into a bonus pool for distribution to employees, or be declared as profit (that is, net income) and made available to shareholders as dividends or retained as additional shareholders equity. The chart shows that no matter how bad or good the industry profit environment the banks arranged the bonus pool so that employees received at least 65 per cent of revenues after non-wages costs. As a consequence, shareholders took less than a third of the dollars available to them and employees pocketed the balance. In addition, of course, a slice of the revenues that was counted as expense went on the legendary entertainment enjoyed by bank employees and was further profit lost to shareholders. Roughly speaking, for every extra dollar in revenue that the investment banks earned during the boom period of 2003–7, they passed 17 cents as income to employees but just seven cents to shareholders.

Some insights into the banks' thinking on compensation practices are given in a presentation on Goldman Sachs' website.[20] Goldman uses a measure termed compensation ratio, which equals employee compensation and benefits as a proportion of net revenues (non-interest income plus interest income less interest expense). This confirms my perspective by showing that compensation and benefits during 2000–10 grew at the same rate as revenues so the compensation ratio averaged 48 per cent, admittedly with a lower ratio in the last few years.

There is no doubt that employees must be adequately compensated: the real issue becomes how much of any surplus they should take. Shareholders could rightly expect a disproportionate share of revenue upside because these higher profits are only possible after their equity has built the franchise and asset base of the bank. Boards, though, do not seem to agree and massage earnings so that employees reap much of the benefit. Suggesting this is a serious agency problem is data for 2008 which was a bad year when the banks wrote off GFC losses and profits tumbled. Employees did not share in this pain, though, as their average compensation remained above pre-GFC levels, while shareholders saw only losses. Again we see shareholders shield employees from pain.

Thus comparing bank profit (which is potential shareholder income) and employee incomes shows another example of how banks ensure themselves an almost fixed split of revenue despite changes in the industry environment. Here we see US investment banks consistently paying twice as much to employees as to shareholders. Earlier data revealed that banks in Australia and the United States consistently took almost half of interest income and paid the rest to lenders. The fixed nature of these shares seems surprising in light of the dramatic shifts in economic conditions, strategies of other banks, and the industry environment which would be expected to show up as variation in the shares of employee compensation and shareholder profits. The roughly constant takes are not indicative of a competitive industry, which brings us back to questioning whether the drag from FIs is excessive.

Do finance experts display skill in forecasting markets?

So far my analysis of banks' drag on investor income has ignored any value that might be added by their skill, particularly the ability to provide good advice to investors. Importantly, the key feature of value-adding advice is the ability to accurately look ahead because finance is all about the future. That is, it seeks to identify assets and securities that will perform well (or badly, and so to be avoided). In addition, application of key finance theories relies heavily on the use of *expected* returns and risks of individual securities and links between them. Without the ability to forecast, market equilibrium and rationality are logically impossible; and investment is little more than gambling. By implication, then, forecasting skill is an important factor in determining how much profit banks are entitled to.

At first blush, many investors may wonder whether banks do have forecasting skill because its absence would help explain why the industry has had so little success in managing the walls of money. So let us examine whether finance experts have skill in being able to forecast future movements in security prices and markets generally.

A high-level evaluation of financial experts' ability starts with their forecasts of the economy, particularly periods of negative growth which are most serious for investors. An example is given by Loungani (2001) who found 72 years of negative growth in 63 industrialised countries between 1989 and 1999, and then, using forecasts of real GDP, looked at when the experts identified the recessions: two were predicted in April of the previous year; and four in October of the previous year. But as late as April of the year in which recession occurred, more than two-thirds had not been identified by economists. That is, on two out of three occasions when an economy suffers a year of negative growth, it is not picked up by the consensus of economists until at least four months into the recession year. This is hardly an indicator of skill.

Turning to markets, as one would expect the accuracy of forecasts is a well-tested question with a long history of published evidence. More than an economist's lifetime ago, Alfred Cowles (1933) established the still commonly accepted position with a negative answer to the title of his article 'Can Stock Market Forecasters Forecast?'. There has not been a serious challenge since to this conclusion, which once led Princeton professors William J. Baumol and Burton Malkiel to argue that 'the value of investment advice is virtually zero'. A few examples from different markets suffice to make their point.

Newcastle University professor Steve Easton analysed experts' forecasts of the Australian dollar exchange rate and concluded that only one out of 15 forecasters could outperform a simple no-change prediction (Easton and Lalor, 1995). A similar study of USD exchange rate forecasts by Blue Chip found that they 'are generally unable to accurately predict directional change and are thus of no value to a user' (Baghestania, 2010). That is, currency experts cannot outperform a coin toss.

Another interesting test can be applied to equities (which are the most important market for investors) as there are many forecasts published in the popular media around the beginning of each year. In Australia, the Fairfax newspapers poll about 20 economists and other market analysts from the country's universities, research houses and banks, and publish their forecasts of a variety of economic and financial measures as part of a long-running Economic Survey.

My own review of the average prediction of these financial experts over the last decade was sobering. First, they predicted a rising market in each year, which is hardly very discriminatory but did get the direction right in 6 out of 10 years. But if markets moved randomly up and down, you would expect success like this to arise by chance in 38 per cent of decades. Again we see that using the consensus of these experts to invest is only marginally better than tossing a coin! For those interested in precision, the average absolute error of forecasts is 16.5 per cent.

There is much other similar evidence of finance inexpertise, and for over 80 years it has been clear that well-resourced, experienced market analysts can barely match predictions from a coin toss. A good summary of what we know about the forecasting skills of financial experts was given by Don Argus, former chairman of BHP Billiton and National Australia Bank (*The Weekend Australian*, 23 February 2013): 'A healthy dose of common sense and historical perspective is vital when evaluating the sophisticated mathematical models that guide so much of our economic life.'

This raises the interesting question: if finance 'experts' are so consistently not, how do they survive? Obviously because at least some investors listen to them. So what motivates investors to take advice that is almost certainly useless? The answer, of course, is speculative; but an insight is provided in a study by Önkal *et al.* (2009)

who find that people prefer stock forecasts from experts rather than a statistical technique (even though they must know that the human forecasts are at least cognisant of some mechanical analysis). The authors hypothesise that this reflects a human need to believe that the world can be understood rationally and so is predictable. As Bertrand Russell (1919) said, people believe what they hope for: in finance, as in so many other areas of life, hope trumps experience every time!

The dubious basis of active investment management

Another perspective on financial experts' skill comes from examination of the performance of active investment managers. They are the classic stock pickers who seek to identify securities that will over- or underperform the market, and follow these decisions to populate portfolios of the mutual funds which now own close to half of many markets (Aggarwal *et al.*, 2011).

The overwhelming consensus of research literature is that the average return from actively managed mutual funds is no better than that of the market. Even the top-performing funds show no replicable skill because returns do not persist from one year to the next. Thus it can actually be a successful strategy to follow poorly performing funds because their performance frequently turns around. These results are evidence that few active managers have skill, and are consistent with the comment to me from a research house manager that 'there is less genuine investment talent out there than people realise'.

During my interviews, several fund managers told me they had calculated the proportion of their investment decisions that proved profitable and each was just below 60 per cent. A New York equity manager told me of their 'really good US portfolio' where 57 per cent of ideas outperform the S&P 500. In his view, managers way overestimate the proportion of times they are right.

A New York lawyer was more colourful about the behaviour of fund managers:

> Value investors have a cold, analytical approach that is socially discomforting. Quants are the smartest, dumb people on the planet: they perceive that numbers written on paper have power; once a number is written down, the risk is erased and all uncertainty disappears.

A significant contributor to money managers' low value add is that a surprising number simply do not know what they are doing. The magnitude of gaps in their knowledge was driven home to me when reviewing a proposal brought forward in 2007 by a leading Australian investment house for a property fund in Malaysia. The investment outlook appeared favourable, but foreign investors could not own property in Malaysia, and so the fund intended to transfer legal ownership of its properties to Merrill Lynch whilst keeping the economic benefits. I suggested this would be quite expensive given that it had to be backed by regulatory capital, but the fund manager, who himself was making the presentation, said it would only cost about 10–20 basis points. 'Then it cannot be on Merrill's balance sheet,' I suggested. 'Who will be the owner?' After a long silence, consternation grew and he said they would have to get back to me. The presentation predictably terminated almost immediately, along with any interest we might have had. The staggering thing, though, was that the manager's understanding of the core features of his property fund was so shallow that he had agreed to turn over title of its assets to an unknown party.

Another afternoon I sat in New York with the chatty manager of a global thematic fund who expanded on the macrotrends that drove his strategy. One involved managing complexity which he had identified after meeting with companies that were facing challenges in how to handle far-flung markets and operations. Although he painted this as a fresh insight, a moment's thought shows that numerous companies are selling enterprise-wide systems to meet just this need (in fact, IBM, SAP and so on were on his list of target investments). And a Google search of the phrase 'managing complexity' brought 350,000 hits, including a 2007 paper that began: 'Complexity is today often considered the latest business buzzword.' Not much innovative thought here! Another topic he raved about was the emerging surplus of natural gas in the United States, and it quickly emerged he thought this was the same product as the gas used to fuel cars and fill barbeque bottles (which is propane or butane, not natural gas which is largely methane). Again not a very deep understanding of what he was doing.

How can such yawning gaps in knowledge persist? My experience is that money managers are rarely challenged, and so there is no process in place to identify any weakness in their assumptions (which must doom their conclusions). This is not helped by the fact that most employees of financial institutions are young, have a short-term perspective and are encouraged to herd. This leads to trend following and market over-reaction that sees decisions whipsawed and promotes high volatility, which, as we saw above, benefits the financial institutions. Analysts' unwillingness to peer too hard into gritty detail can see them obsess over what firms report (through financials, press releases and so on) and neglect what is not reported. This leaves them blind to emerging problems, which explains why their skills are rarely used creatively by the firms they study. If analysts had skills of value in analysing companies, they could expect to be headhunted for board positions and senior strategy roles: few are.

A complementary contributor to fund underperformance is that returns are often of less importance to their managers than is the task of attracting new clients. The principal source of income for most funds is from fees related to the value of funds under management, rather than anything linked to investor returns. Thus, for a fund manager to be financially successful requires building the quantum of funds under management, which in turn relies on attracting sufficient investors who believe that the manager has skill in leveraging a driver of prices.

This can see a fund's manager spending more time on marketing than research. Most of those chief investment officers (CIOs) that I spoke to complained they spend half their time in client meetings rather than investing, and so their presentation skills can be more important than investment ability. Obviously from the investor's perspective, choosing CIOs on these bases does not always ensure skill in making superior investment decisions, or in recruiting good subordinates who can independently run the investment business while the manager is off doing the marketing. As a New York equity manager explained succinctly to me: 'In money management you sell a process, and its integrity and the character of returns.' Performance comes a distant second in too many cases.

Because out-performance is so hard to deliver and sustain, funds can prefer to focus investor attention on a strategy that they claim will deliver good returns. All too often, the proposed strategy may be plausible, but, like the thematic guy above, has dubious links to results.

An example is the classic marketing pitch which sustains flows into emerging market funds. It is based on the link between economic growth and equity performance, and predicts that rapid growth in developing economies will bring better investment returns. Reality is that this economy equities link is a porky, no matter how appealing or intuitively obvious it might seem. That is because the consensus of economic studies is that high economic growth does not translate into good investment returns (e.g. Ritter, 2005). Moreover, the real profits in developing economies are not made by the listed stocks that most funds access, but in private, unlisted firms. Simply throwing money at countries whose economies are expected to grow fast (whether emerging markets or not) may make intuitive sense, but history suggests it will be a poor investment.

An alternative explanation of poor fund performance that is kinder to their managers is provided by Berk and Green (2004) who suggest that at least some active managers do add value, but they expropriate it in higher fees. The authors explain the lack of persistence in performance by the fact that investors chase returns, and so funds under management move in line with previous performance. Thus a good performance by a fund leads to increased investor inflows. Although this is good for the institution's earnings, these additional funds must be invested in less-preferred securities which will lower fund return. Whatever the reason, though, active investment funds can prove a poor choice.

Fund managers that I interviewed largely agreed that the *average* manager might not add value (although assuring me that their process did). But a London fund-of-funds manager quipped acidly: 'If I were brutally honest about funds management, it's a low value added industry.' He argued that it has the hallmarks of a cottage industry. The main motivation is to gather assets rather than secure good performance. Groupthink is rife because competition drives funds to herd. He told me he finds it ironic that fund managers say they look for well-run companies to invest in, but the funds themselves are so badly run.

Sadly the funds management industry seems structured so funds capture much of the rent, which delivers Ferraris to fund managers and average returns to investors. The dubious benefits of investing in actively managed funds bolsters the case that the average fund investor is an idiot to pay for active management which cannot be delivered (see Gruber, 1996).

Finance lends itself to conspiracy theories

Given the obvious importance of finance to all the world's citizens and the industry's shortcomings, it is not surprising to have seen a proliferation of sinister interpretations, especially suggestions of malicious conspiracies.

Prominent amongst the conspiracy theorists is Professor Carroll Quigley (1910–77) who taught history at Georgetown University and was acknowledged as a mentor by Bill Clinton.[21] Many of Quigley's ideas were set out in his 1966 book *Tragedy and Hope* where he wrote (pages 323–4) that leading financiers sought 'nothing less than to create a world system of financial control in private hands able to dominate the political system of each country and the economy of the world as a whole'. He suggested the world's central banks would use the Bank for International Settlements in Basle as a cover and secretly manipulate their global economic power to benefit financiers.

Reality, of course, is that reputable researchers do not believe in a conspiracy to control the financial system and enrich conspirators at the expense of everyone else. Nor am I a conspiracy nut, figuring that it is too hard to effectively organise a genuine conspiracy because they are so complicated, and prefer to believe that stuff-ups are more likely explanations of puzzling events or situations.

Apart from stuff-ups, an alternative explanation for conspiracy-like abuses in finance is that they are manifestations of individuals' greed. Some people in finance can be classified as glib marketers, driven analysts or ruthless deal makers who think like the investment banker who told me over a drink that 'we only eat what we kill'. In my experience these people totally ignore the big picture because they are rewarded deal-by-deal in what *The Economist* (21 January 2012) referred to as 'the one-night stands of finance'. They are focused solely on their own gain, and do not have the scope or vision to be interested in group activities which are key for the conspiracy-minded. The focus on immediate returns by many in finance leads to the common complaint by New York cabbies that young bankers don't tip because they never expect to see them again. A New York equity manager told me what happens when this attitude is aggregated to the bank level: 'Banks strategise for good medium-term returns: they are happy if they have six or eight great years between each financial explosion.'

A New York securities lawyer had a different interpretation of the behaviour of Wall Street by seeing deep-rooted causes of the finance industry's problems, which he blamed on Sigmund Freud and modern psychology that promoted the concept that self-actualisation is good. This was interpreted by finance sector workers in light of modern economic theory that looks solely at the efficiency of transactions. They support incentive compensation which delivers massive individual and firm returns on the basis that self-actualisation is an economic good because it promotes efficiency.

The net is that quite decent people promote a moral construct which allows immoral colleagues to pillage clients. Thus the finance industry is structured and operates so that conspiracy ideas can survive.

Conclusion

This chapter offered a couple of messages. First, since the 1970s the finance industry has seen regular waves of incremental investments, some of them one-offs such as commodity-driven sovereign wealth funds, and some more permanent such as an influx of working women and increased retirement savings. Although each provided great opportunities for investors to obtain good returns, most proved stillborn. Little of the earnings potential from the walls of money was tapped efficiently, but went to build new products with, as we will see later, excessive risks and asset price inflation, or was captured by employees of financial institutions. The final message is that the finance industry is highly concentrated, with a handful of banks that are able to set its structure and arrange their affairs to secure advantage through changing environments so they can distribute revenues for the benefit of employees. As a result, almost irrespective of the environment, banks take a roughly fixed share of investment revenues to the detriment of investors, and give employees a disproportionate share of these revenues to the detriment of shareholders.

Through the 2000s, financial institutions grew dramatically. But much of this was funded by debt, which leveraged profits, as did expropriation of return generated by risk taking with investors' funds. As pointed out in a report from the London School of Economics (Turner *et al.*, 2010: 87), the fact that bank profits outpaced revenues suggests the finance industry 'underwent a productivity miracle from the 1980s onwards'. In fact, though, much of the growth came from risk taking through higher leverage and new products which became so high that disaster was inevitable.

What is the alternative? One is for the finance industry to be more creative. It certainly has adequate human resources because high salaries attract many of the world's brightest people. The title of the chronicle of Enron's spectacular downfall – *The Smartest Guys in the Room* – is apt. The walls of money represent a surfeit of demand for investment, which calls for innovation in identifying additional investment opportunities. These new products can be obtained from pushing or pulling. Pushing new products identifies opportunities and develops products to promote them. It involves picking winners, or at least the best ideas. The alternative is more passive and allows innovation to bubble up, provides the capital to support ideas development, and lets them grow organically.

A good example of opportunities that are wasted is apparent to anybody who drives, flies or uses mobile electronics as they know that the infrastructure supporting these technologies is fully taxed. This is true in every country with an expanding economy. Quite simply, the pace of infrastructure renewal has lagged so badly that a report by the OECD puts the need for new infrastructure investment at $US 3 trillion per year,[22] which seems like an ideal sink for funds. Sadly, though, the finance industry blew this opportunity after the mid-1990s by exploiting the information asymmetry between security manufacturers/marketers and investors who were interested in infrastructure as an asset class. Its solution was public–private partnerships (PPPs) but these rorted the system and brought sub-optimum funding for governments and disastrous returns to investors. Investor appetite has been blunted. This feeling, of course, has been reinforced and compounded by other products that burned investors by pushing them into overpriced securities ranging from dot.com IPOs to dud asset classes like CDOs and sub-prime mortgages.

Given all the shortcomings discussed above, it is not surprising that finance fails to meet its core mission of efficiently and cost-effectively providing funds to finance the strategies and growth of firms and government and securing optimum returns for investors.

Notes

1　See: www.census.gov/compendia/statab/2012/tables/12s1216.pdf; and www.world-exchanges.org/statistics/annual/2010/equity-markets/domestic-market-capitalization

2　SWF Institute. www.swfinstitute.org/fund-rankings

3　www.federalreserve.gov/releases/h15/data.htm

4　OECD real GDP change was negative in each of the four quarters to March 2009 (http://stats.oecd.org/#).

5　Sources: US Federal Reserve, *Flow of Funds Accounts of the United States* (www.federalreserve.gov/releases/Z1/Current/z1r-4.pdf), Table D3; and Bureau of Economic Analysis (www.bea.gov/national/index.htm#gdp).

6　Sources: Total credit market debt outstanding: US Federal Reserve, *Flow of Funds Accounts of the United States*, Table D3; US equity market capitalisation: World Federation of Exchanges, *2012 WFE Market Highlights* (www.world-exchanges.org); Commodity production is agriculture, minerals and fuels (Tables 844, 907, *Statistical Abstract of the United States 2012*); futures markets: Bank for International Settlements, *Exchange Traded Derivatives Statistics* (www.bis.org/statistics/extderiv.htm); derivatives: OCC Quarterly, *Report on Bank Trading and Derivatives Activities* (www.occ.gov/topics/capital-markets/financial-markets/trading/derivatives/dq412.pdf, page 12).

7　As an aside, readers with an econometrics background will wonder whether female workforce participation and real house prices co-integrate. This refers to the fact that each is a time series, so there is concern that the two are simply growing over time due to common factors that influence them both such as a larger economy or population, which would mean the apparent relationship between them is spurious. This problem was tackled by Paul Engle and Sir Clive Granger and its resolution earned them Nobel Prizes. They developed the concept of co-integration, which means that two variables have a linear relationship that is independent of their time series properties, and is demonstrated by mean reversion of the residuals from regression of one variable on the other (Engle and Granger, 1987). In this case, house prices and FWP do co-integrate, so readers need have no concern that their apparent co-movement may be spurious.

8　Bloomberg, 17 April 2008. www.bloomberg.com/apps/news?pid=newsarchive&sid=aLSge4iZvG3g

9　http://hsgac.senate.gov/public/_files/052008Masters.pdf and http://hsgac.senate.gov/public/_files/062408Masters.pdf. See also Masters, M. W. and White, A. K. 2008. The accidental hunt brothers, Special Report. www.accidentalhuntbrothers.com/?p=67

10　Available at www.census.gov/compendia/statab/2012/tables/12s1216.pdf. See Table 1216.

11　See Investment Company Fact Book at www.ici.org/pdf/2011_factbook.pdf and www.world-exchanges.org/statistics/annual/2010/equity-markets/domestic-market-capitalization

12　Table L213 of the US Federal Reserve's *Flow of Funds Accounts of the United States*, available at www.federalreserve.gov/releases/z1/current/data.htm; and Bureau of Economic Analysis, *Income and Product Accounts Tables*, Table 6.16D.

13 Bureau of Economic Analysis, *Income and Employment by Industry* and *Value Added by Industry* (www.bea.gov).

14 Sourced from Reserve Bank of Australia, *Statistical Tables*, F04 and F05. www.rba.gov.au/statistics/tables/index.html#money_credit

15 Companies are classified by NAICS sector: Banks – 5221; Investment banks – 5231; Funds – 525; Other – 5239. These cover SIC codes 60, 61, 62 and 67.

16 Treasury securities and corporate debt outstanding $32.7 trillion; market value of equities $24.4 trillion. From US Federal Reserve, *Flow of Funds Accounts of the United States*, Tables L4 and L213. www.federalreserve.gov/releases/Z1/Current/z1r-4.pdf

17 www.occ.gov/topics/capital-markets/financial-markets/trading/derivatives/dq211.pdf

18 Monthly Banking Statistics at www.apra.gov.au/adi/Publications/Pages/monthly-banking-statistics.aspx

19 Available at www.nytimes.com/2012/03/14/opinion/why-i-am-leaving-goldman-sachs.html

20 www2.goldmansachs.com/investor-relations/corporate-governance/corporate-governance-documents/compensation-practices.pdf

21 During his speech accepting the Democratic Party's presidential nomination in 1992. See www.4president.org/speeches/billclinton1992acceptance.htm

22 www.oecd.org/dataoecd/24/1/39996026.pdf   and   www.imf.org/external/pubs/ft/weo/2011/02/weodata/index.aspx

4

RISK! WHAT RISK CAN THERE POSSIBLY BE?

> Except for the palatial offices, nothing is what it appears in finance.
>
> Anonymous trader

The nature, causes and consequences of corporate and investor risk are one of my research passions, and much of my thinking is set out in a recent book, *Risk Strategies: Dialling up Optimum Firm Risk* (Coleman, 2009). This chapter develops concepts from that book to analyse risk in the world of finance.

Managers in most industries spend a great deal of time worrying about risks, which they see as having many aspects and contributors: to their business and employees; for their customers; following corporate strategy; and from competitors, government and other outside influences. Firms think of risk as an adverse impact on their income, and sometimes, particularly in industries such as manufacturing or energy, as misfortune for their neighbours or environment. Risk is broad based and ever present. A fund manager in New York who thinks along these lines told me: 'I constantly worry that we have got something wrong.'

Because firms spend so much time identifying and managing their risks, they are generally well recognised and communicated. Biotech researchers, for instance, will parrot the sober warning that just 1-in-5,000 drug discoveries becomes a blockbuster, and it takes up to 18 years and over $1 billion to get to market. Companies in dangerous industries know that – even with the best safety programmes – human error occasionally kicks in and they will have a fatality: in the United States, for instance, one miner is killed for every ten million man hours worked.[1]

But risk in finance – like everything else in the industry – is quite different to that in the rest of the world. First, finance customers are almost unique in facing concentration risk, whereby they are reliant on one firm or at best a few firms to manage their assets and transactions. Banks encourage all of us to set up recurring electronic payments and direct deposits of income so it becomes impractical to change banks. It is impractical, too, to diversify investment advice and other financial services. Thus bank customers and investors have a totally different and far more risky set of constraints than supermarket shoppers.

Another difference is that finance does not clearly communicate its risks, preferring mystique bordering on secrecy. Financial institutions never tell their clients the truth, which today is: 'Investors, based on our performance in the last decade, you are unlikely to significantly increase the value of your investment.' They never admit what we saw in the previous chapter which is that higher volatility or market risk increases their profits, and so banks have a vested interest in lifting market uncertainty for their customers. And to cap this off, finance prefers to report risk using irrelevant measures such as value at risk (VaR: of which more later in this chapter), or multiple measures over different periods that are confusing. Risk in finance is so poorly understood that the industry has managed to direct investors' attention away from the likelihood of poor returns.

Finally, as we saw in the previous chapter, banks tend to insulate themselves and their employees from risks arising through changes in markets and business environment. Effectively the finance industry has structured itself so that investors bear *all* the risks, except in times of crisis when exposure spills over to the economy more generally. Employees of banks are handsomely rewarded, with additional benefits when profits rise (even if the surge is quite beyond their influence such as in times of rising commodity or security prices). Investment advisers receive fees based on funds under management, and regulators are salaried. Everybody except the investor is dealing with other people's money, so their compensation is always generous, even when returns are negative. All risks fall on investors and taxpayers.

The risks of bank organisational structure

To quantify risks in the finance industry, let us start with a macro view. Figure 4.1 plots the annual frequency of bankruptcies of US financial institutions.[2] They come in waves, and peaked during 1990–2, 1998–2002, and on a tsunami scale in 2008–10.

Although these crises are typically shrugged off as aberrations, the chart shows that financial risk – in this case as evidenced by bankruptcy of US financial institutions – is always with us. The United States sees at least one bank failure each year, and the frequency of financial crises has doubled since the onset of deregulation after 1970 (Allen *et al.*, 2009).

Financial institutions do not become bankrupt by chance, and almost by definition the bankruptcy peaks reflect systemic crises. The two latest, which occurred after the terrorist attacks on 9 September 2001 and the peak in financial stocks in late 2007, have been compared, respectively, to the Japanese attack on Pearl Harbor in 1941 and the NYSE collapse on Black Tuesday 1929, as if two of the greatest shocks in US history recurred within just a few years. Financial risk is endemic and getting worse: investors ignore it at their peril.

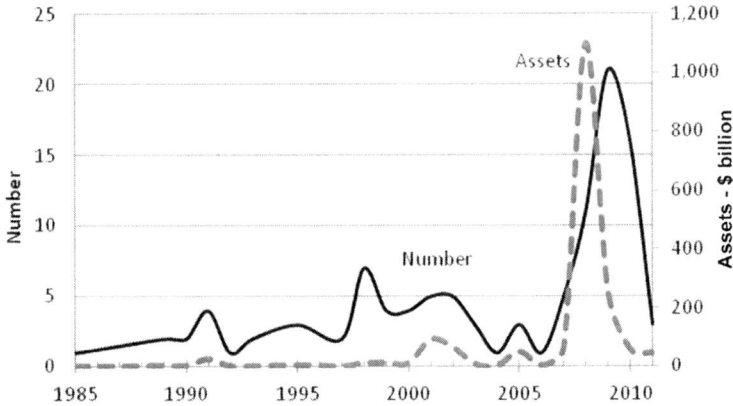

FIGURE 4.1 US financial institution bankruptcies

The flimsy nature of risk models

What leads to such financial risk that banks regularly fail? Certainly regulators are frequently blamed. But their role is no more than to monitor and constrain risks by others, and they do not initiate or take risks. They operate after the event with minimal opportunity to avoid collapses, and are always playing catch up, so it is unrealistic to expect that regulators can eliminate investor risks. I cover regulators' functions and strategy in Chapter 7, and in this chapter want to pursue financial risk from the perspective of risk takers who directly cause collapses.

The concept of financial risk and tools for its management grew out of the classic book entitled *Portfolio Selection* by Harry Markowitz (1959), which popularised the definition of financial risk as the statistical uncertainty or standard deviation of security returns. The driver was that returns have a known probability distribution based on history, and so are amenable to precise calculation and mathematical modelling. The book also highlighted the premise of diversification in which a basket of securities is of less risk than just a few stocks. These ideas led to the concept of financial risk management, which optimises an investor's portfolio by diversifying its composition to achieve maximum return for a given level of risk or uncertainty.

The finance view contrasts sharply with risk in other fields where it is a largely qualitative judgement about the possibility and quantum of a loss. This is close to what Frank Knight (1921) called uncertainty, which sees the future as indeterminate because it will be shaped not just by unknowable data but also by people's future decisions and actions. This is why most people outside finance believe that except in the case of repetitive processes such as manufacturing or credit approvals uncertainty cannot be measured, only estimated using perception and judgement that invite debate and controversy.

Unlike other industries, finance follows its quantitative nature and reports risk as a numerical measure, steadfastly faithful to Markowitz's half-century-old idea of it as statistical uncertainty in the value of a security, asset or portfolio. The most commonly used technique is a measure called value-at-risk (VaR) which expresses the probability of a given loss over a stated period: a portfolio, for instance, might have a 5 per cent probability of losing $1 million on any trading day.

As an example, consider how Goldman Sachs describes its use of VaR (page 103 of the 2009 10-K):

> VaR is the potential loss in value of trading positions due to adverse market movements over a defined time horizon with a specified confidence level. For the VaR numbers reported, a one-day time horizon and a 95% confidence level were used. This means that there is a 1 in 20 chance that daily trading net revenues will fall below the expected daily trading net revenues by an amount at least as large as the reported VaR.

There are no other details of the calculation methodology such as the nature, frequency or time period of data used to calculate VaR; nor details of trading positions included in the calculation.

VaR calculations are developed by sophisticated models and so give a lot of comfort to their users. Advocates stress the benefits from systematising risk and the critical thinking and extensive data collection that are required. Use of a single number to encapsulate so many complexities is also attractive to senior executives and regulators. Thus VaR looked like a powerful risk management tool when invented in the 1990s. Sadly it is riven by defects.

First, the structure of statistical measures such as VaR is inevitably limited. Each relies on the assumption that markets will deliver an expected return over the long term. This is the rationale for slogans along the lines that 'It's not market timing that's important, but time in the market'. What VaR does is to measure short-term deviations from this mean, usually looking ahead by a single day, and never more than a few weeks.

Although VaR may be informative for portfolio managers who want to stay close to the returns of their peer group, it conveys limited information for investors, particularly because it buries tails. Returns on most securities are roughly normally distributed, and when plotted give the familiar bell curve. VaR concentrates on the 95 or 99 per cent of days that lie within the main body of the bell curve: thus it focuses on what is *likely* to happen on most days. VaR ignores the uncommon days that comprise the tails which hold periods of major falls (and rises) in the market and hence the risks that worry investors.

Simply knowing the probability of a given short-term fluctuation tells average investors nothing about the real risk facing them, which is the probability that the portfolio's performance will be below a target level. Investors are concerned about the long term: how much could I lose over the next five years, or until retirement? As a New York fund manager told me:

> If you invest for the long term for retirement or a child's education, you have a 20-year view or more: why do you care about daily volatility? Nobody can think that a short-term measure like VaR is useful over the long term.

Financial risk management also tends to ignore what it terms systematic risk, which is the possibility that the whole market underperforms. For example, the major US stock market index, the S&P 500, was virtually flat from 1965 to 1978, and range traded from 1997 to at least 2013. Overall market risks are dismissed because everybody faces them equally, and so they tend not to trouble fund managers or regulators (at least not in their professional lives).

Another shortcoming of VaR models is that they assume that risk characteristics calculated from historical data will persist. To the contrary, there is no evidence that historical data in combination with even the best econometric techniques have anything more than trivial ability to forecast security performance. This is particularly true of returns, which at most have weak auto-correlation over days and mean reversion over years (Cochrane, 1999). Although forecasts of risk have more success, even the most sophisticated models cannot predict more than 30–40 per cent of variation in the next day's volatility, and this drops below 20 per cent beyond about ten days (Andersen et al., 2003). Over horizons greater than a week or two, investors cannot form expectations of risk and return distributions that are superior to a naive strategy, such as tossing a coin or taking the current value.

This defect in the models is made worse by the fact that returns are not random but tend to have runs. This is recognised in many finance studies that show markets and individual securities have price momentum: they tend to move in the same direction for extended periods. This is logical: individual firms, for instance, have periods of good or bad results depending on the skill and strategies of their managers and the nature of their industry.

A New York equity manager told me of his pet theory that momentum comes from attitudes towards risk. The demand for risky assets is driven by the degree of risk aversion: when the discount rate goes down, prices rise, risk falls and people buy into the rallies. He didn't know the driver of these money flows, but recognised that price momentum is one of the most persistent market anomalies. Experienced investors know that one bad period is not the end of their losses.

But VaR is blind to momentum because it sees returns as random, and models markets as a game of chance that has a known distribution like roulette. Random outcomes from a known distribution mean that each individual outcome is uncertain. Will the portfolio value rise or fall today? Will the ball drop on red or black? The result over time is statistically known. This is captured in the concept of random walk that is used to describe markets, which means that today's value equals yesterday's value plus or minus a random move. The defect, of course, is that each spin of the roulette wheel may be independent, but this is not true of markets where outcomes over successive days, months or years are not statistically independent and we see runs. For risk managers, momentum in markets means that days of losses can cluster and VaR's assumption of randomness in the data will give overly optimistic projections.

Another reason why successive market moves are linked is that investors respond to other investors' actions. This is what George Soros (1994) termed his Theory of Reflexivity where systems with thinking participants are not passive but set up a two-way feedback mechanism between actual events and participants' expectations. Because markets have thinking participants who react to events, they are reflexive and their future value is indeterminate. This harks back to the argument of Lord Keynes that investment success comes from outguessing other investors, and points to the need for qualitative assessment of risk and possible shocks.

Although feedback from decisions is inherent in markets and their risks, VaR is a normative model adapted from the physical sciences where analysts rely upon total separation between events and observations and can ignore human or social factors such as biases and behavioural pressures. Observing the Moon with a telescope or even blasting a rocket at it brings no response. The opposite, of course, is true of markets with their thinking participants and reactive behaviours.

Similarly VaR incorporates the idea of diversification so that risk is reduced because uncorrelated portfolio components move in different directions, such as gold and banks or manufacturing and mining. In the jargon, VaR models assume that covariance matrices are stable. In reality they are not, because sharp moves in a major market pull other markets along with them.

Thus historical data are no guide to the future, most especially in the tails. In short, adherents of risk models pin their faith on nothing more than continuation of a good fit to past data, which they should know is improbable. This makes risk models of some use in monitoring so that regulators and firm management can keep an eye on what is happening; but they are of limited value in choosing investments.

The most important defect in VaR from an investor's perspective is that it does not measure their biggest risk which is a significant and prolonged loss of value from investing in the wrong asset class or security. A New York equity manager explained how this arises with his observation that 'risk is the failure to recognise when your heuristics are no longer working'. Successful investing requires a paradigm that matches the market psychology, and VaR is totally blind to this.

A minor, but often significant, issue with VaR models is that their design and operation are not standardised. Thus, even though the Basel Committee on Banking Supervision recommends that banks use them in determining market risk, 'no particular type of model is prescribed'.[3] It seems ridiculous that banks are able to develop their own proprietary risk models for reporting purposes, and that they can report what they choose to regulators and investors. But just this happens because calculations by financial institutions of their VaR are not in a standardised format and so companies' VaRs are difficult to compare. In the United States, for instance, Citigroup and Bank of America report VaR at the 99 per cent confidence interval, whereas Morgan Stanley along with JP Morgan Chase and Goldman Sachs report at the 95 per cent confidence level.[4] For equivalent trading positions, 99% VaR is about half as large again as 95% VaR, so the difference is not trivial.

Banks also have freedom to choose the dataset on which to base their VaR calculations. The Basel Committee guideline merely says: 'The choice of historical observation period (sample period) for calculating value-at-risk will be constrained to a minimum length of one year.'[5] Typically banks use a two-year dataset, which means that the models quickly forget market crashes. During the GFC, for instance, volatility of the S&P 500 was about twice its long-term average. But this had fallen out of VaR models by 2011, and banks' reports of their VaR now ignore the possibility of another GFC. Investors should not be comforted by this.

Despite the precision and scientific perspective that risk managers effect, they have nothing more to go on than historical data that has limited use in predicting the unknowable future: all too often market cycles and crashes catch them unawares.

These criticisms of VaR are well recognised. So why do finance professionals rely so heavily on it? There are two reasons. The first is that VaR and similar techniques quantify the market risk of portfolios and financial institutions. This is particularly attractive to regulators and senior executives who wish to monitor the numerous complex exposures that are embedded deep in the firm from their offices. It is also essential in a complex environment where a bank may have literally thousands of financial risks and must be able to track its total exposure. To those interested in oversight or the big picture, VaR may be imperfect, but it is a better measure than nothing.

The second group that welcomes VaR are the traders and portfolio managers who obtain clear limits to the risks that they can take. Previously they were constrained by position limits: they could not invest more than a given sum, and had other bounds such as stop losses and concentration limits. Modern risk models are quite different: they give traders a risk budget rather than a position limit, and the new approach to risk management often provides much greater latitude for them to act. This is the subject of the following section.

Risk management increases risk taking

As suggested above, a counter-intuitive consequence of improved tools to manage risk is that they can actually lead to higher risk and greater volatility in markets.

One way for this to occur lies in the nature of VaR that allows fund managers to game the risk models and take on bigger positions (and risks) than would previously have been allowed. Consider, for instance, the manager of a long-only equity fund with assets of $100 million which has a one-day 5 per cent VaR of $3 million (which means $3 million, or 3 per cent, is the fund's maximum expected loss on 95 per cent of days). If the manager now morphs the fund into a long–short equity style, he can increase the long position to $150 million and take on a short position of $50 million in stocks that have similar volatility and link to market moves while still keeping the VaR at $3 million providing the broad composition of the portfolios remains unchanged. This is because the model figures the losses and gains on the $50 million short position will offset gains and losses on $50 million of the long position. Thus it sees a net of $100 million invested and VaR remains the same.

Although VaR says risk has not changed, this contrasts sharply with the 'old' limits where portfolio risk would have risen by half in line with the aggregate size of the positions. Under them, a holding of $150 million is half as risky again as $100 million. So, even though manual scrutiny and intuition might suggest that the fund has become much more risky, its VaR on a PC screen has not changed.

Why would traders and portfolio managers want to game the risk models? Quite simply so they can increase their exposure and thus possibly make a higher return which would bring them a bigger bonus under the standard incentive compensation arrangements in most funds.

A second reason why modern risk management tools lift risk arises in the trading strategy of hedge funds and investment banks. They rely on borrowing or leverage whose level is pro-cyclical so that it increases as the market moves up, and *vice versa* (Adrian and Shin, 2008).

Some simple math show how this might unfold. Consider a leveraged investor such as a hedge fund which borrows so that it makes $2 of investments for every $1 in funds under management. With investor funds of $50, the manager will build a portfolio of $100. Should the market rise by 10 per cent, the portfolio value goes to $110, debt stays at $50 and investor funds go to $60. Thus the manager could borrow another $10 and increase the fund size to $120 without changing leverage. The result of a 10 per cent market rise is that this leveraged investor could lift holdings by up to 20 per cent. Thus as asset prices rise, leveraged investors borrow more and use the proceeds to buy more assets which leads to an upward-sloping demand curve that accelerates price rises. Exactly the opposite happens with a downturn in asset prices because leveraged investors are forced to liquidate assets.

The result is the mirror image of undergraduate economics teaching where demand curves slope down and supply curves slope up. This centuries-old intuition holds that rising prices stifle demand and encourage supply, but it offers little to explain the behaviour of contemporary financial markets. VaR limits and investor leverage reverse normal supply–demand responses and exacerbate market price moves, with a sequential nature that explains momentum in many markets.

To see how this operates, consider Goldman Sachs which reports quarterly data on VaRs by asset category since 2000 in its 10-Qs (and year-end data in its 10-Ks and ARS – Annual Report to Stockholders). Figure 4.2 plots Goldman's trading

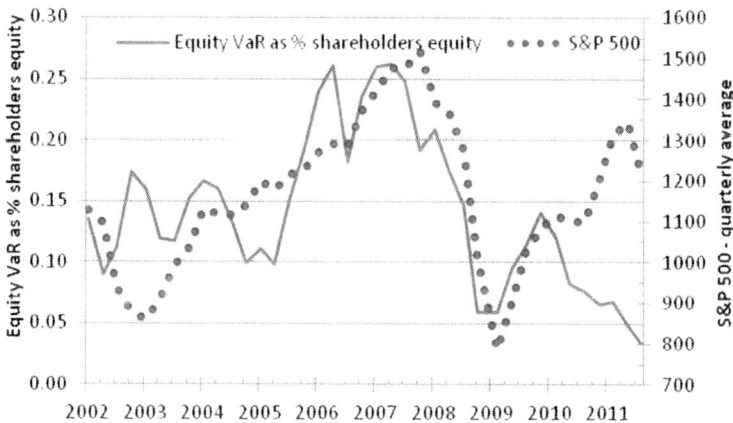

FIGURE 4.2 Goldman Sachs equity VaR and S&P 500 Index

position to show that equity VaR moves in line with the market, so that a rising S&P 500 induces Goldman to increase its risk relative to shareholders funds. The negative consequence of pro-cyclical leverage is that assets can quickly evaporate. This can be dramatic, and an article in the *Financial Times* reports that a Goldman Sachs fund lost 30 per cent of its value in a week and forced the firm to inject $2 billion of its own money to shore up investor confidence.[6]

My interviews with fund managers found that most now believe that the slope of the demand curve for stocks is up rather than down. A South African manager agreed that using leverage means that the portfolio moves with the market, betting bigger. An Istanbul equity manager pointed out that margins for most investors are very thin, but they can be magnified by leverage. This strategy has now become the psychology of the moment: because the largest traders use leverage, others are forced to follow. This turns conventional economic theory on its head so that when prices rise funds buy more stocks and actually chase the market.

The negative of using high leverage is that – if you are out of synch with the market – you can get hurt very badly, even if you are fundamentally correct. Investment managers that I interviewed all recognised that leverage is potentially profitable, but is of such high risk that it has a deleterious effect on returns over the medium term. They blamed lax monetary policy for excessive leverage by large investors, with several observing that regulation allows leverage to be too high. They felt it had brought bubbles in markets that collapsed, and so set up the familiar boom–bust–boom cycle.

Where were risk managers during the global credit crunch?

Despite the limitations of VaR and other measures of risk, they are accurate, reliable and available in real time. Thus they have considerable utility and are in widespread use by large financial institutions.[7] Given all the tools and resources available to risk managers, why did they (and regulators) miss signals ahead of the GFC?

An interesting insight to the frailties of risk management comes from an article in *The Economist* (August 2008) entitled 'Confessions of a Risk Manager',[8] which points to two flaws in banks' risk management processes. The first was that risk managers concentrated too much attention on financial products that the ratings agencies defined as high risk. The agencies – led by Standard & Poor's and Moody's – have specialists who evaluate the risk of financial products and then publish them on a standard scale, with AAA being the highest rating/lowest risk and then down to D, which is in default of its obligations, typically after missing a scheduled payment such as interest.

This anonymous risk manager admitted that it was not a surprise to many of his peers that their bank took large losses on credit derivatives during the GFC when liquidity dried up and prices collapsed. The surprise was that it occurred with so many higher-rated, investment-grade securities. The risk managers had accepted the rating agencies' opinions on the basis that they knew best, and assumed there would always be a market for investment-grade securities so they could liquidate positions as necessary. Thus they had worried about the lower-rated, sub-investment-grade holdings. In the end, of course, higher-rated credit derivatives collapsed, too, with losses so large as to threaten the whole financial system.

The second flaw was that – because risk managers' role was to serve as gatekeepers to the business lines' decisions – they came under intense pressure to approve the highest-risk products because they attract the highest fees and marketers want to sell as many as possible. As structures of various credit derivatives became more complicated through the 2000s, the returns got higher and – intuitively – so did the risks. The business lines wanted to write more business to increase revenues and bonuses, and saw the concerns and limits from risk managers as obstructive and pressed them hard for approvals.

This risk manager's ruminations are consistent with the main feature of the GFC which was that it took most investors into new territory, where – like all innovations in finance – risks were under-appreciated. Perhaps the greatest lesson from the GFC is that booms of the 2005–7 scale which rely on new products (in this case credit derivatives) take everyone into the unknown. This offers great attractions from what *could* be found there: in finance terms, the lack of track record and shallow understanding of new products gives them optionality. Like an out of the money option on stocks, this uncertainty offers an (admittedly small) probability of huge return, which is why innovations of this type prove attractive to many investors: the market could make them a fortune.

That is what happened in the GFC to so many investors, especially the notionally most sophisticated. Instead of worrying that what they didn't know could hurt them, they hoped that it could benefit them. This is why the business lines put so much pressure on risk managers to approve exposures to credit derivatives.[9]

Fund managers I spoke to echoed many of these comments. One in Istanbul had previously worked in his firm's risk management department, and described the process of continuous reporting to the CEO and CIO of each portfolio's VaR, volatility and contribution by component. This tracked the risk that was being taken in each portfolio to secure the returns reported. The risk manager, though, has a passive role in reporting by relying on historical results: reports cannot look forward, only limit risks for portfolio managers if performance falls below target. The risk managers have a strong role in compliance by monitoring positions against limits in policy statements, but because all their information is historical they can only be reactive.

A London equity fund manager complained that all his firm's quantitative models broke down during the market turmoil in 2007–8. For him they are fine during the 99 per cent of times when the market is normal, but they cannot handle the tails. They cannot project turning points or high volatility, the sort of events that he and other fund managers worry about. By the time the models have caught up with the market it is too late for them to be of value. Like most of his colleagues, he was very sceptical about the utility of risk management.

Biases in the data

We have already discussed the limitations of historical data in forecasting future returns and volatility: because there is little correlation across different periods between either returns or volatility of equities and other securities, projections from history are problematic. Even so, historical data are an important guide to many investors and this has led to proliferation of financial databases. Although users of the data should be resigned to accepting their questionable forecasting ability, many probably assume they still provide robust platforms to support analyses of historical performance of markets, funds and other investments by academics and practitioners.

Sadly, however, reality is that much of this historical data is unreliable. This is because many datasets have considerable upward bias, often due to under-appreciated mechanical issues: as a result the historical returns of markets can be overstated.

The most common bias to historical data involves survivorship: markets that fail and funds that cease reporting drop out, and so the return given by the database is inevitably biased upwards because most data reports the performance of surviving, successful constituents.

The effects of survivorship bias are clear in the interesting review of 'Global Stock Markets in the Twentieth Century' which analyses data during 1921–96 for 39 stock markets (Jorion and Goetzmann, 1999). One conclusion is that returns are highest in longer-lived markets: the 11 countries with continuous data during the study period had a mean annual real return of 1.9 per cent, whereas the figure for all countries was −0.5. The US and UK markets, which are most often used to justify equity investments, are the longest lived of all, and had exceptional average annual returns of 4.3 and 2.4 per cent, respectively.

History shows that investors in any country face a once-in-a-century risk of substantial loss through prolonged closure of its stock market. A common contributor to cessation of trading is war or financial crisis which have a debilitating impact and can become chronic.

A tangible example of how survivorship affects data is to compare the long-term experience of investors in Australia and Argentina: each country spans much of the southern hemisphere, is highly urbanised after being settled by Europeans, and has a stellar agricultural and mining history. In the early nineteenth century, the geography, economy and population of the two countries looked similar; so, too, was their wealth, based on historical statistics published by the OECD which report that the per capita gross domestic products of Argentina and Australia were close in the range $US1,300–1,550.

Despite striking similarities two centuries ago, the countries have since followed quite different paths. By 1900 the figures for GDP per capita in Argentina and Australia were $2,756 and $4,299, respectively; and in 2000 they had widened further to $8,544 and $21,883 (Maddison, 2003). There is similar divergence in performance of their stock markets with respective USD compound annual returns during 1930–95 of −1.4 and +6.3 per cent. Thus the seemingly similar young countries started with roughly the same living standard and economy 200 years ago, but Australians are now two-and-a-half times more wealthy and had a much better performing stock market.

By concentrating on the track record of successful markets, real investment return is biased up (and risk biased down), sometimes quite sharply.

A second type of upward bias in historical finance data comes from backfill, and arises when a security (most often a mutual fund) is added to a database. A fund is typically only added to a database after some period of successful operation, usually a couple of years, and because hard data is available prior to the date of addition to the database this is usually incorporated, too. But, because the decision to incorporate a fund in the database is contingent on proven good performance, this also builds an upwards bias into returns.

Backfill bias can be substantial, and a good perspective is given by Aggarwal and Jorion (2010) in an article in *Financial Analysts Journal* about the TASS (Tremont Advisory Shareholder Services) database which is widely used to measure hedge fund performance. The TASS database goes back to 1977, and in 1999 was purchased by Tremont which had its own database and invited member funds to be included in the TASS database. The predictable result was that additions to the new database were all funds that had a record of operating successfully prior to 1999–2000. Thus the new fund database was biased by inclusion of survivors with strong performance history (a backfill issue). The authors calculated that annual returns during 1994–2001 for the Tremont funds in the database averaged 1.6 per cent, whereas those that had been added selectively from the TASS database averaged annual returns of 10.3 per cent. Adding strength to concerns that this performance discrepancy is artificial, there were negligible performance differences between the two groups during 2002–8.

Whilst these biases can be dismissed as mechanical, they do influence investor decisions. The need for caution over survivorship bias comes from the fact that it is not only military and political winners who write the history, because financial winners do so, too. Nobody uses the experience of Argentina as an indicator of likely economic or stock market performance: they select data from Australia, Britain, the United States and other successful countries. Investors who look to history as a guide to future returns need to be alert to risk from bias in the data.

Counterparty and operational risks are always with us

Risk management software became increasingly sophisticated through the 2000s, and this encouraged fund managers to embrace the concept of risk budgets. That is, they would adopt limits according to the statistical risks of the portfolio. Most financial institutions appointed risk managers to maintain and monitor these programmes, and they became responsible for reporting risk parameters and ensuring there were no breaches to position limits. After about 2004, more and more of the presentations that I saw from fund managers had heavy emphasis on computer-based risk management, and provided considerable detail of their controls.

But it seemed that – as mechanical controls – strengthened less and less attention was being paid to traditional human-intensive counterparty and operational risks. Several examples of this have already been discussed. And, of course, most explanations for the GFC blame it on weak processes, rather than technical failures.

This resonated with me when a New York equity manager shared an unusual, longer-term perspective on the growth of risk management with the observation that there have been rolling crises every seven years or so for the last 30 years. He felt that crises are caused by the illusion of control which indicates that you can learn from history. As we try to solve the last problem, which during the GFC was misunderstanding the true risk of complex securities, we set ourselves up for the next crisis.

The persistence of financial crises even as risk management techniques evolve should caution that we can lose sight of two crisis triggers that seem to recur. The first is bad investment decisions. Put simply, transactions have winners and losers, and loss can be high from wrong choice of an investment, particularly when it is leveraged through debt or a derivative bought on margin.

The second, and for large investors probably more significant, source of loss is counterparty risk. This is inherent in virtually all investments because they involve giving up cash now for the right to receive a future cash flow: investors can only obtain returns through the successful performance of an investee or other creditor. Inherent in investment, then, is counterparty risk or the possibility of payment default, particularly by the issuer of a debt security which has committed to pay back its face value on the maturity date. Credit or counterparty risk is so serious in finance that it is the single-greatest cause of bank failure.

Counterparty problems are chronic with over-the-counter (OTC) derivatives which are private, minimally regulated deals.[10] Investors who wish to use the leverage inherent in derivatives can choose to trade either through a futures exchange or directly with a bank or other financial institution (i.e. OTC). Notionally the costs of equivalent transactions should be similar for the two approaches, although futures markets trade standardised securities where pricing is competitive, whilst OTC products can be tailored to investor needs and so create margining opportunities for their issuer. The most important difference between OTC and exchange-traded products, though, is in counterparty risk. The counterparty with futures contracts is the exchange, which imposes margin requirements on both parties to ensure adequate capital is always available to meet repayments. OTC products, by contrast, only offer recourse to the issuer and so settlement relies on their capital adequacy.

The second aspect of counterparty risk is monitoring exposures, which is most complicated for non-bank investors because the finance industry is structured to make it hard for outsiders to become directly involved in transactions. Non-bank investors looking to buy securities and non-bank firms which seek funding by selling securities do so through advisers, agents and other intermediaries: these outsiders must rely on finance insiders to select and monitor counterparties, and the performance of agents is a significant risk.

A good example of agency and counterparty risk for outsider investors came with the sale of complex credit derivatives during 2002–7 by a number of banks, especially Lehman Brothers. The products proved so flawed that 72 clients of the Australian Lehman subsidiary (who were mainly local governments and charities) sued the bank for $250 million. Their case said they accepted Lehman's advice because 'they wanted someone who knew more about money than them to look after their money'.[11] Like many marketers, Lehman seems to have assumed the roles of both adviser and seller. The risks of this should have been clear to even less sophisticated investors who would be more sceptical in other transactions ('Do I look really good in this?'), but suspended disbelief and took investment advice from product marketers who clearly knew far more about the transaction.

The message is that counterparties in finance take on many guises. Their range is so wide that Australian market commentator Marcus Padley observed pithily in his newspaper column: 'Most financial professionals exist to connect you with a service or product.'[12] Counterparty risk is so pervasive and potentially serious that investors should understand the risks of each of their counterparties and monitor exposures for threats of loss. Obviously, though, that is impractical, so investors should be sceptical of all advice.

Whilst this may appear cynical, a London fund-of-funds manager reiterated the obvious point that 'running money is a business'. Thus finance firms are not altruistic, but face commercial imperatives and must respond in kind. If competitors offer soft commissions to clients or suppliers or pay investment platforms for the shelf space to include them, then all other funds must follow. If competitors offer rosy-glasses assessments, it is hard to tell clients not to trade.

Another traditional risk is the possibility that a given transaction may not be accurately executed. This is termed operational risk, and defined by the Basel Committee on Banking Supervision (BCBS) (2001: 94) as 'the risk of loss resulting from inadequate or failed internal processes, people and systems, or from external events'.

It is interesting that finance tends to ignore operational risk. Thus a Working Paper from Wharton entitled *The Place of Risk Management in Financial Institutions* sniffs that 'operating problems are small probability events for well-run organizations' (Oldfield and Santomero, 1997: 12); and a comprehensive review of risk management in banking by Bessis (1998) devotes just a few pages to operational risks.

In fact operational risk is both ever-present and significant. BCBS polled a range of banks on its incidence, and 63 banks reported about 37,000 events. On average, each bank faced a loss of more than $10,000 *every* trading day, with most either external fraud, largely in the retail area, or process failures in trading or retail banking. About 99 per cent of losses were less than $1 million, so on any day banks have a 1 per cent chance of losing $1 million due to an operational deficiency (which is equivalent to a $1 million 99 per cent VaR from operational risk). Because the frequency of operational risk is related to transaction volumes, the VaR for large banks would be proportionately higher, although is still only a fraction of their market risk (which is around \$200 million per day at the 99 per cent level for big investment banks like Citigroup).

Risks from investment manager underperformance

Investment is so complicated that most private investors conclude they lack the skill and resources to make their own decisions. The finance industry has so successfully parlayed this logical argument that managers of investment funds now make most investment decisions. For instance, in the United States mutual funds and other investment institutions (mainly public and private pension funds, life insurance companies, and exchange-traded funds) owned 47 per cent of the market value of listed equities at the end of 2012,[13] with similar scales of holdings in Canada, northern Europe (Norway, Sweden), the United Kingdom and elsewhere (Aggarwal et al., 2011). With funds owning close to half of most markets, investment has been institutionalised and this sets up several important risks for investors.

Because most investors save through funds, their principal choice is not what securities to buy, but what funds to invest in. These two decisions have very different bases. Deciding on what shares or bonds to buy involves judgements about the future profits of a company, its competitive position and strategies, the skills of its managers, and risks from actions of its customers, competitors and regulators. Choosing a mutual fund involves judgements about the fund's objectives, the investment skills of its managers, and the risk that the fund will not operate as promised.

From a practical point of view, it is impossible for the average investor to monitor any fund's activities. Certainly most report performance daily. But few funds publish their holdings in real time, and so it is impractical to identify what contributed to results. This practice is defended on the basis that selection of investments represents proprietary skill, but it is hard to see why it matters who knows what a fund has already bought. In fact, if the fund has skill, other investors will follow its lead and so increase the profit from any transaction.

The most obvious risk from investing in a fund is that it collapses. Studies of hedge funds show that about 12 per cent fail annually during their early years, so that only a third survive for more than a decade (Grecu et al., 2007). Mutual funds are somewhat more robust with about two-thirds surviving for at least a decade (Bu and Lacey, 2009). Whilst fund termination does not necessarily mean loss of the total investment, funds generally do not stop operation because they have been performing well! For investors who entrust their savings to fund managers, it should be sobering to realise that between one- and two-thirds of them could be out of business within a decade. In this case it makes sense to diversify and avoid concentration risk.

Another risk from relying on a manager's investment decisions is that they may not remain true to label. Finance loves clear labels, for example describing investment funds as balanced, growth, value, emerging markets and so on. It is, however, beyond the capability of most investors to monitor compliance of their fund with its investment objectives, and so they run the risk that the fund will not maintain its stated strategy if the market goes against it.

There is also a set of risks from criminal behaviour within funds and these are discussed in the following chapter.

The final risk for retail investors in managed funds arises because funds concentrate attention on their large clients. Most of their revenue comes from fees that are a proportion of fund size (rather than from fund performance), which tends to skew operations towards capture and servicing of the large, most profitable clients. These large investors consider themselves sophisticated, which means that they want to kick the tyres before they put in money, and will expect face time with the chief investment officer. The latter can find himself (there are still very few women in this role) spending far more time in front of clients than on research. All investors suffer, especially if this leads the manager to take his or her eye off the ball.

Moral hazard is rife in finance

Moral hazard arises when a third party reduces the risk from any action and hence changes the decision maker's risk propensity. The classic example is car insurance, which removes or reduces the financial liability of drivers from an accident and so can induce some to take less care. A good finance example is given by an observation in *The Economist* (21 May 2005) that tax deductibility of interest expense encourages taxpayers to 'take bigger risks than they would if left to their own devices'. Reverse moral hazard arises when the risk of an action is increased by a third party such as making it illegal and people become less willing to undertake it.

Moral hazard is rife in finance, largely because of the separation of skill and responsibility, so that investors bear all the losses and their skilled agents such as fund managers and brokers only profit from investments (with very limited exposure to loss). Investors effectively give their agents call options linked to investments' return, which skews the risk–return relationship and can induce high-risk propensity in some agents. Investors, in fact, create moral hazard for themselves by working through agents who are protected from loss and differentially rewarded by the greater possible returns in risky investments.

Moral hazard can also arise because of the asymmetry of information available to small and large investors, so that the purported knowledge of a large, presumably more skilled institution can induce an investor to take risks. A good example was discussed earlier where Lehman Brothers marketed CDOs in Australia to less-sophisticated investors who accepted the obviously conflicted advice because they wanted someone smarter than them to look after their money.

Even market regulation can promote moral hazard if it lulls investors into believing their money is safer than it actually is and thus lowers the apparent risk of an investment. The best example is government agencies that insure investors against losses. In the United States, the Federal Deposit Insurance Corporation (FDIC) provides protection for deposits of up to $250,000 in over 7,000 member banks. A similar type of moral hazard arises in banks and other firms when governments appear willing to bail out those that fail. Executives become confident that their losses will be covered and this can induce them to take on risk. This has been a major criticism of actions by the US Federal Reserve and other regulators that have provided financial support to failing firms and banks during financial crises.

Another source of regulatory moral hazard is approval by regulators of securities such as complex derivatives that leads investors to think they are safe, and so buy them and take on their risks.

Monetary policy is a recurring source of moral hazard for investors because central banks appear reluctant to see a decline in asset prices for fear of the knock-on effect to consumption and economic activity. A good example was belief during the late 1990s that the boom in global equities would persist because of the 'Greenspan Put' (Miller et al., 2002). This assumed that US Federal Reserve Chairman Alan Greenspan was so concerned over fall-out from collapse of the irrationally exuberant US stock market that he would prevent it by pre-emptive reductions in interest rates. Investors in equities felt this provided a floor under the price of their shares, much as can be achieved by a put option.

Monetary policy since about 1990 does seem to have had an eye to preserving stock prices. This can be seen in Figure 4.3 which plots moves in the US federal funds interest rate and the S&P 500 Index: every time the equity market weakened, the Fed moved its key interest rate down to stimulate recovery.

This equity-friendly policy of the US and other central banks has not been benign, however, because the artificial distortion it brought to markets obscured the true prices of stocks as set by sustainable supply–demand and economic fundamentals. Bubbles emerged, only to collapse, and the policy backfired. Moreover, the policy was asymmetric so that central banks were slow to constrain asset price bubbles, but used accommodating monetary policy to avoid or cushion asset price collapses. This boom-acceptance and bust-opposition broke the essential nexus between investors' long-term confidence in markets and their respect for its risks,

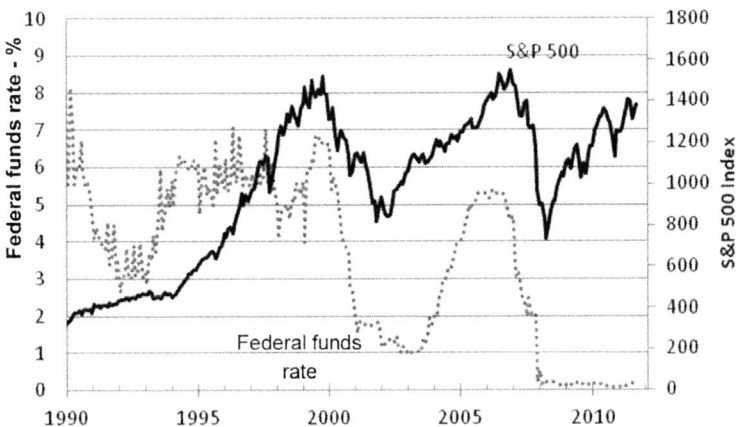

FIGURE 4.3 US federal funds rate and S&P 500

especially the warning that gains come only with an attendant possibility of loss. For several decades, serial equity booms and busts pointed out the obvious fact that misguided monetary policy is the cause of most market bubbles and crashes.[14]

How stupid do they think we are?

Around 2.40 pm on Thursday 6 May 2010, the US equity market fell by 6 per cent in 15 minutes. According to a report by the SEC (2010), it had been drifting down through the day on high volume over concerns at Greece's debt crisis. Then at 2.32 pm a trader at mutual fund Waddell & Reed[15] placed an order to sell 75,000 E-Mini S&P contracts on the Chicago Mercantile Exchange (CME) as a hedge on an existing physical position. The trade was valued at around $4 billion and was executed by computer within 20 minutes. At this time there were only $2.7 billion in unfilled buy orders for the contract, so liquidity quickly vanished and prices rapidly declined. Starting at 2.41 pm, programme traders began selling into the price decline and the bellwether S&P 500 futures contract dropped 5 per cent. A few minutes later, the CME intervened and paused trading in the E-Mini contract, after which prices stabilised and then fortunately recovered.

This 'flash crash' was blamed on rogue computer trading and quickly dismissed. A New York equity manager patronisingly explained to me that most market players use trading algorithms, and they all ended up trying to sell the same inventory about the same time. It just snowballed on itself. For him and most others it was an extraordinary event, not to be repeated, and so its occurrence has all but disappeared from view.

But this was a huge market move, wiping out about $1 trillion in investor savings, admittedly temporarily. Also, if it could happen once, it could happen again; and perhaps that loss may not be reversed. Surely such a unique and serious event should be fully understood?

Well, the SEC launched an investigation which took five months. Its report effects a largely mechanical perspective, detailing what happened and when, but not why. Was the flash crash deliberate manipulation, an accident, or just coincidence? The SEC makes no comment. Looking ahead, it announced that in response to the crash SEC 'staff worked with the exchanges and FINRA to promptly implement a circuit breaker pilot program for trading in individual securities'. In effect the SEC produced an inconclusive, do-nothing report.

Has anybody else come up with a decent answer? Not really. Since the flash crash, pathetically few analyses have appeared. One, though, by Chris Rose (2011) was unequivocal: 'It is increasingly looking as if the crash of May 6th was not an accident.' He pointed to the range of tricks available with computers to manipulate the market, and noted that similar flash crashes had occurred earlier and looked like dry runs. This makes one of the SEC's lessons learned particularly interesting: 'Under stressed market conditions, the automated execution of a large sell order can trigger extreme price movements.' Is this a one-line primer on how to make a fortune through market manipulation?

Roswell all over again! So, exactly what happened? And, if the market had been manipulated, what would the motive be?

The most obvious objective of manipulators would be to make a profit by placing big bets on a market decline and then triggering it. The best way to make these bets would be to sell S&P 500 futures contracts and/or buy put options on the S&P 500. If this occurred around the flash crash, what would we expect to see? Most likely, an increase in volume of futures and options positions over a few days leading up to the morning of 6 May 2010, which would be closed out as soon as practicable after the market fall. This, of course, is facilitated by executing the manipulation around mid-week.

Table 4.1 uses daily data from Datastream to look at moves in key contracts around the flash crash. The most interesting feature is the size of futures and options trading in the two days before the crash. The volume of mini contracts was about twice the average for the first four months of the year, and amongst the largest of the year. Similarly the trading volume for S&P 500 put options on 4 and 5 May was well above average: the 36,000 contracts on 5 May was the third highest for the year-to-date.

The table *could* be interpreted to suggest that informed traders had positioned themselves ahead of the market fall. That is, they had bought put option contracts and sold S&P mini contracts. It is beyond my scope here to pursue this issue any further, hence the emphasis on 'could' above. It is interesting, though, that the SEC did not look at trading volumes in the days leading up to the crash.

Could markets get sucked into economic warfare?

Discussion of the flash crash assumed that the objective of market manipulation is profit, but it could also be executed with malicious intent. The rationale for this can be seen in Figure 4.4 which shows that the US economy dropped into recession shortly after the market collapses in 2000 and 2008. Recessions bring job loss, corporate failures and other trauma, often including changes of government. This makes it plausible for foes of a country or group of countries to launch a debilitating economic attack through the stock market (or currency, debt or other market).

This risk is so large for the economy and investors that it is receiving credible evaluation in several countries. For instance, a document entitled *Economic Warfare: Risks and Responses*[16] was prepared for the US Department of Defense by a consultant

Table 4.1 Futures trading around the 2010 flash crash

2010	S&P Futures Index	Futures contracts volume	S&P mini contracts volume	Futures call option volume	Futures put option volume
Av January–April	1,138.3	27,009.1	2,098,204.6	14,242.9	21,561.8
3 May	1,198.6	16,440.0	1,798,536.0	13,152.0	14,481.0
4 May	1,172.4	30,456.0	3,558,639.0	9,908.0	29,474.0
5 May	1,163.9	30,366.0	3,062,139.0	24,949.0	35,926.0
6 May	**1,122.4**	**54,701.0**	**5,683,315.0**	**19,854.0**	**32,114.0**
Av 7–31 May	1,110.5	32,423.9	3,142,809.3	21,566.6	34,519.4

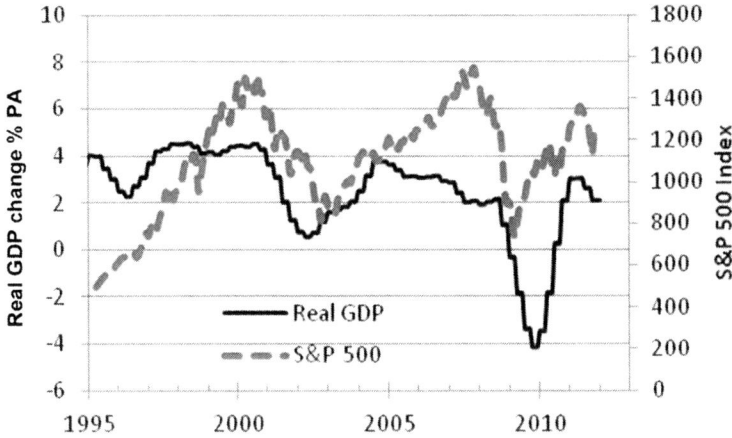

FIGURE 4.4 US real GDP and S&P 500

to the Irregular Warfare Support Program. It goes so far as to argue that a three-phase economic attack had been launched on the United States in 2007. This began with a tripling of oil prices with proceeds used to manipulate the stock market and bring on recession in the United States and Europe.

Manipulation of the global oil market would be within the capability of major oil producers. For a start, the world's ten largest oil companies (each of which is state-owned) control more than three-quarters of global oil supplies.[17] Moreover, it seems pretty clear that the oil price was manipulated during 2005–11 by traders taking large long positions in the futures market.

It also seems pretty clear that the prices of many bank shares were manipulated during mid-2008. An article published by Bloomberg describes how the share prices of Bear Stearns and Lehman Brothers were pushed so far down that the once-venerable firms collapsed.[18] The basic technique is to place large orders for sale of shares to induce a fall in the stock price. This can be done at no cost by an unscrupulous seller (using a credulous broker) who places the sell order, watches the price fall, and then simply evaporates before the sold shares must be transferred three days later. This practice of defaulting on short sales is known as naked short selling (selling shares you do not own) and fail-to-deliver (not settling an agreed trade).

In the case of Bear Stearns, failed trades peaked at 1.2 million shares on the day after JP Morgan announced it would buy the bank (17 March 2008), indicating that there had been a large volume of naked short sales in the previous few days. With collapse of Lehman, the naked short selling was accompanied by false rumours that it was to be sold to Barclays plc for 25 per cent under the share price, and that several fund managers had stopped dealing with it. Two days after Lehman filed for bankruptcy, failed trades comprised a quarter of all sales of the firm's stock. According to one estimate, these bear raids accounted for around half the fall in Lehman and Bear Stearns' stock price (with the unstated point that the balance was due to losses from mismanagement).

The 'how' of this manipulation also seems clear. The *Economic Warfare* report notes that two previously unremarkable small brokers emerged in 2007–8 as major traders in financial firms, lifting volume from 350,000 shares per month in 2006 to over eight billion shares by September 2008. This included over one billion Lehman shares in the lead-up to its collapse, with trades peaking at 640,000 shares per hour in October 2008. Turnover of the firms during this period was equal to about half the outstanding shares on the NYSE, and adding strength to the oil link they were also the largest traders of energy stocks.

The report does not suggest that the brokers themselves launched the raids. Rather, that they offered what is called sponsored access where they rent out their broking rights and equipment to traders who do not have to pass through standard regulatory checks and registrations (although you might wonder why a prudent broker would sponsor a large trader that is not subject to regulation).

The *Economic Warfare* report considers who could have perpetrated the market attacks. Hedge funds are dismissed as simply taking advantage of trends, despite $1+ billion gains during the GFC by four leading funds. A more likely possibility is the Russian mafia and Latin American drug cartels, given the testimony by whistle-blowers to Congress that they were involved in the $50 billion Madoff Ponzi scheme.[19] Top of the list of suspects, though, are oil-rich countries, even if the evidence against them is circumstantial. The inference is that oil-financed groups (in the Middle East and Venezuela) are attacking Western interests through economic means as part of an ongoing terrorist war that is consistent with Sharia and socialist-inspired attacks on capitalism.

The third phase of the purported attack would take advantage of developed economies' foreign debt. For instance, foreign entities hold about a third of US government debt[20] and almost as much of UK government debt.[21] The thought is that malicious foreign debt holders would flood the US and/or UK market by selling their holdings of bonds, which would drive down their price, spike interest rates and tank the currency with knock-on threats to sovereignty. At the time of writing, the third phase has nowhere become evident.

Conclusion

Quantification of risk has become a popular pastime for finance practitioners, to the extent that some manage risk rather than return, almost as if they believe that risk brings its own reward. They are part of the tradition that has seen a scientific basis to markets that began with the analytical achievements of celebrity economist Irving Fisher that led him to proclaim just before the 1929 crash that the market had reached a permanently high plateau. Analytical finance techniques performed little better ahead of the many subsequent crashes, when blind optimism was in plentiful supply. Bloomberg, for instance, reported (27 June 2007) statements by Merrill Lynch's CEO, Freddie Mac's Treasurer and Lehman's CFO that rising problems in the mortgage market did not pose wider risks to other markets.[22]

In 2008, risk models humiliated their advocates just as so many other finance concepts have let them down. No investor should doubt that markets remain highly risky. This chapter has concentrated on risks inherent in the structure of the finance industry and on systemic risks. We have ignored risks from criminal behaviour by those in the industry which are sufficient to merit the following chapter.

Notes

1 US Department of Labor, *Injury Trends in Mining*. www.msha.gov/mshainfo/factsheets/mshafct2.htm
2 UCLA-LoPucki Bankruptcy Research Database. http://lopucki.law.ucla.edu/index.htm
3 'Revisions to the Basel II Market Risk Framework', January 2009. www.bis.org/publ/bcbs148.pdf; and December 2010 update at www.bis.org/publ/bcbs193.pdf
4 www.occ.gov/topics/capital-markets/financial-markets/trading/derivatives/dq311.pdf
5 'Revisions to the Basel II Market Risk Framework', January 2009. www.bis.org/publ/bcbs148.pdf
6 'Goldman Pays the Price of Being Big', *Financial Times*, 13 August 2007.
7 See 'How Pension Funds Manage Investment Risks: A Global Survey'. http://papers.ssrn.com/sol3/papers.cfm?abstract_id=1687774
8 www.economist.com/node/11897037
9 See an interesting timeline of write-offs at www.creditwritedowns.com/credit-crisis-timeline
10 At the time of writing details of regulation have not been finalised: see Commodity Futures Trading Commission proposed standards for derivatives clearing organisations at www.cftc.gov/ucm/groups/public/@lrfederalregister/documents/file/2013-19845a.pdf
11 'Councils and Lehman Brothers Fight It Out in Court over Risky Investments', ABC Radio, *PM*, 31 May 2011. www.abc.net.au/pm/content/2011/s3232047.htm
12 *The Age*, 12 September 2009. www.theage.com.au/business/a-second-essay-on-share-market-mythbusting-20090911-fkwb.html
13 Table L.213 of the *Flow of Funds Accounts of the United States* published by the US Federal Reserve at www.federalreserve.gov
14 A good discussion of this can be found in Allen *et al.* (2009).
15 www.reuters.com/article/2010/10/01/financial-regulation-flashcrash-idUKN0114164220101001
16 www.archive.org/details/EconomicWarfare-RisksAndResponsesByKevinD.Freeman
17 'State Capitalism', *The Economist*, 21 January 2012, Special Report, page 6.
18 Gary Matsumoto, 19 March 2009, 'Naked Short Sales Hint Fraud in Bringing Down Lehman'. www.bloomberg.com
19 www.house.gov/apps/list/hearing/financialsvcs_dem/markopolos020409.pdf
20 As at September 2013, the value of outstanding US Treasury securities was $16.7 trillion (Treasury, *Monthly Statement of the Public Debt of the United States*, www.treasurydirect.gov), and $5.65 trillion or 32 per cent was held by foreigners led by China and Japan with about 7 per cent each, and oil exporters with 2 per cent (Treasury, *Major Foreign Holders of Treasury Securities*, www.treasury).
21 UK Debt Management Office, *Quarterly Review* (www.dmo.gov.uk).
22 In like mind, Rick Newman of *US News* (3 September 2009) reports '10 Gaffes by Doomed CEOs'. http://money.usnews.com

5

CROOKS, SCAMS AND BIASES

The grease of finance

Everybody knows that the dice are loaded ... The poor stay poor, the rich get rich.
That's how it goes, everybody knows.

Leonard Cohen, 1988. *Everybody Knows*

This chapter is not complimentary about some people in the finance industry. At the outset, let me state unequivocally that the points below relate only to a very small proportion of those who work in the industry, no more than a few per cent. The great majority of people I know in finance – both in academia and industry – are intelligent and hardworking, and take pride in delivering a quality product. This chapter is not about them, but about the few scumbags who damage the industry's name.

Money is the most powerful of all motivators, and is the core commodity of finance. So it is not surprising that the finance industry attracts more than its fair share of people exhibiting greed and worse who bring with them the stench of corruption. These few can execute rip-offs that are so extraordinary as to enter the lexicon as bywords – such as Ponzi – for financial double-dealing. Offenders in finance often seem to act as if they are above the law and exempt from the constraints that shackle mere mortals, and presumably are hardened to the damage they do to others. All too often, their actions are facilitated by benign regulators and compliant observers.

Greed, incompetence and dishonesty can survive in finance because most research and practice relies on the honesty of individuals. The same reliance is also placed, of course, on rationality of investors and efficiency of markets. Breakdown in each assumption proves fatal to investment theories and strategies, and affects the wealth of honest investors.

Examples of criminal behaviour and offences in finance

Some years ago I was waiting outside a board room to make a presentation and fell into conversation with the company's security chief. A burly ex-policeman whose nerves had made him uncharacteristically garrulous, he used a nearby whiteboard to make a point about honesty and drew a vertical box with horizontal strips at its top and bottom. Pointing to the thick strip at the top he said: 'These are always honest. This thin strip at the bottom is always crooked. And that lot in the middle is opportunistic!' Cynical? Certainly; but it may be a useful model as we step through the actions of finance criminals.

Although there are no relevant statistics, anecdotes abound of criminal individuals in the finance sector, so let us consider a few examples.

To narrow the analysis, let me focus on one well-known and globally successful firm: Macquarie Bank is an Australian finance house which generated such rent from its financial innovations that it became known as the millionaires factory. Despite the bank's success, press releases from the website of the regulator Australian Securities and Investments Commission (ASIC; www.asic.gov.au) list a number of successful actions against the bank and its 20,000 employees.

In 2002 a former executive director was convicted of insider trading and jailed for two years.[1] In 2007 a private client adviser transferred losses of $210,000 from his girlfriend's trading account to another client's superannuation fund, and received an 18-month prison sentence.[2] In 2010 a broker was jailed for two years after pleading guilty to eight counts of market manipulation.[3] In 2011 a portfolio manager who had been head hunted by the bank was jailed for 18 months after making a profit of $1.5 million from insider trading.[4] In 2013 ASIC reported that a two-year investigation had 'found some recurring compliance deficiencies' in a bank subsidiary.[5]

In addition to ASIC actions, the bank was reprimanded in 2010 by the Hong Kong Securities and Futures Commission for failing to exercise due care in relation to a commission rebate scheme on warrants it issued.[6] Away from work, bank employees have been found to have been involved in other questionable activities. In 2005 an employee pleaded guilty to larceny by finding after failing to report his discovery of $250,000 in cash in a bag in a laneway.[7] In 2012, a senior managing director based in New York was ordered off a Qantas flight for alleged disruptive behaviour.[8]

Finance prosecutions also involve individual serial offenders. Take, for example, Donald Johnson, a senior Nasdaq official who used inside knowledge gained on the job to illegally trade. He had previously worked as a nurse, during which time he was discharged from the Army Reserves for using stolen narcotics in an army hospital.[9] *Forbes* reported that just before joining Nasdaq, Johnson had his nursing licence revoked after admitting stealing and using schedule II drugs (which include opiates and stimulants) at Fairfax Hospital where he then worked.[10]

Central players in many infamous financial scandals also had previous criminal behaviour. And it is common to find that individuals who are banned by regulators from finance activities – serving as a company director or financial adviser, for instance – have previously received a similar ban.

What motivates financial criminals?

Perhaps not surprisingly, the research literature offers pretty thin answers to the question of what motivates financial criminals.

One relevant paper reports an extensive interview with Sherron Watkins, who was vice president of accounting at Enron up to 2002 and used her ringside seat to draw some insightful conclusions (Beenen and Pinto, 2009). According to Watkins, individual leadership (in terms of the presence or not of an ethical lodestone) is very important in promoting or tolerating wrong doing. When smart young men of decent background see the rules relaxed, they run amok. According to her, the Enron collapse 'would never have happened' if Jeff Skilling had not been President and COO. 'The reason was Skilling's leadership. He was charismatic and intimidating. He was very hypnotic, and convincing. He is sharp and could sell anything.' She described Skilling as Machiavellian and willing to punish dissenters.

Another perspective on the motivation of financial criminals is an analysis by Drennan (2004) of the high-profile 1990s collapses of British institutions Mirror Newspapers and Barings Bank. He found that each failure was caused by the unethical behaviour of an individual, although others in senior positions may have had knowledge of much of their activities. Those involved were Robert Maxwell and Nick Leeson, respectively, and although poles apart in status as executive chairman and Singapore trader they shared important traits. Maxwell had a decade-long record of questionable practices, and in 1971 was described in a UK Department of Trade and Industry report as 'not a person who can be relied on to exercise proper stewardship of a publicly quoted company'. Leeson was forced to withdraw an application for UK registration as a securities dealer in 1992 after lying on the application form about debts against him; and was charged in Singapore with exposing himself. Maxwell was highly charismatic, but also bullied his family and employees to secure blind obedience. Leeson, too, could be very aggressive (at least when drunk). Both came from poor backgrounds, proved secretive and took financial risks that failed.

Studies of finance criminals suggest that they share several common traits. Observers describe them as having a winning smile, captivating body language and fast talk: they are extroverts who are superficially charming and successful. This makes it interesting that similar descriptors are used by Robert Hare (1994) in *Psychology Today* to describe other people's perception of the typical psychopath. Despite their attractive facades, psychopaths inside are cold, calculating and ruthless, and this enables them to lie, cheat and manipulate others for their own ends. They are not strongly motivated by money, but thrills: they have a need for excitement and live life on the edge, which can induce them to create situations of high risk. In organisations, psychopaths have endearing personalities, display enthusiasm and extroversion, and rarely evidence any self-doubt, which makes them good in the crises they create. These attributes also help them leap over setbacks and gain the confidence of people who should see through them, but instead will often propel them to senior positions.

As an aside, many of the attributes of psychopaths are attractive to organisations, and there would be few managers who would not display some of them at times. So it can be hard to identify truly dangerous psychopaths, at least until they overstep the line. This makes it important to recall that organisational drift often precedes corporate failure, frequently in employees' criminal conduct.

Because finance offers so many opportunities for daring innovation and rewards, psychopaths inevitably find the industry irresistible. According to a paper by Clive Baddy (2011) in the *Journal of Business Ethics*, there were so many psychopaths working in financial institutions during the 2000s that their self-serving actions were a major cause of the GFC. According to Baddy, they would be unconcerned at the carnage they create, lack any regrets over losses by clients or counterparties, lie about events, and blame others. Psychopaths have no conscience, few emotions, and no feelings or empathy for people affected by their actions. This explains the theme of many newspaper headlines along the lines that 'Wall Street shows no remorse'. Another psychopathic feature of white-collar criminals is that most do not believe they did anything wrong, and half of those sentenced to prison successfully deny any crime in a lie detector test. Perhaps worst of all, many psychopaths who lost their jobs in the GFC employed their charm to secure lucrative policy roles advising on how to avoid future crises.

The possibility that financial crimes are driven by the psychopathy of investors' agents has significant implications for regulation of the finance industry. Most obviously these criminals are not misguided individuals or people out of their depth who deserve sympathy. Nor can their mistakes be remedied by imposing limits on behaviour and promoting good governance. Psychopaths are driven to create value for themselves; they do not have a moral compass but possess a criminal mind and mendacious spirit. The only thing that will deter them is a high probability of being punished for destructive behaviour.

Surely the big banks are not corrupt!

The finance industry goes to considerable lengths to avoid the appearance of chronic problems. Each time a criminal case emerges around financial markets, it is accompanied by soothing statements suggesting that it is a one-off event perpetrated by a scoundrel who was acting alone. In fact rogue, which the *Oxford Dictionary* defines as 'an elephant or other large wild animal living apart from the herd and having savage or destructive tendencies', is the common description of bank employees involved in unauthorised activities. The title of a film about Nick Leeson was *Rogue Trader*. The implication is that crimes perpetrated within financial institutions involve the unapproved actions of some kind of psychotic individual that do not reflect a broader problem that might affect the safety and returns of investor funds.

One pointer to the possibility of broader-based corruption can be seen in one of the least-remarked features of the finance industry – its concentration. Just five financial institutions comprising traditional banks JP Morgan Chase, Bank of America and Citigroup and investment banks Goldman Sachs and Morgan Stanley control most of everything in US markets and a few more like Barclays, Credit Suisse, Deutsche Bank and UBS have similar control over other major markets. Thus the integrity of the finance industry is bound up in the governance and behaviour of the nine large banks: if any is corrupt, then the problem starts to look endemic.

So, could corruption be systematic? Obviously there are no statistics on this, nor is it a topic of polite conversation. But successful actions by regulators against the big banks provide enough evidence to have some suspicions.

Consider Morgan Stanley which bought physical precious metals (gold, silver, platinum and palladium bars and coins) on instructions from 20,000 clients between 1986 and 2007, and naturally charged them the costs of storage and insurance. It turned out, however, that the clients did not actually own anything specific or identifiable, but 'at best had an unallocated precious metal investment'. Instead of backing the clients' orders with physical metal, Morgan Stanley either bought futures contracts or had taken the exposure on its own account. It paid $4.4 million to settle a class action.[11]

In short Morgan Stanley accepted orders from its clients to buy precious metals on their behalf, but never bought the metal. It then charged the clients to store and insure bullion and coins that never existed! These investors presumably had no faith in futures markets or bank counterparties and elected to hold physical bullion. The differences between physical precious metals and paper derivatives were not trivial for investors who believe that owning precious metals can protect them in the event of a collapse of the economic system (although, to me, the only real stores of wealth then would be tinned food and the weapons to protect it).

This is not an isolated incident because it is common to see large banks heavily fined for what are serious crimes against their clients' interests. In an article headed 'Wall Street Fine Tracker' *Forbes* listed fines levied during 2004 against America's largest financial institutions that totalled $4.5 billion.[12] Citigroup paid $2.7 billion to settle a class action suit in relation to the collapse of WorldCom; and another $70 million to settle Federal Reserve allegations of improper lending practices. Bank of America paid $375 million to settle allegations that it allowed favoured mutual funds to trade after the market had closed and to execute market-timing trades, which take advantage of temporary price misalignments by rapidly shifting in and out of mutual funds. UBS was fined $100 million by the Federal Reserve for executing transactions with countries subject to US trade sanctions including Cuba, Libya and Iran. Just to show employees were not immune from abuse, Morgan Stanley paid $54 million to settle a sex discrimination suit filed by the US Equal Employment Opportunity Commission. These came on top of $4.2 billion in fines levied in 2003 and $3.0 billion in 2002. *Forbes* continued to pursue this issue, including the cover story 'The Sleaziest Show on Earth' (24 May 2004). An important aspect of these fines is that they all occurred before the GFC broke.

Huge fines of financial institutions remain chronic. In 2009 JP Morgan Chase paid $772 million to settle a case brought by the SEC alleging that $8 million in secret payments had gone to the close friends of the commissioners of Jefferson County, Alabama, to facilitate a bond issue.[13] In 2009 JP Morgan Securities was fined $175,000 by the NYSE for front running and mis-reporting transactions.[14] In 2013, the bank agreed to pay a total of $920 million in fines following losses by traders in London.[15] In 2013 the bank paid $13 billion to settle claims by the Justice Department and other authorities that it had misrepresented RMBS transactions.[16]

In 2008 the SEC accused Citigroup and UBS of misrepresenting auction-rate securities (which are bonds whose interest rate is reset at regular auctions) as safe and liquid and obtained fines of $100 million and $43 million, respectively.[17]

Goldman Sachs, too, has been the subject of a number of large fines. In 2012 the Commodity Futures Trading Commission (CFTC) fined it $1.5 million for internal-control failures that were exploited by a trader who lost $8.3 billion.[18] CFTC levied a fine of $7 million in 2013 for another failure of supervision.[19] In 2010 the bank paid $550 million to settle a case brought by the SEC for misleading clients about the nature of a CDO.[20]

Many of the banks' actions involve giving special treatment to large clients who lift their transaction volume and hence generate more fees for the bank at no risk of loss. One popular scam has been front running, in which a broker or institution enters its own proprietary trades immediately after a large order is placed by a client (but before it is executed) so they profit from the price rise it brings. These and similar offences result in lower returns for investors, which is effectively theft by the bank from its clients. Eliot Spitzer, who was Attorney General of New York during 1999–2006 and responsible for many of the successful prosecutions, argued that there are 'widespread illegal trading schemes' that could cost investors more than $4 billion a year.[21]

The big banks do not just practise corruption on their own, but will join in quite complex conspiracies. A good example came to light in mid-2012 when Barclays bank was fined £290 million by UK and US authorities for manipulating LIBOR (the London Interbank Offered Rate, which is an interest rate for lending between banks in US dollars) since at least 2006, and possibly as far back as the early 1990s.[22] The rate is set by the British Bankers' Association based on reports submitted by member banks. Barclays submitted rates that were lower than actual to indicate that it could borrow more cheaply and hence was of lower risk than it actually was. This issue has significant implications for the many finance benchmarks which are developed by private bodies. Adding fuel to allegations by conspiracy buffs and critics of regulators, years before the scandal broke *The Wall Street Journal* (16 April 2008) published an article questioning the reliability of LIBOR, which prompted only cursory scrutiny from the US Federal Reserve, the Bank of England and other regulators.

No investment manager raised these issues during my interviews, save to observe that investment banks are a risky investment choice. A New York securities lawyer, though, asked, perhaps rhetorically: 'What other industry could survive countless claims of serial offence against its customers? No other industry cheats its own customers so badly as to attract fines of hundreds of millions.' He went on somewhat resignedly: 'Congress believes that banks are necessary, and problems are part of their price.'

The destructive web of hidden commissions and charges

I recently made a rare visit to my bank at the university to deposit some foreign currency cheques, and the teller politely offered to set up an appointment for me to obtain advice from the bank's financial planner. On the face of it this seems like good service. But in fact the teller – without warning me – receives a few dollars as payment for every customer who takes up the offer.

This may appear a trivial example, but it evidences how far the tentacles of hidden incentives have spread through the finance industry. Financial advisers receive commissions when their clients first buy a product, and often receive trailing commissions, too, that come for years afterwards. Virtually all payments to the various advisers and agents who represent the public face of finance are based on transaction volumes, not success for the investor. It is worth restating the caution: 'Most financial professionals exist to connect you with a service or product',[23] and that these professionals are compensated by the volume of transactions, that is, how much investors turn over, and not the return to investors.

Put differently, there is often no alignment of goals between investors and those who offer them advice and assistance. This makes commission risk a major issue for investors, especially as it is hard to spot because so many are hidden.

Incentives encourage financial advisers to favour particular service providers, with less consideration of what is best for clients. The classic example comes via what the industry coyly calls soft commissions, which are non-cash payments in a variety of guises. In the case of individual advisers they span the range from football tickets to family holidays; for firms they typically take the form of free services or equipment.

The rationale for payments to individuals is clear: to influence them in selection of business partners. The amounts involved can be large. In 2000, for instance, the America's Cup was held in Auckland which was only the second non-US venue for this event in over a century. Corporate entertainment was lavish, and many Australian banks invited clients and a partner to journey to New Zealand and watch the race in style at the banks' expense. My employer at the time had a sensible policy that employees could only accept entertainment that could be reciprocated, which limited us to dinners and local sporting and cultural events, so I politely rebuffed invitations to Auckland. Many others, though, did not.

Soft commissions to firms are usually designed to increase income, and this is most easily achieved by providing a product or service such as information terminals and risk management systems, or free research materials. The client saves money by avoiding the cost of purchasing the equipment or staffing a research department, and shows its gratitude by using the services of the bank or broker. Also common is the practice of paying kickbacks in exchange for business, often in the form of volume discounts.

The size and extent of these soft dollar practices was revealed by Benn Steil in a colourful Op-Ed in the *Financial Times*.[24] As one example, he described the practice of some fund managers who took advantage of their ability to directly charge investors' accounts with transaction costs such as buying and selling shares. This can be exploited by an unscrupulous fund manager which may pay a high fee to a broker for share transactions rather than negotiating a discount, and then receive services from the broker (perhaps research), preferential access to hot IPOs, or even a cash rebate. The net is to charge a higher transaction cost to investors and pass a benefit to the investor's agent or adviser. Steil estimated that the cost of this scam alone may be as much as 1 per cent per year of funds under management.

Research reports *are* independent. Aren't they?

A barrier to efficient investment by outsiders is information asymmetry: small investors, for instance, do not have the contacts and research capabilities of their large counterparts and so have limited scope to gain deep understanding of any investment. The good news, though, is that they can access numerous research reports about the prospects of various asset classes and drill down into likely performance of individual stocks, bonds and funds. Arguably these reports fall into three categories. The first is prepared by a firm or fund seeking investments and is designed to foster positive market and investor reaction. The second is provided by sell-side analysts in stockbrokers and investment banks who want to encourage investors to trade and hence generate profit from commissions. The third category of reports comes out of research houses which produce them for profit.

Surely Chinese Walls, ethics and analyst reputation make research reports reasonably balanced? Not so according to a paper by the Australian Securities and Investments Commission (ASIC) entitled 'Strengthening the Regulation of Research Report Providers'.[25] ASIC was motivated by failure during the GFC of investment products that had recently been highly rated by research houses, and focused on conflicts of interest that might have compromised reports' integrity. ASIC looked to research houses knowing that they function as a gatekeeper because their approval of a product is required before many institutional investors will include it in their investment stable and financial advisers will recommend it to their clients. ASIC wondered whether 'revenue model' conflicts of interest arise because of the usual practice where the product issuer pays for research houses' reports and product ratings.

When explaining revenue model conflicts to my class, I use familiar terms. Assume you respond to an advertisement for a used car and the vendor provides you with a mechanical report that it has commissioned and paid for. How much weight do you place on the report? Well that is what happens when companies issue bonds or entrepreneurs launch opportunities to invest. They pay a ratings agency to provide a report about their product. How much weight should you place on *this* report?

ASIC does not name names, but high-profile litigation provides examples. One case involved Bathurst Council in central New South Wales which bought a $A1 million Community Income Constant Proportion Debt Obligation Note (don't even try to work out what that is) through Royal Bank of Scotland in late 2006. At the time, the note was rated AAA by Standard & Poor's, but less than two years later the council was told that the note was being unwound and it would receive only $A67,043.[26] A second lawsuit in Australia united 72 councils and charities that had bought collateralised debt obligations (CDOs) that were widely marketed by a Lehman Brothers subsidiary. These securitised asset-backed loans such as those for houses and cars and had been assigned an AAA-rating; but defaults led to write-down of values. Demonstrating that misunderstanding the risks of these products was not confined to naive investors, National Australia Bank (NAB) built a $A1.2 billion portfolio of AAA-rated CDOs, and then reported in May 2008 that it would write off 90 per cent of its value.[27]

Nor was the problem of unreliable ratings confined to Australia. Bloomberg, for instance, ran a farsighted article during May 2007 entitled 'CDO Boom Masks Subprime Losses, Abetted by S&P, Moody's, Fitch'.[28] Three-quarters of the global CDO market was in the US, with virtually all of these derivatives sold over the counter. The CDOs incorporated diverse assets and – because of their complexity and general lack of information – investors relied heavily on the published opinions of rating agencies. The latter painted a rosy picture of this asset class and in 2006 rated more than 90 per cent of the $60 billion in CDO sales at above investment grade (that is, BBB or higher). The dark side of the picture was that the market had exploded through the mid-2000s, so that almost half the income of rating agencies came from rating CDOs and similar products. Revenue model conflicts grew even more intense when the ratings agencies began to work with the issuers of the CDOs to design them to get the most favourable ratings. Unbeknown to most investors, the ratings of complex securities such as CDOs were impossibly conflicted in the lead-up to the GFC.

This Bloomberg article appeared months before the GFC began to get serious, and it set out clear evidence of the conflicts behind many security ratings which questioned the validity of their valuations and threats to the financial position of holders, especially large banks and funds. The depth of uncertainties behind valuations of complex securities was there for all to see, and was rammed home when the article described a CDO issue of $340 million in late 2000 by Credit Suisse Group that was rated AAA by S&P, Moody's and Fitch, but had since lost a third of its value.

Ratings agencies are not the only notionally independent analysts to receive criticism, as there has been a fair volume of allegations that sell-side analysts in broking houses and investment banks lack independence and offer biased advice. Reflecting such doubts, *Fortune* ran a front cover (21 May 2001) asking 'Can We Ever Trust Wall Street Again?'. Articles under near-identical headlines that question analysts' credibility and integrity have since run on *BBC News* (13 February 2002) and in *The Wall Street Journal* (8 February 2010).[29]

Sell-side analysts appear to be bedevilled by revenue conflicts. Their opinions are most valued by retail investors who have limited resources to analyse investments and want unbiased advice, but make up only a small portion of the income of analysts' employers. Most revenue comes from corporate advice, proprietary trading and services to institutional clients who have their own analytical capability but want corroborating opinions. In practice it is probably unrealistic for retail investors to expect to be able to obtain any truly unbiased research.

Unholy alliances between universities and finance firms

Where ratings agencies and sell-side analysts have obvious revenue conflicts, academics have a high public trust factor. This should make them ideal for evaluating financial products, so it is surprising to sometimes find that their opinions, too, may not always be to the advantage of outsiders such as retail investors. It seems that some academics can internalise the views and opinions of actual or potential patrons in industry and shape their conclusions accordingly.

Barry Eichengreen, Professor of Economics and Political Science at the University of California, Berkeley, alluded to this in an article in *The National Interest* (May 2009). He pointed out that top academics enjoy participating in off-site client meetings organised by banks at ski and beach resorts, especially when 'generous speaker's fees are available to those prepared to drink the Kool-Aid'.[30] These sessions were not for everyone, but attendance did give prestige to academics who could successfully participate.

One of my favourite examples of an academic drinking the Kool-Aid involved a paper published in the prestigious *Journal of Applied Corporate Finance* entitled 'Transforming Enron: The Value of Active Management'. Written jointly by Enron's Director of Research and a Baylor University finance professor (Kaminski and Martin, 2001), it details how 'Enron's management has turned a $200 million regulated natural gas pipeline owner into a $100 billion new economy trading powerhouse' and argued that its competitive strength and strategies gained respect from Wall Street and the financial press. The article was published in the journal's winter 2001 edition, right around the time of Enron's December 2001 collapse in what was then America's biggest bankruptcy.

This example is particularly instructive because it came in the wake of media reports that were becoming ever less favourable to the energy giant. Although as late as mid-2000 *The Economist* magazine ran a laudatory article hailing Enron's CEO Ken Lay as a business visionary, many prudent analysts and observers had serious doubts about his business model. For instance, prominent Americans including former Treasury Secretary Robert Rubin did not take up offers to join the Board.[31] Reporters at *Forbes*, *Fortune* and other magazines raised serious doubts about Enron practices. And an article in *The New Yorker* reported that a group of Cornell University business school students had studied Enron as a term project in 1998 and concluded that the company was a Sell (Gladwell, 2007). The true state of Enron was apparent before it failed, although it took skill, persistence and independence of thought to get to the truth, which, of course, is a responsibility that Wall Street analysts failed to accept.

A disappointing aspect of the relationship between finance academics and the industry they educate and research is a reluctance by many to engage in debate over public policy or major issues involving finance. Occasionally an academic or someone from a think tank, research firm or pressure group will speak out. But most commentary on finance topics comes from bank spokespeople, and financial expertise in the mainstream media – newspapers, radio and TV – is virtually the exclusive province of bank economists. Usually a little nerdish, bank economists are pervasive and pop up to provide a reassuring explanation of seemingly complex moves in markets. No doubt they are easily accessible to the media, have good television faces (and radio voices), and are eminently credentialed. But most have conflicts of interest because their prime responsibility is to protect the interests of their employer (bank) and not provide independent counsel.

By contrast, finance academics are much less conflicted, but few are willing to even comment on the finance industry, much less offer criticism or unpalatable solutions to problems. It was most noticeable during the GFC: in country after country, no more than a handful of academics made any meaningful public input to discussion on appropriate policy responses. The newspapers, airwaves and government lobbies were filled with the opinions and prescriptions of bank economists who were firm that only government bailouts could prevent meltdown of the financial system. Nobody asked why representatives of those who had caused the GFC had such a stranglehold on interpreting it and recommending policy.

The only discussion that I could find of this point is a 2010 conference paper by academic Todd Bridgman who summarised his opinion in the title: 'Laughing All the Way to the Bank: How New Zealand's Banks Dominated Public Debate on the Global Financial Crisis and Why It Matters'.[32] He pointed out that New Zealand academics have a statutory obligation under the Education Act to serve as the critics and conscience of society, but during the GFC (which hit New Zealand hard with the collapse of over 30 finance companies) they were conspicuous by their silence.

One of Bridgman's explanations for academics' silence is that they are not encouraged or rewarded by their universities for engaging in public debate (but rather are pushed towards academic research which receives virtually no public recognition). He also pointed to the cosy link between bank economists and the media which is promoted by the scale of bank advertising especially on TV and facilitated by the availability for interview of media-savvy bank economists.

The absence of an academic–investor nexus is consistent with weak incentives for academics to contribute to public policy, or to share their expertise more broadly. Few corporate boards, for instance, include academics, nor do the senior ranks of regulators. Whatever the cause, it is a sad waste that academics offer so little finance counsel to the community.

Where is governance in finance?

Governance, and its handmaiden ethics, receive only limited attention in finance even though most firm collapses can be traced to their absence. Governance is the process that ensures investors receive a reasonable return. It is driven by a board that is able to think independently, especially of company executives, and which will set and promote the right objectives for the firm. Strong governance relies on directors with skill, energy and backbones.

A good example of how little respect at least some senior finance executives have for good governance is given by the pre-GFC composition of the board of Lehman Brothers.[33] That board was overseeing developments that would lead to Lehman's collapse in 2008, and in 2006 comprised 11 directors, ten of them non-executives. Four of the non-executive directors were aged over 75, and their number included a Broadway producer, an ex-CEO of Sotheby's auction house, a retired US navy admiral, retired CEOs of construction, mobile telephone, computer and television companies, and a former actress.

The last was Dina Merrill, the 84-year-old daughter of a stockbroker and whose sixth birthday fell on Black Tuesday 1929 which ushered in the Great Depression. The party that night must have been pretty subdued. Merrill became an actress, and her only commercial board apart from Lehman was RKO Pictures Inc, which is best known as the source of late-night cable movies. Amongst her other attributes, she starred alongside Mickey Rooney in the 1958 movie *A Nice Little Bank that Should Be Robbed*, and two years later made the cover of *Life* magazine.

The key takeaway from looking at Lehman directors' CVs is that only two of the ten non-executive directors had any skill related to finance. What possessed one of the world's great risk machines to structure such a board? Lehman obviously was not seeking skill, energy and backbones!

Is the Lehman attitude an outlier, or representative of governance in general? It is hard to tell because only a few insider reports have emerged of how boards operate. One is provided by Daniel Schwartz (1977) in his review of board activities leading up to the shock collapse in 1970 of Penn Central Transportation Company. The company had been formed in 1968 following a merger between New York Central and Pennsylvania railroad companies. The study attributed Penn Central's bankruptcy to the board's underestimation of difficulties in completing the merger (which is a common cause of corporate failure). It found that 'the officers [of the corporation] were engaged in an exercise of poor management while the outside directors blandly stood by'. Like Lehman's outside directors, few of those at Penn Central had any relevant industry experience, and thus failed 'to search for adequate information, to ask the necessary questions and to be cognizant of potential problems'.

Perhaps the hands-off attitudes of directors is more common than we know. Some years ago I was appointed to an honorary position on the board of a local hospital. It was run by an enthusiastic MBA and we hit it off, so I asked him for a tour. We spent several hours together, doing the rounds of wards, visiting each of the campuses, chatting to staff and reviewing his budgets and reports. I have always enjoyed this kind of industrial tourism, thanked him warmly at the conclusion, and apologised for taking up his time. 'Not at all,' he replied. 'You are the first director that has ever asked for a tour.' A similar example of disengaged executives is Merrill Lynch CEO Stan O'Neal, who became increasingly isolated as the sub-prime crisis unfolded during 2007 to the extent of taking a golf vacation (McLean and Nocera, 2010: 314).

The interesting aspect of failed companies such as Penn Central, Lehman Brothers and Enron is that the structure of their boards superficially reflected best practice. They put in place good governance measures such as independent com-mittees and had a majority of non-executives with diverse backgrounds. It was not so much the composition of the board that let them down, but the *process* followed, because the directors did not (or could not?) use the tools available to adequately monitor management.

Although it is fine to lament the absence of good governance and ethics amongst firms and funds, a bar to promoting it is that there is not much evidence that investors reward it. For instance, Margolis and Walsh (2003) reviewed 109 academic articles published between 1972 and 2002 that examined the impact on companies' financial performance of their corporate social performance, which was variously measured using Social Indexes and *Fortune* reputation rankings, environ-mental and social disclosures, lawsuits and awards. Half the studies pointed to a positive relationship, whilst the other half found a negative, mixed or no relation-ship. A recent synthesis of studies by Orlitzky (2008: 127) concluded there was 'a positive, but also highly variable, relationship between corporate citizenship and corporate financial performance'. This is reminiscent of what the Roman satirist Juvenal said of virtue: *laudatur et elget* (it receives praise but is left out in the cold). Even when everybody seems enthusiastic about ethics, good governance or corpo-rate citizenship, it is hard to motivate a firm to adopt best practices in these areas if investors do not value them.

The lack of substantive interest in ethics, sustainability and similar issues was reflected in my fund manager interviews. All managers were aware of these influ-ences on investment, but felt that their clients only paid lip service to them. A fund manager in Melbourne stated proudly that his firm had signed up to the United Nations Principles of Responsible Investing; but then somewhat sheepishly admit-ted that the bar was so low they had not needed to change any of their policies or processes. An Istanbul fund manager expressed frustration that discussion by his peers of ethics – even at meetings of local Chartered Financial Analysts (CFA) – was only superficial. Everybody seems to be talking about it, but few intend to do much in a real sense.

Why do financial brands have so little value?

The last two chapters have discussed the risks in finance, and many of these relate to incompetence, bias or theft by financial institutions. In the jargon, there is reason to suspect that any FI could be a lemon for its customers or shareholders. A successful response to the lemons problem in tainted industries has been for ethical leaders to emerge and distinguish themselves by building a trusted brand or image. It is interesting that finance does not (yet?) have a Coke, Apple or Mazda.[34]

Based on a ranking of the globe's top 100 brands by consultant Interbrand before the GFC fall out,[35] the leading financial services firms are American Express (ranked at number 23), JP Morgan Chase (28) and HSBC (32); only 11 other financial services firms appear on the list. Where just 14 financial institutions make the top 100 based on brand, their economic importance is far greater and a *Forbes* ranking of the world's largest public companies includes 36 finance firms in the top 100 (with JP Morgan Chase and HSBC ranking first and second, and seven others in the top 20).[36]

Branding's importance seems linked to consumer expectations of greater security: PayPal, for instance, has been a critical factor in the success of on-line retailer eBay because it provides secure forms of payment. Intuitively, then, one would expect that financial institutions would make a strong effort to promote their image and brand given that trust is essential to meeting their core objective, which is to link investors who have cash to invest to governments and firms that need money. Each party has a strong interest in helping to increase the size of the cake (which is made up of returns from use of the investors' money).

But the finance industry's poor image suggests a lack of mutual co-operation that is emphasised by cases of secrecy, abuse of power and information asymmetry. Even though branding has had a neglected place, when a bank with the reputation and significance of Bear Stearns or Lehman Brothers can fail almost instantly, investors would flock to a bank with a robust reputation, much as they do when choosing a car, soft drink or laptop.

Conclusion: finance is exempt from market discipline

A tenet of finance theory is that the market disciplines weak and inefficient companies and investors. This epitomises the best of capitalism's philosophy that better managers are always available to take over poorly performing firms and restructure them to improve performance. This complements that other great philosophical advantage of liberal societies which is democracy. Although free markets and democracy do not necessarily deliver the best financial system and government, they do allow incompetent managers or representatives to be bloodlessly removed and make way for better successors.

Obviously the finance industry is not structured along these ideal lines. It is common, for instance, to pay high salaries to senior executives with the justification that they align their interests with those of shareholders only to see them align their interests with weak corporate values and rationalise that criminal behaviour is not. Big bonuses lead to inappropriate deals, and – with penalties for independent thinking – encourage people to turn a blind eye. This totally refutes a zero tolerance policy for breaches of controls and ethics (especially by star performers), and rejects a mechanism for collecting and managing bad news.

Sadly truth in parts of the modern finance industry is a long way from the disciplined ideal. Markets bring discipline, equity, efficiency? You cannot be serious!

Notes

1 www.asic.gov.au/asic/asic.nsf/byheadline/02%2F331+Simon+Gautier+Hannes+found+guilty?openDocument
2 www.asic.gov.au/asic/asic.nsf/byheadline/07-300+Former+Macquarie+Bank+client+adviser+sentenced?openDocument
3 www.asic.gov.au/asic/asic.nsf/byheadline/10-49AD++Former+Macquarie+broker+pleads+guilty+to+market+manipulation+charges?openDocument
4 www.asic.gov.au/asic/asic.nsf/byheadline/11-69AD+Former+fund+manager+imprisoned+for+insider+trading+involving+front+running?openDocument
5 www.asic.gov.au/asic/asic.nsf/byheadline/13-010MR+ASIC+accepts+enforceable+undertaking+from+Macquarie+Equities+Ltd?openDocument
6 www.sfc.hk/sfcPressRelease/EN/sfcOpenDocServlet?docno=10PR48
7 SMH, 11 October 2005. www.smh.com.au/news/national/banker-bag-man-pleads-guilty/2005/10/11/1128796507054.html
8 www.smh.com.au/business/disruptive-behaviour--macquarie-exec-ordered-off-qantas-plane-20120607-1zxiq.html
9 See 'Insider Trader at Nasdaq Had Drug-Abuse Record', *The Wall Street Journal*, 10 June 2011. http://online.wsj.com/article/SB10001424052702304259304576373731829124842.htm
10 www.forbes.com/sites/corporateresolutions/2011/06/16/nasdaqs-in-house-fraud-another-example-of-the-importance-of-background-checks
11 United States District Court Southern District of New York. www.gcginc.com/cases/pdf/SLB/SLBNotice.pdf
12 www.forbes.com/2002/10/24/cx_aw_1024fine.html
13 www.sec.gov/news/press/2009/2009-232.htm
14 www.nyse.com/DiscAxn/discAxn_08_2009.html
15 www.sec.gov/News/PressRelease/Detail/PressRelease/1370539819965
16 www.justice.gov/opa/pr/2013/November/13-ag-1237.html
17 www.sec.gov/news/digest/2008/dig121108.htm
18 www.cftc.gov/PressRoom/PressReleases/pr6450-12
19 www.cftc.gov/PressRoom/PressReleases/pr6206-12
20 www.sec.gov/news/press/2010/2010-123.htm
21 www.ag.ny.gov/press-release/state-investigation-reveals-mutual-fund-fraud
22 www.cftc.gov/PressRoom/PressReleases/pr6289-12
23 *The Age*, 12 September 2009, at www.theage.com.au/business/a-second-essay-on-sharemarket-mythbusting-20090911-fkwb.html
24 'Get Tough on Soft Commissions', *Financial Times*, 21 December 2004. www.cfr.org/corruption-and-bribery/get-tough-soft-commissions/p7575
25 Published 16 November 2011 at www.asic.gov.au
26 'S&P's AAA Ratings for CDOs Sold to Australian Towns Will Be Issue for Trial', Bloomberg, 3 October 2011. Available at www.bloomberg.com/news/2011-10-02/s-p-faces-australia-trial-over-ratings-of-cdos-sold-to-towns.html
27 Transcript of interview with NAB CEO at www.abc.net.au/insidebusiness/content/2007/s2315640.htm
28 Richard Tomlinson and David Evans, 31 May 2007. www.bloomberg.com/apps/news?pid=newsarchive&sid=ajs7BqG4_X8I
29 http://news.bbc.co.uk/2/hi/talking_point/1806311.stm; http://articles.moneycentral.msn.com/learn-how-to-invest/will-we-ever-again-trust-wall-street.aspx
30 This refers to the drinks laced with cyanide that Jim Jones gave to his followers in Guyana in 1978 which brought mass suicide ahead of the arrival of a US Congressional investigation team.

31 http://edition.cnn.com/2002/ALLPOLITICS/02/21/enron.lay.rubin
32 An updated version was later published as Bridgman (2010).
33 Form DEF 14A Proxy Statement for LEHMQ dated 27 February 2006. www.sec.gov/Archives/edgar/data/806085/000104746906002510/a2167808zdef14a.htm
34 The weak image of financial institutions seems to reflect lack of trust and low public opinion of business in general. For instance, a 2009 survey of US opinion by the Pew Research Center (www.people-press.org/files/legacy-pdf/528.pdf) found that business executives ranked lowest on their contribution to society's well-being with just 21 per cent of respondents putting it at 'a lot', whereas scientists, teachers and the military each scored over 70 per cent.
35 See www.interbrand.com/en/best-global-brands/best-global-brands-2008/best-global-brands-2011.aspx
36 See www.forbes.com/lists/2012/18/global2000_2011.html

6

HOW DOES FINANCE REALLY WORK?

> According to an old poker joke, if you look around the table and you can't spot the sucker, then the sucker is probably you.

It should be clear from the discussion above that nobody really knows very much about what drives markets. One can readily empathise with John Maynard Keynes (1936) who suggested they were speculative in the same way as casinos. He also equated markets with bets on the outcomes of beauty pageants where the object is to pick which contestant will be chosen as the winner. This must have been a common perception at that time as Ben Graham and David Dodd (1934) reflected similar sentiments in their classic *Security Analysis* with the observation that the market is a voting machine, not a weighing machine. Markets, then, are not only speculative, but speculative about what other speculators think. You can ponder that for hours. Because successful investment requires outguessing other investors' guesses, investors inevitably lose value in the chase for each other's tails.

What sets the price of a security?

In investment there are three core decisions: by investors in relation to the quantum of investment and its allocation across assets; by fund managers in relation to purchase of securities using funds under management; and by corporate managers in allocating operating cash flow between investments, creditors and shareholders. A critical element in each decision is the price of the chosen security or investment.

Since the time of Adam Smith (1776), economic theory has held that prices in physical markets for houses, livestock, copper and so on adjust to establish equilibrium between the flows of orders to buy and sell, and thus clear supplies. Sometimes this is suggested as the driver of financial markets, too: Charles P. Jones (2010) writes in *Investment: Principles and Concepts* that 'prices of stocks traded on the NYSE are determined through supply and demand'.

In practice, though, most finance researchers and practitioners do not think that supply and demand set the value of securities.[1] Rather, they believe that investors follow a unique process and price securities at the present value of expected future cash flows discounted at a rate set by alternative investments, adjusted to take into account their relative risk. Investors sell stocks priced above this value, and buy stocks below it.

This concept was first clearly set out by Ken Boulding (1935) and is probably the most common assumption of all in finance. For instance, the leading textbook by Brealey *et al.* (2012) leads its list of known finance facts with discounted cash flow analysis. Supporters say this means prices are rational, and are independently established by investors' clinical calculus about value. Also, it is linked to the concept of market efficiency that was captured by Burton G. Malkiel (2003) (author of the bestselling *A Random Walk Down Wall Street*) when he defined an efficient market as one that 'does not allow investors to earn above-average returns without accepting above-average risks'. This implies that markets are highly effective in capturing new information and reflecting it in prices, so that true value will win out in the end.

The net is to put the investor in charge of valuations, which is a convenient construction for finance industry professionals because it supports the argument that their skill should be used by less-experienced investors. But as discussed in Chapter 2 the assumption of rational pricing of securities is totally unproven, as is market efficiency. In particular, investors cannot rely on fundamental valuations because these require reliable forecasts of cash flows and market yields, whereas the only comprehensive and accurate price-related information is historical and it has transient predictive power.

Finance, of course, is all about the future, and its most important practical skill is in predicting performance of investments ranging from new mines and factories to stocks and bonds. The problem, though, is that even the best-prepared, forward-looking materials are subject to uncertainty: for instance, it is much easier to announce a new strategy than to implement it; and the environment is rarely stable, especially with market moves. In reality, the most important influences on firm and security prices – market yields and profitability within industry sectors – are unpredictable beyond a few weeks. Forecasts are invariably stymied by events that are impossible to forecast, and the constant flow of new, unexpected information is a stark reminder that it is not practical to form meaningful estimates of future cash flows and risk-adjusted discount rates. It is a bit like driving in a thick fog using a GPS system: you are fairly confident that you know where you are, but you cannot see anything ahead, and so are blind to crashes, obstacles on the road and other threats.

With traditional finance theory providing only weak explanations of decisions to buy and sell securities, it is prudent to seek guidance from the processes that support decisions about other transactions. For instance, most purchases arise because of a need, whether for a washing machine, house or ingredients for dinner, and the available choices are narrowed according to their hedonics (Ford or

Porsche?) and price. Few transactions are decided following detailed financial analysis, even when they occur in settings with the characteristics of markets such as competing suppliers with a range of offer prices (think of the metres-high price boards outside petrol stations) and interactive supply channels with competing buyers and sellers such as eBay or Betfair. A moment's consideration suggests that transactions in markets, too, will have many rational, but not necessarily economic, influences on their supply and demand. It is a puzzle why the decision process underlying financial transactions is assumed to markedly differ from that applied in other settings. In the latter case, non-economic factors largely determine supply and demand for products: prices are set by flows of orders with a mix of qualitative and quantitative drivers, not theory-based calculations of intrinsic value.

Another determinant of security prices that weakens the assumption they are based on value is that orders to buy and sell securities often arise through involuntary factors outside the control of investors. The most obvious are the walls of money discussed in Chapter 3, especially regular savings encouraged by tax-incentivised retirement savings programmes. About $500 billion of annual savings goes into buying US equities, which is roughly double the value of new equity issues, and means that at the margin retirement savings represent the net of shifts in supply and demand for equities. The decisions of retirement savers, then, determine the demand for stocks, whilst price relativities are set by the churning of mutual funds and investors. Importantly this means that net stock demand is blind to prices.

My intuition is that many investors are price takers (not price makers) because their decisions to buy and sell are largely involuntary. Individual investors can have the quantum of their investments set for them such as securitising an expense stream to cover known costs (e.g. house purchase instead of rental), and save for retirement (pension fund) or meet contingent events (e.g. loss of employment). Because assets are mainly acquired in light of expected liabilities, they are involuntarily liquidated when the anticipated or contingent expenses arise. Thus the only discretion that most investors have over financial decisions is in allocating investments between asset classes, and some limited choice over the timing of buy–sell decisions.

Professional fund managers, too, respond involuntarily to fund flows, and this constrains their ability to make strategic choices. Effectively, then, security prices represent the equilibrium between involuntary supply–demand with limited fundamentals-based valuation, and so are subject to bubbles and significant, unexpected moves.

As an aside, it is interesting that cash flows are not only involuntary, but tend to be processed mechanically: investment funds come out of regular pay packets; tax year ends are popular times to rebalance portfolios and sell winners or losers to optimise capital gains taxes; and summer vacations are often quiet on the markets, whilst early autumn is busy after investors come back to work with new resolve (and resolutions). These regular cycles and patterns can make prices partially deterministic, which explains the validity of heuristics ('Sell in May and go away') and technical analysis.

Another interesting involuntary influence on investors is predictable stages in their life cycle, and so demographics are important to security returns. This can be seen in Figure 6.1 that plots the proportion of the US population aged between 15 and 34 years, along with the US ten-year government bond yield. This age bracket comprises three key consumer groups: those in the younger end of the teens and twenties which have high discretionary expenditure, including significant influence over household spending; the middle group includes those setting up homes and filling them with durables and cars; and the older cohort comprises young families with another wave of consumption.

The chart shows the financial sway of history's most prominent cohort of 15–34-year-olds which was the baby boomers who were born between 1946 and 1964 and swept through the population pyramid after the mid-1960s. In the late years of the 1960s and into the 1970s, demand for durables grew. Manufacturers reacted by lifting production capacity and increased borrowing to fund new investment. Similarly household borrowing rose to pay for new homes. Higher demand lifted inflation, and competition for borrowing further lifted interest rates. The second phase began after the 18th birthday parties of the last baby boomers during the early 1980s when durables demand peaked, and this ushered in a period of manufacturing overcapacity that saw jobs and profits decline, and loss of pricing power which led interest rates down. The third phase came when

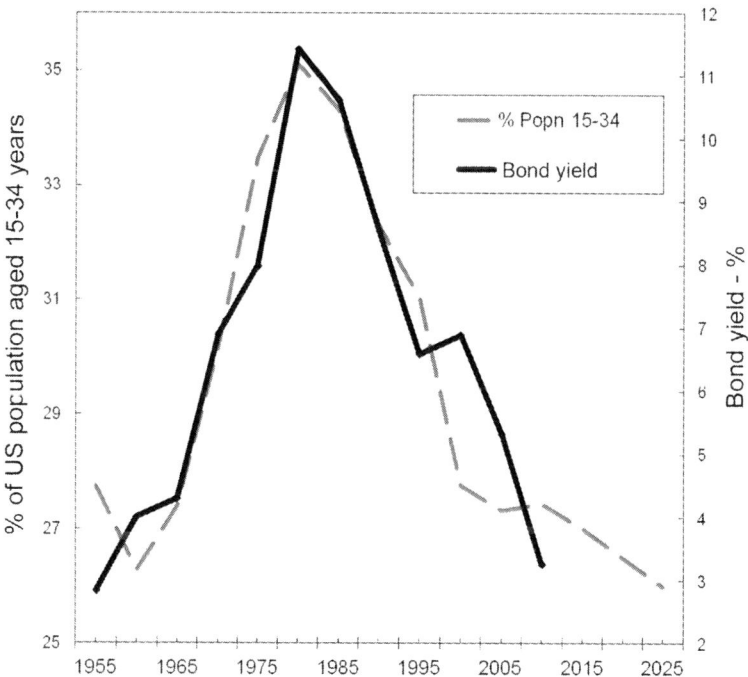

FIGURE 6.1 US bonds and 15–34-year-old population

the baby boomers left the 18–34-year-old cohort in the 1990s and overcapacity tripped re-engineering of whole industries. Savings rose when the high-earning baby boomers began to age (the first turned 45 in 1991), and inflation and interest rates plummeted. Thus US bond yields have moved in lockstep with ageing of the baby boomers.

The unpredictable behaviour of investors

A seemingly obvious, but often over-looked, feature of markets is that they have thinking participants whose actions are important determinants of prices. In particular, people respond to market moves, in line with what George Soros (1994) termed the theory of reflexivity. This expects that markets not only estimate the future but help shape it because their thinking participants respond to events and so induce feedback and non-linearity. The role of investors is similar to that of players in a football game where physics can accurately predict the trajectory of a ball when kicked, but observers know that its actual path will be subject to unpredictable disruption by players which depends on their proximity, psychology, reaction time and so on. Importantly, too, players' actions are related to their ability and desire to influence the score.

Another consequence of the involvement of humans in markets is that they tend to act in anticipation, which can reverse cause and effect. A simple example arises ahead of a firm's scheduled profit announcement: correct anticipation of its content by the majority of traders will see prices move accurately ahead of the announcement. Thus traders produce an effect (say higher prices) in anticipation of the cause (profit increase), and expound the beauty pageant analogy of Keynes (1936) where successful investors do not judge the best investments, but those that other investors believe will be best. Alternatively, information can lag prices, so that price falls bring on bad news, and *vice versa*. Thus analysts typically downgrade firms after they release bad news, which exacerbates the price decline, and information can be pro-cyclical (Cornell, 2001).

Apart from anticipation, investors can be more opportunistic and manipulate markets or trade proprietary information. These lead to abuses that are best evidenced by the eight-to-ten-figure fines imposed on major banks in recent years for defrauding their customers (e.g. Partnoy and Eisinger, 2013).

A further human influence on security prices is that investors, firm managers and other market participants shape the flow of orders and information so that they do not instantly reach the market. Thus, as examples, institutional investors may split large trades into smaller parcels; firms make financial decisions such as dividends and leverage in light of previous decisions, and will execute one-off transactions such as stock issues and mergers at the most propitious time; and analysts revise their opinions of securities in increments (Brown, 2011; Cronqvist *et al.*, 2009). Other staggered flows of price-sensitive information come from the sequential nature of data series such as official interest rates, economic growth and corporate profits which can trend for extended periods. The result is that information does not reach the market completely, but can trickle out over time; nor is it random, but can be serially correlated.

Individual investors face another set of price impacts because each is in a different situation to the market, which sets up asymmetry between their decisions and market behaviour that can appear to be biases. For example, many individual investors realise that they cannot diversify the full range of their assets (including savings, human capital, property and other real assets) or liabilities (including uncertain contingencies) in any meaningful sense. This makes them particularly vulnerable to adverse events, which leads to a natural tendency to be loss averse (Hwang and Satchell, 2010). Because investments are subject to price uncertainty but are intended to meet less variable, inflation-influenced expenses, the degree of loss aversion rises with proximity to the anticipated expenditure because the possibility of recovery from any loss steadily declines. This can appear as a short-term focus. Investors will also pay a premium for protection against severe loss, which is why real put options such as insurance sell at well above their economic value. Individual investors, then, practise asset-liability management to harmonise the market sensitivity, duration and currency of their investments and expected liabilities.

Further, many investments are intended to meet domestic liabilities, and so there is a preference for assets in the currency of liabilities (which explains the near-universal home country bias in investments).

Other perfectly rational decisions by investors can be misinterpreted as biases. As examples, investors in equities establish relative valuations based on heuristics such as price–earnings ratio; choose sell–buy points based on historical price highs and lows; follow market momentum and the decisions of other investors, especially company officers and analysts; and favour economic and industry themes, and particular firm traits such as size and ESG (environmental, sustainability and governance attributes). Over and above that, inherited traits and personality explain a significant portion of variation in investors' financial decisions (Cesarini *et al.*, 2010); whilst other decisions have psychological bases that are at best only minimally predictable (Kahneman, 2011).

It is not just individual investors who face involuntary influences because corporates do, too. Like individuals' investments, their assets are securitised liabilities in that they are intended to generate income to meet payments to contributors of debt and equity. Financial decisions must respond to exogenously driven cash flows (operating cash = net investment + net debt repayment + net payout), and are smoothed to avoid signalling caprice or policy change. Thus corporate managers face bounds on decisions such as leverage and payout because of previous choices, analysts' expectations, demanding clienteles and competitor policy.

Another strong exogenous influence on firms is pervasive moral hazard, which arises when outside actors induce firms to take higher risks than they would if left alone. Powerful contributors to moral hazard are analysts' expectations and competitive pressure. Also important to moral hazard is the prevalence of out-of-the-money options in at-risk compensation packages for senior executives that increases their risk propensity (Dass *et al.*, 2008).

Even though there are constraints on the decisions of managers in investment funds and corporations, they do have some discretion as agents. Most protect their human capital by acting as stewards (Tosi *et al.*, 2003) and optimise value for investors and shareholders. Also, because managers are engaged in tournament-type competition against fellow employees and competitors, they tend to herd. As a result, non-financial rationales can dominate managers' notionally financial decisions and add further appearance of bias.

Overall, exogenous factors mean financial decisions incorporate objectives other than unconditional value maximisation. Fund managers and firm executives make decisions in light of the weight of money, either as investor contributions or firm cash flow, and are usually price takers. Thus assets have no fundamental value but are priced to achieve equilibrium between largely involuntary flows of funds and securities.

The past *is* a good guide to the future

The idea that the market provides the best indicator of true value dates to at least thirteenth-century philosopher Thomas Aquinas, and many investors take the past as a guide to the future in constant challenge to the ubiquitous fine-print warning against doing so. Consider some examples of where knowledgeable and sophisticated investors rely on historical price data to make buy/sell decisions.

First, a study of almost 700 fund managers across five countries found that the vast majority use technical analysis or some form of charting that uses historical prices to predict future prices. For short-term decisions with horizons up to a month, it is the most important form of decision analysis (Menkhoff, 2010). This was confirmed by most of the fund managers I spoke to. One in Istanbul told me that before starting to manage money he did not believe in technical analysis based on historical data, but has learned that he cannot ignore it.

Another example where experienced investors make reference to historical prices comes from a study of trades in options that a technology firm granted to its employees as part of their compensation (Heath *et al.*, 1999). This found that the firm's executives who should be its most knowledgeable investors tend to exercise options around an historical high in its stock price. In similar vein, Baker *et al.* (2009) found that bid prices in acquisitions cluster around targets' highest price in the previous 52 weeks. In each case, parties with the most information about a firm – its own employees and prospective managers – anchor their valuations around historical prices. Put differently, their best estimate of an attractive future price for any stock is its highest price during the last year or so.

There is also a lot of anecdotal evidence that big figures are important in markets. These are notable price levels – 10,000 on the Dow, a gold price of $1,000 per ounce and similar – that attract investor attention. In a typical study, Jason Mitchell (2001) sets out examples of clustering and price barriers around numbers with symbolism, many of them tied to the decimal system. He concludes that round numbers become simple rules of thumb to measure value, and are used strategically in setting price targets.

Somewhat more unusually, some statistical analyses identify influences on investors from historical data that seem to be quite unrelated to markets. For instance, there are well-documented statistical relationships between stock prices and phases of the moon (Yuan *et al.*, 2006) and the onset of daylight savings (Kamstra *et al.*, 2000). I leave it to readers to decide if this data mining is coincidence or reality.

Finance theorists deny any validity for historical price information because it violates the assumption of efficient markets, where rational investors ensure that publicly available information is continually reflected in prices. This means that no public information – most certainly not historical prices – can have any predictive value. But investors – particularly those running mutual funds or trading in volumes that have measurable market impact – are not likely to be irrational when they make decisions, nor to repeatedly follow behaviours that are sub-optimum. Moreover, they routinely use other information that is already in the public arena such as company reports. This raises a paradox: whereas finance theorists see no merit in historic price data, they believe that other publicly available information sets the fundamental value of securities.

The fact that experienced investors use price data alongside research materials implies they do not believe either has been fully incorporated in prices. Historical data has price value.

Do markets mean revert?

An important question in finance is the extent to which markets mean revert, or move around a long-term average value or trend. The answer cannot be unequivocal because there are two types of datasets in finance.

The first type of financial dataset is the more common and involves a price-based measure such as commodity prices and stock market indexes. Their value changes with moves in the cost basis of the measure, part of which arises from inflation. Many analysts believe that these measures are indeterminate, random walks so that for a security:

$$\text{Price}_t = \text{Price}_{t-1} + \varepsilon_t.$$

where ε is a random, normally distributed value. That is, the price today equals yesterday's price plus a random move.

For econometricians this kind of relationship is called non-stationary because it is not anchored to a mean or average value, and so drifts. Non-stationary datasets pose particular analytical problems because their level is a function of time. Thus when one dataset that evolves over time is regressed on another non-stationary dataset (such as inflation, household disposable income, population), any statistical link identified between them may be due to their shared time base rather than an intrinsic relationship, and so could be spurious.

The second type of dataset is dimensionless and measures some financial parameter that does not have an absolute scale or unit of measurement. Good examples are returns on shares (which come from changes in price-based measures), and ratios such as price-to-earnings or dividend yield. These are generally stationary and stay within a range, and so mean revert.

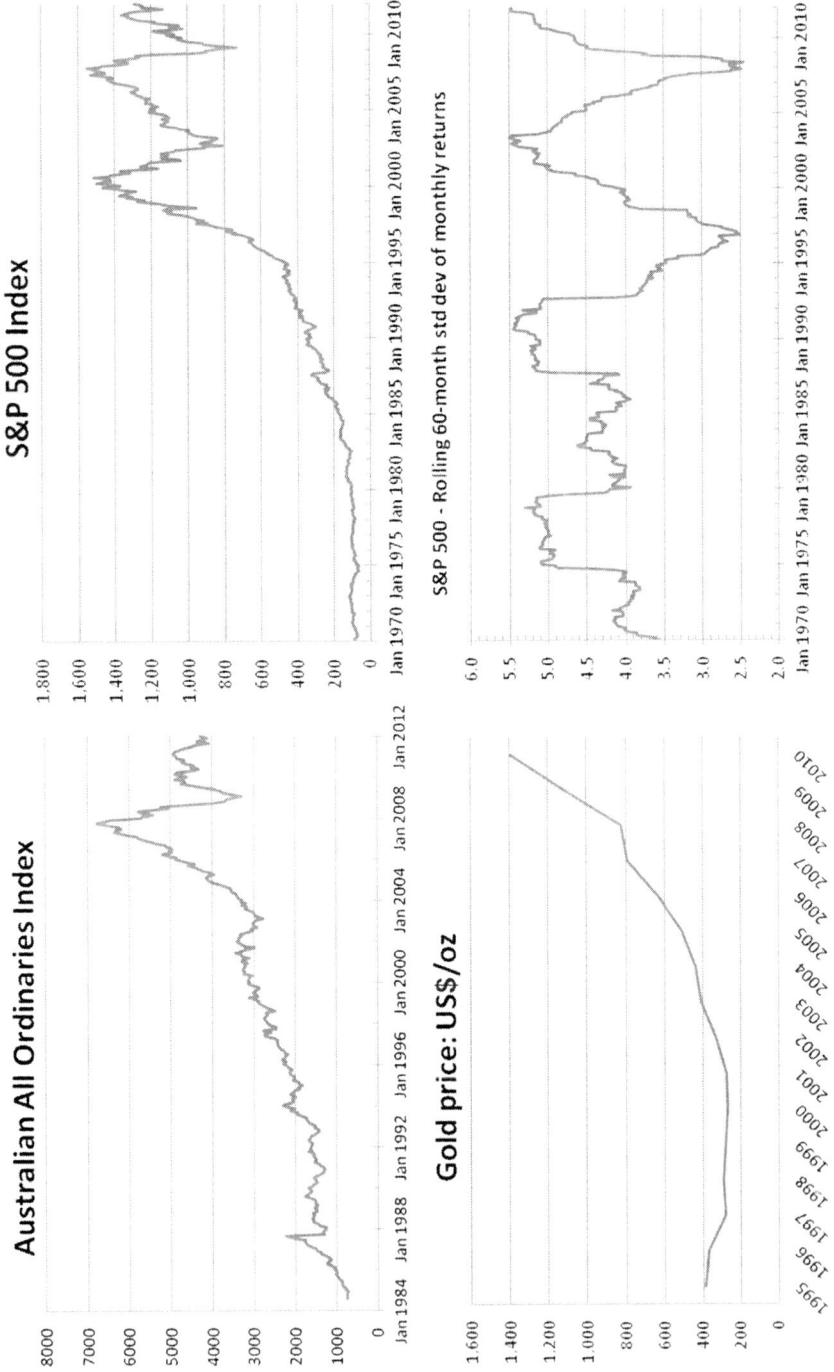

FIGURE 6.2 Plots of All Ordinaries and S&P 500 Indexes, gold price and S&P volatility

The distinction between stationary and non-stationary datasets is not always clear. In Figure 6.2, for instance, the Australian All Ordinaries Index appears non-stationary because it has drifted upwards in a roughly straight line for 30+ years (with excursions above trend in 1987 and 2005–7). But the nature of the US S&P 500 Index is not so certain as it has been range bound since the late 1990s (although it trended up until then). In the lower part of the figure, the gold price appears non-stationary, whilst the dimensionless standard deviation of the S&P 500 is stationary.

The beauty of a stationary measure is that its extremes are obvious and – even without understanding the factors that determine their value – give a guide that helps avoid the worst investor mistakes, which are buying high and selling low. Non-stationary measures, by contrast, can head in the same direction for long periods, during which trend following is a successful strategy. Eventually, of course, the trend falters or even reverses: the S&P Index is a good example. But what about gold? Will it go to $3,000 as the gold bugs predict, or mean revert and crash back towards its $500–800 cost of production?

Sensible investment requires deciding whether the measure you are following is stationary or not.

The best way to trade a non-stationary measure is by following price momentum, and this has been a reliable technical indicator, especially during the bubble periods of recent decades. Alternatively an investor may rely on dimensionless measures that almost certainly mean revert, and trade around their extremes. This explains use of the classic valuation measures – particularly ratios of stock price-to-book value, price-to-earnings and price-to-dividends – which are stationary.

An interesting issue with markets that mean revert is what makes them change direction. The answer is the same as that which flips the outlook of all forward-looking decision makers such as entrepreneurs, inventors and explorers: expectations shift following some catalyst. Many changes in direction are characterised by a metaphor. Exploration, for instance, has often been seen as triumph of the successful explorers' nation – much as sport is today – and the conquest of new lands from Antarctica to the Moon and Olympic medal tallies are linked to the abilities of a whole economy. Markets perform in similar fashion, so that exchange rates have come to be seen as a barometer of national economic success, and interest rates as an inverse measure of government financial skill. The catalyst to flip direction arises in factors such as re-evaluation of government skill or policy, or the long-term prospects of an industry (where expected improvements typically attract the label new) or economy (with labels such as power house or resurgent). Other times, markets will change direction because of sentiment which is cyclical: this is the analytical equivalent of the old contrarian adage that when the bellhops are buying shares, it's time to sell.

Almost without exception the fund managers that I spoke to believe in mean reversion of markets. They see indexes and established stocks as trading within a range, often quite broad and with considerable volatility at times. This leads to a common strategy of overloading on well-priced securities at the bottom of their historical range, and taking profits around historical highs.

Do dud firms throw off warning signs?

It is certainly nice for any investor to correctly identify a good-performing firm, but it is equally important to avoid the duds. Fortunately there is quite a lot of guidance on how to spot them. This has mostly come in the wake of corporate implosions through the last few decades when post-audits were routinely conducted to determine their causes (although none has demonstrated success in stamping out recurrences).

One of the first comprehensive evaluations of contributors to corporate failure came in 1991. This was the year when the Bank of Credit and Commerce International (BCCI) rocked London with the world's (then) worst financial scandal by failing after a '$20-billion-plus heist' which included allegations of money laundering, bribery, terrorism and a host of other offences (Beaty and Gwynne, 1993). Later that year came another massive shock when publisher Robert Maxwell drowned off the Canary Islands in mysterious circumstances, and it was revealed that he had been siphoning funds from his company's pension plans to pay down debt. The London Stock Exchange reacted by commissioning Sir Adrian Cadbury to prepare the first of a string of similar investigations.

Distilling the findings of the Cadbury, Turnbull and other reports suggests that companies at risk of collapse share a number of features that should be apparent to outsiders. The most prominent is a dominant chairman or CEO, often seen in a high and gushing media profile. A typical example was provided by *The Economist* (1 June 2000) in a laudatory article on Enron's CEO only 18 months before the company collapsed. It hailed Ken Lay as a business visionary under the headline 'The Energetic Messiah', and after reporting that Lay was a friend of jailed Drexel Burnham Lambert junk bond trader Michael Milken, who had had an equally high media profile, closed with the observation: 'The arrogant Drexel collapsed in a heap of bad debts and ignominy. For all of its arrogance, Enron is hardly likely to share that fate: but hubris can lead to nemesis, even so.'[2]

Being hailed as brilliant is not always a good thing. A few years after McKinsey consultants Peters and Waterman (1982) published *In Search of Excellence* about America's best-run companies, *Business Week* ran a cover story, 'Who's Excellent Now?' (5 November 1984), which pointed out that many of the companies had failed to keep up with changes in their markets, especially Atari, Delta Airlines, Digital Equipment, Hewlett-Packard and Texas Instruments. In a pointer to the importance of governance, the article blamed the companies' strategic shortcomings on poor organisational structures and processes.

Hubris brought nemesis for many in the GFC, most prominently the head of Lehman Brothers which collapsed in 2008.[3] Dick Fuld became Lehman CEO when the company relisted in 1994, and was Wall Street's longest-tenured CEO in 2006 when *Institutional Investor* magazine named him as America's top chief executive in the private sector. In March 2008, just six months before Lehman's collapse, *Barron's* included Fuld in its list of the world's 30 best CEOs, dubbed him Mr Wall Street, and praised him for transforming 'a bond shop into an elite investment bank'.

This pattern of hubris-brings-disaster is so common that a report by the International Federation of Accountants (2003) traced many corporate failures to

'dominant, charismatic chief executives who were able to wield unchallenged influence and authority over the other senior executives and board directors'. It seems that
CEOs who encourage cult followings come to suffer from some combination of
excessive overconfidence and lack of attention to their business, which leads to con-
flict with lesser mortals such as members of the board. Failing companies often do
not look like a smoothly operating five-ring circus, but a trapeze act featuring headline grabbing Lone Rangers who are more interested in applause than shareholder
value.

A second recurring feature of failed companies is the sudden emergence of a
shortage of human and financial resources that is most commonly brought on by
a poorly executed, major acquisition. These typically occur because too little attention is paid to how much to pay for the acquisition, and inadequate resources are
applied to post-deal challenges, such as blending of systems and culture, restructuring and business optimisation. The company's financial resources become stretched
by the excessive acquisition price, and its internal resources are chewed up by the
effort required to fix chronic problems. Failure becomes inescapable.

Finally, in looking for differences between duds and more successful firms, they
often seem to boil down to mistakes not made. Although there may not be much
to distinguish between good investment ideas, each is streets ahead of bad ideas.

An alternative approach to investing

Most days something happens in the marketplace to challenge finance theory and
investors' preconceptions. Not surprisingly, a large number of investors see markets
as complex, chaotic and unpredictable, and seek something to believe in, perhaps
as a means of making sense of uncertainty.

This search for order is most obvious in finance newspapers and investment
magazines which are full of tips, systems and tempting advertisements offering ways
to get rich. Some systems even guarantee their results. Australia's Securities and
Investments Commission, for instance, took court action to stop a company called
Safety in the Market from advertising that its $A995 computer system would allow
users to profitably trade commodities, currencies and stocks.[4]

Get-rich-quick schemes do not work, and there are really only a few ways to
make money in markets. The first is limited to a small group of people who have
innate skill in identifying opportunities. They tend to have decades of relevant experience and appear to be intuitive modellers who continually absorb huge amounts of
data, process it through a finely tuned experience-based paradigm, and come out
with what appears to be consistently good advice. Others work in a confined space
such as a market sector like mining or pharmaceuticals, or perhaps a country – China
is currently popular – where they know players' track records, can keep abreast of
developments and leverage their particular insights. They identify securities that are
mispriced, and hold them until the security moves to its correct level.

The second way to make money in markets is to provide a service to investors.
A good example is information broking which made a fortune for New York
Mayor Bloomberg through his eponymous company. Other examples are investors

with skill who prefer to capitalise on it by running a fund and using commissions to skim some of the benefits of their skill, knowing it is investors' funds at risk. These are brokers, not dreamers.

In addition, of course, many investors with a wobbly moral compass do so by breaking the law. This can be through notionally victimless (and seemingly low-risk) insider trading, which we discuss in the following chapter. Or it can be more traditionally criminal as discussed in Chapter 5.

For readers seeking to improve their investment decisions, a good place to start is to read the interesting paper by Chicago professor John Cochrane (1999) entitled 'New Facts in Finance' which summarises recent academic research into investment. Cochrane is emphatic that high returns can only be achieved at high risk of loss: investors know they can obtain the market return at low cost and risk, and should think carefully before doing anything different.

Given earlier discussion of investment analysts' conflicts and limited skill, it is no surprise to find that one of the few accepted facts in finance is that the average managed investment fund adds little value. This is because it is fundamentally hard for the average fund to beat the Index (which is a typical performance benchmark) when around half is owned by funds. Moreover, much of any advantage from skill is eroded by expenses and fees that average around 1.6 per cent (Wermers, 2000), and are even higher for better-performing funds. Evidence that funds cannot beat the Index suggests that investors who want their money managed should consider simply accepting the return of the Index through a fund that mimics its constituents. Despite the seeming advantages of this approach, Morningstar (2012) reports that passive-equity mutual funds that invest according to the Index have just 15 per cent of the market, and this has only grown slightly from 10 per cent in 2000.

Despite reason to doubt the ability of analysts, a study by Jegadeesh *et al.* (2004) found that investors can profit from them by following changes in the consensus of analysts' recommendations, and also favourable recommendations for stocks that have established upward price trends and low price-to-book ratios. The net is to acknowledge that analysts' estimates of value are weak, but then pursue price momentum by following trends in their opinion, and validate their opinions using value indicators.

With the dice seeming loaded against the average investor, what can he or she do? A start is to adopt the posture of successful investors which involves a mixture of good ideas, innovative research, respect for market lore and deep cynicism.

A second step is to dismiss as nonsense the finance precept that no investing edge can be obtained by using publicly available data. One basic approach follows simple trading rules. It is recognised, for instance, that dividend ratios predict equity returns (Goyal and Welch, 2003), as do other empirical regularities. Use of such heuristics is the only generic technique for non-professional investors to beat the market.

An approach followed by Warren Buffett, Peter Lynch and other legendary investors is to buy value. They spend much effort in forming a proper, long-term valuation of a firm and buying it at significant margin below that price. This is commonly traced back to the principles set out by Ben Graham (1949) decades ago in his book *The Intelligent Investor* (which is still in print). Buying value typically goes against the crowd. It requires patience and the ability to dismiss fads and bubbles with the *sang froid* exhibited by Warren Buffett when he refused to invest in any business he could not understand and thus famously stayed out of the dot. com boom.

As an aside, most admirers of Graham overlook the fact that he was fairly pessimistic about the average analyst's prospects of making much money. He concentrated more on companies whose price was beaten down towards liquidation value, especially those which he termed cigar butts that were a good short-term investment because they still had a few puffs left in them. A subset of value investors is the disciplined group that adopts a contrarian strategy that rejects over-hyped conventional thinking and relies on mean reversion (Lakonishok *et al.*, 1994). A simple application is to invest in last year's losing asset class, which often does well.

In similar vein, investors with knowledge of a particular sector can leverage it to pick outperforming companies. An experienced geologist, for instance, has insights into the abilities of exploration managers and the prospectivity of their tenements which may provide an edge in identifying best in class.

Another approach builds on my argument in the Introduction that the strategy adopted by commercial banks accepts their lack of expertise in predicting markets and concentrates on generating profits from transactions. The merchants of finance – the banks, brokers and investment houses which dominate the industry – make most of their money from executing financial transactions rather than investing. Retail banks, for instance, arrange loans that charge a margin above their costs of funding. Brokers profit from commissions on transactions they execute for investors. Investment banks make their money through advising on acquisitions and asset sales, issuing equity and arranging debt. Investment funds take a commission on funds under management.

It seems that the best and brightest in finance make good incomes through fees they charge for assisting investors who they encourage to pursue a strategy of seeking profit by predicting future security prices. Put differently, finance experts prefer to sell their transactional capability rather than trading any claimed expertise for their own benefit. This is not surprising as intuitively one would expect that anyone who could forecast markets would use it to trade for themselves in relative anonymity.

Astute readers will identify a similarly low-risk, high-return strategy through investing disproportionately in banks. By extension, it could be equally attractive to invest in other transaction-based activities such as manufacture and sale of consumer staples (e.g. food and liquor), retailing, and property management (rather than ownership). The intuition is that nobody can forecast anything with reasonable accuracy and so investments relying on market prediction or strategy-based activities have unpredictable outcomes. By contrast, services-concentrated portfolios assume that consumers will eat, drink and seek shelter irrespective of market conditions and rely on this natural hedge to reduce the possibility of loss.

Few investors can access the real wealth opportunities

If markets are loaded against outside investors, where can they turn? The most obvious answer is to look for opportunities in privately owned firms through venture capital. These companies are at least partially isolated from the finance industry because they are not yet listed on stock exchanges and thus do not attract scrutiny from mainstream analysts, nor the media (Shojai and Preece, 2001).

Unlisted firms are not necessarily less successful than listed firms, nor inferior investments: just – in many cases – cheaper to buy. Many are better long-term performers because real fortunes are made by entrepreneurs who have a good business model and take well-judged risks. The successful entrepreneurs then extract rent from their skill and risk taking by selling a well-established business to investors. By the time these firms are listed, they have reasonably well-understood cash flows that are of low risk and hence provide only modest returns.

The most obvious evidence to support a strategy of investing in unlisted firms comes from experience of wealth creation in new markets as diverse as US railroad expansion following the Civil War and the 1990s internet boom. The railroad barons and dot.com founders made fortunes from selling their creations, whilst those who invested after the firms went public were typically disappointed. Today in developing economies, most money from investment is made through backing private entrepreneurs.

Some insights into alternative investments came from my discussion with the manager of a London private equity fund. The big difference between his fund and listed equity is that private equity investors are effectively an inside buyer. He has a team of people crawling over the business for months, so they know more than any analyst can find out about a public company. In addition, they can identify risks and mitigate them in a sale and purchase agreement. For instance, there might be concerns about defection of a major customer, tax liabilities, or environmental exposures. The venture capital buyer simply requires an indemnity and warranty so that previous owners take the risk: the buyer, for instance, may agree a price of (say) $100, but only pay $80 and provide the balance after it is clear the risk has gone away. Thus the contract shares risk from information asymmetry, which makes the buying decision the major benefit of private equity. In addition, private investors can take large, often majority, positions which give them a real say in the running of the business.

Another private equity investor in New York pointed out the low level of competition in the sector. His group is able to seek out potential assets, often where the owner is looking for partial exit and a value-adding partner. This gives a better buy price, and also the opportunity to restructure the business: neither is available to listed equity.

What goes on in the investment banks?

As mentioned earlier, I spent six weeks during the second quarter of 2012 interviewing 34 fund managers in Istanbul, London and New York. After scrutinising this concentrated horizontal sample of investment managers, it was hard not to draw comparisons and conclusions.

I came away from Wall Street with at least partial confirmation of much of the criticism of its denizens. A number of fund managers appeared arrogant and self-centred to the point of belittling clients. My visit came a few weeks after Goldman Sachs employee Greg Smith reported that his colleagues refer to clients as Muppets: nobody called me that, but several behaved as if that's how they viewed me.

My first interview was in a magnificent meeting room and finally began after my hosts arrived ten minutes late without apology. During an interesting one-hour session, the two managing directors repeatedly began their responses with 'This may sound arrogant, but ...', before both ostentatiously rushed off to catch planes across the Atlantic and the country.

My contact at another firm assured me that he had set up two meetings with New York managers. I arrived for my first interview only to find that I was not on the manager's calendar, so he knew nothing about me. Even so, he agreed to meet (greeting me courteously, if cautiously), but so obviously treated the contact as inappropriate that I left after a few minutes. Prior to the second interview I received an apology from my contact and assurance that all had been fixed. I arrived a few minutes before the second interview, discovered again that I was not on the security list, and left rather than endure another embarrassing attempt to insert myself where I was not wanted.

Other interviewees were not as arrogant or rude, but few gave the impression that they could really add any value through the investment strategies they led. For instance, during a three-hour session with a global name, I was totally under-whelmed by its money managers' presentations of their favoured investment strategies. The first was built around a strong statistical link between the price of shares today and the consensus forecast of next year's earnings, which seemed little more than a tautology to me. The second involved building a portfolio incorporating in-house global themes, such as growing complexity of firms as globalisation spread. This led to investing in companies such as SAP, IBM and Oracle that offered accounting and other enterprise software, but the manager could not articulate a link between the theme and prices of these companies' shares.

Managers' answers to my questions were often shallow, indicating a lack of introspection about their processes or a salesman's falsity; description of their investment strategy was superficial, amounting to little more than an assurance of buying low and selling high; and most approaches had little evidence of innovation in thought or process that might distinguish them. Few displayed any indication that they had reflected on their task or outcomes. Few confessed to any limitations despite the very fine line between success and failure and the industry's poor mean returns. This was exacerbated by the universal reliance on salary as a performance yardstick.

My Wall Street visit, in particular, left me with the impression that many money managers are like spoilt children, with no manners, team spirit or consideration for others. They live transaction-by-transaction and possess an immense conviction of their own merit (the 'big swinging dicks'). Although financial crises have become recurring characteristics of markets and are catastrophes for clients, money managers see them as mere blips in their personal income streams, and professional irritants because clients take funds away in a retreat to cash. Most interviewees in

New York provided archetypal examples of the worst features of unbridled capitalism, which is reinforced in books on the GFC such as *All the Devils are Here* (McLean and Nocera, 2010) that confirm investment managers understood the risks they were taking with investor and shareholder funds.

Attitudes in London provided a stark contrast to New York as interviewees had a much more collegiate approach within their organisations and towards clients. Following the financial crisis, most seemed to have thought deeply about changes in markets, and what led to the losses. This was evident in numerous reflective comments by most of the interviewees. Experience had humbled their knowledge, and determined them not to repeat the experience, although it had made them uncertain about what investment strategies could work. London had a much more obvious European-style socialist and collectivist approach than New York, and money managers seem a lot more introspective and determined to find solutions for investors.

Conclusion

There is little doubt that the inner workings of finance are opaque. Perhaps the best evidence is the number of new investment approaches that burst on the scene offering great promise, only to burn up like the proverbial shooting star. For instance, in the 1980s chaos theory emerged as an explanation of markets; then behavioural finance took hold as a way to explain investor irrationality; sustainability, ethics and governance arrived in the 1990s; as did a host of other innovative concepts in between and since. It is telling that none has secured support, and markets remain ambiguous.

Notes

1 See, for instance, Harford and Kaul (2005) and Maher *et al.* (2008).
2 *The Economist* is known for howlers on its front covers, and a detailed list is provided by Sullivan (1999). My favourite example is the 1999 cover story entitled 'Drowning in Oil' which predicted that oil prices would continue to head down below their $10 per barrel level just before they began a dizzying rise to $150! However, other well-regarded magazines can be just as bad. For instance, a cover story entitled 'The Crazy Things People Say to Justify Stock Prices' appeared in *Forbes* in 1992 when the US S&P 500 was under a quarter of its March 2000 peak (Baldwin, 1992).
3 'Bleeding Green: The Fall of Fuld', 6 October 2008. Available at http://abcnews.go.com/Business/Economy/story?id=5951669&page=2
4 'ASIC Commences Proceedings against "Safety in the Market"', 8 December 2010. Press release available at www.asic.gov.au

7

THE MIXED RECORD OF FINANCE REGULATION

Q: What do you get when you cross a Mafia don with a bond salesman?

A: A CDO[1] dealer: someone who makes you an offer you can't understand.
Joke doing the rounds of financial markets during the GFC

Investors face risks from failure of markets, banks and firms. Apart from the media and investors' own resources, the only protection comes through bodies that regulate financial services and corporations, and their activities are the subject of this chapter.

Finance is probably the most heavily regulated of all industries, even by comparison with such inherently dangerous activities as nuclear power and licit narcotics cultivation. Monetary authorities – such as the European Central Bank and the United States Federal Reserve – fix official interest rates, and hence strongly influence the price of finance's key commodity, which is money. In most countries, obtaining a banking licence is bureaucratically complex; and anticompetitive legislation to prevent mergers between banks is common. Reporting of financial institutions' activities and condition is continuous and extensive, with banks required to provide regular detailed reports to industry regulators. The latter's powers are sweeping, and enable them to step in with little outside restraint and direct banks' activities.

Successful investment requires knowledge, experience and effort. These are not shared equally between investors, but each anticipates an equal opportunity to make good returns. Regulators are expected to maintain a level playing field by removing impediments such as corrupt managers who destroy their firms; insiders who illegally use private knowledge for profit; large investors who manipulate markets for their own benefit; and availability of excessively risky securities.

Despite expensive and intrusive corporations regulation, the industry has been marked by chronic crises and scandals ranging from excessive risk taking in corporate strategy to fraud by banks. Direct regulation of banks and other firms does not have a good record. So let us examine the (largely anecdotal) evidence to see how effective regulators are in outlawing practices in markets, banks and firms that are potentially so threatening to the interest of investors.

Ever-worsening cycles of bankruptcy

The most obvious evidence of weak regulation is that – since national regulators adopted a concerted global approach after the 1970s – there has been an international financial crisis roughly every seven to ten years. The effect on firms is shown in Figure 7.1 which plots the frequency of bankruptcy by US companies with assets in excess of $1 billion,[2] and clearly shows the roughly decadal cycle of corporate collapses.

Failures during 1989–91 include Continental Airlines, Drexel Burnham Lambert, Texaco and Washington Bancorporation; and amongst companies that collapsed during 2001–2 were Bethlehem Steel, Enron, Loews Cineplex and WorldCom. The latest wave, of course, is the 2008–11 global financial crisis (GFC), where the best-known failures included General Motors, Lehman Brothers and Merrill Lynch. The GFC's most troubling aspect for me is how its bankruptcies slotted – almost like clockwork – into the roughly ten-year cycle of major corporate collapses.

Another disturbing feature of the figure is that each new wave is increasingly damaging, with a growing number of large bankruptcies. Further compounding the concern is that other developed economies as far apart as Australia and Britain experience similar waves of corporate collapses (Clarke, 2004). Nor is this a new

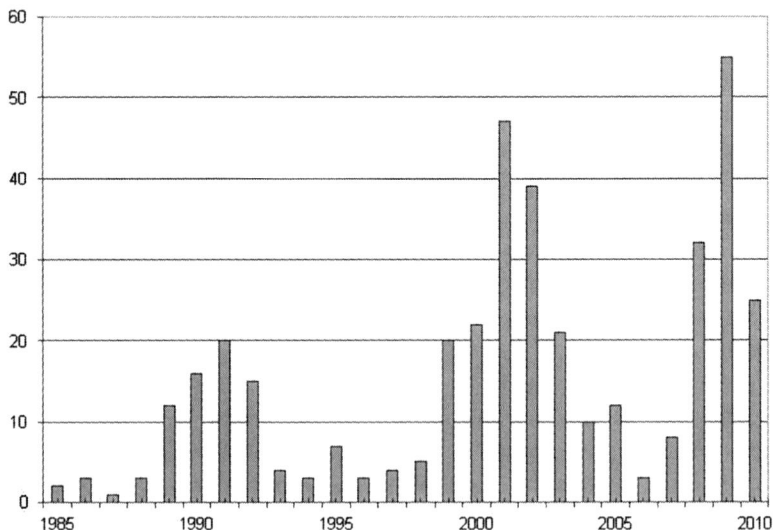

FIGURE 7.1 Frequency of large US bankruptcies

phenomenon: Britain, for example, saw a market crash or panic in virtually every decade of the nineteenth century (Fox, 2009). This regular cycle of collapse of large firms is the most obvious evidence of chronic deficiencies in corporations legislation.

It is important to recognize that most failures of large companies are not due to acts-of-god or crippling competition, but occur because of inadequate strategies and weak processes that were the responsibility of management and should have become apparent to diligent directors and been brought under control. Study after study shows that bankruptcy can be traced to a few key generic causes: poor internal processes, particularly the inability to produce accurate financial accounts; failure to understand the implications of financial activities, particularly hedging and use of derivatives; poorly executed strategies, particularly acquisitions; unskilled directors and disengaged chief executives; and excessive debt.

Whatever the cause of corporate collapse, the effect is that companies become unable to meet their financial obligations. Government can come under strong pressure to pay these costs and must strike the right balance in how much to impose on the rest of the electorate (Thurow, 1981). When the affected group is sufficiently large or politically influential, the company becomes too big to be left to fail and its liabilities are met by the taxpayer.

When government bears costs arising from erroneous corporate behaviour, it may induce moral hazard that encourages future risks: executives gain confidence that government will step in if a serious loss emerges in their firm, and so may take greater risks than they would do otherwise. Sometimes large investors actually encourage companies to take on greater risk knowing that their own exposure is small. Anecdotal evidence and popular sentiment endorse this intuition, but it also has research support: Gropp *et al.* (2010), for instance, analysed the strategies of a large number of banks in OECD countries and found that bail out of a bank induces its competitors to take more risks. This suggestion that corporate collapses and government bailouts feed back to promote future risk in surviving firms is consistent with evidence that collapses come in regular waves.

It is also significant that finance is invariably involved when any firm collapses. Most obviously this includes failure of financial institutions, with recent examples of Lehman Brothers and Merrill Lynch, and historical failures such as Drexel Burnham Lambert and Washington Bancorporation. But finance is involved in many other bankruptcies, especially of large corporations, through misreporting in financial accounts (as in the case of Enron, WorldCom) or financial mismanagement (Continental, Texaco). Also, of course, bankruptcy of any listed firm usually means that investors lose heavily.

Thus corporate failure is a large and steadily intensifying financial problem.

Did people or processes cause the GFC?

Before even thinking about remedies to improve regulation of banks and other corporates, we need to understand how regulations interact with markets to bring on recurring financial crises.

In seeking the causes of financial crises, it is sobering for me to recall a simple study that I made soon after the 1987 stock market crash by reading the findings of the four US inquiries that were set up in its wake. Each was staffed by people with intimate knowledge of the industry and they studied recent, well-documented events (not the future, or distant past). Although the inquiries identified many factors that *might* have affected the market, none could link them to the decisions of investors. Even today the cause of the 1987 Crash remains in dispute, and the economics literature still cannot explain why stock prices shift so abruptly (Cooper *et al.*, 2008).

As an aside, dispute over the genesis of even the best-documented events is actually quite common. My favourite example is recounted by Barbara Tuchman (1962) in her brilliant history *The Guns of August* and involves a German general who was asked how the First World War started, to which he replied, 'Ach, if we only knew!'

The poor track record of financial economists and others in unravelling historically significant events cautions against over-quick prescriptions of the GFC's causes. In fact an interesting paper by Mark Jickling (2009) of the Congressional Research Service has a table that sets out 26 causes! This includes the conventional wisdom of short-term pay incentives for executives in funds and companies, weak regulation and excessive leverage. But it also includes the Black Swan Theory (a once-in-a-century event with uniquely rare causes), excessive use of OTC derivatives (whose risk was unknowable), and human frailty (poor decision making). In similar vein, MIT Professor Andrew Lo (2012) has synthesised the conclusions of a variety of books about the GFC and identified a bewildering array of possible causes.

The outsider consensus is that the GFC was caused by a failure of regulation, which can be traced back to changes in US financial markets legislation during 2000. This moved the industry towards self-regulation, which University of California Professor of Economics Barry Eichengreen derided in *The National Interest* (May 2009): 'Relying on institutional investors to self-regulate is the economic equivalent of letting children decide their own diets.' According to Professor Wray (2009) of the University of Missouri, the reasons why Congress ignored any doubts about the risks of winding back prudent restraints was because 'support of these changes generated huge campaign contributions for political candidates'. The banks presumably expected that self-regulation would be profitable for them.

Of course, it was not deregulation *per se* that brought on the GFC, but decisions by banks and other large investors to take on much more risky strategies, particularly securitisation of a wide variety of loans and rapid growth of derivatives based around interest rates and credit risk. As a result, the face, or notional, value of interest rate derivatives in G10 countries grew from $94 trillion in 2000 to peak at $683 trillion in mid-2008, before dropping and not reaching a new high until 2013 (BIS, 2012 and previous). Most of this was traded on margin, so there was pervasive leverage.

The principal objective of leverage is to boost profit through building a larger portfolio. To see how this operates, consider a house purchase: if mortgages are not available, a house must be bought for cash. With mortgages, though, a deposit of only 10–30 per cent is required to buy a house, not the full price. Thus mortgage lending creates more buyers, and this increase in demand raises the price of houses. Other assets are no different. If investors can borrow to buy shares or can purchase derivatives on margin, they buy more and/or pay more for them. This will obviously boost investors' profits, providing, of course, that the expected return exceeds the loan interest rate. And that is a big proviso.

The risk of borrowing is that – just as it can increase the price of assets and hence their return – it exacerbates losses in a falling market. This is because leveraged investors see the value of their holding fall but not the value of their debt, which forces some to sell assets and accelerates the price fall. So leverage and easy liquidity may initially boost markets; but they make the eventual decline more pronounced.

To set the scene for further discussion, recall that in Chapter 3 we discussed the wall of money from debt and innovation in credit markets. In the US since 1980, borrowings have risen about twice as fast as the economy, mainly in the financial sector where debt rose 23-fold to be larger than each of households, government and other business. This was then leveraged by over-the-counter debt derivatives whose face value is five times the size of all US debt.

The situation was even more stretched in late 2007, and leverage inherent in strategies built around debt derivatives made many securities look like a Ponzi scheme because rising prices gave investors (especially large funds and banks) more borrowing capacity, and so they bought more derivatives. As investors became increasingly leveraged to derivatives of increasingly questionable value, everyone seemed tacitly aware of the risks involved. The best example of this for me came in fund manager presentations that I saw after the early 2000s: more and more of their time was spent in explaining how they controlled risk.

Investing borrowed money in securities that return more than the cost of borrowing is obviously profitable, and leverage can generate good returns even from thin margins. Banks' profits through this period were high, and they clearly secured the expected benefits of self-regulation. As discussed in Chapter 3, the finance industry's share of all US firms' profits rose from 25 per cent in the decade before deregulation to average 33 per cent in the following decade. Through this time, finance contributed a steady 20 per cent of US GDP. Reflecting the shift, financial sector stock prices doubled in the eight years after deregulation was foreshadowed in 1999, while the market as a whole barely budged.

However, like the best Ponzi schemes, everything was fine only as long as everything appeared fine. Expectations of perpetually rising asset prices were brought to an abrupt halt after the US federal funds interest rate doubled in 2005–6: house prices peaked and unemployment began to rise; mortgage defaults rose as the economy slowed; financial stocks fell after late 2007; and in September 2008 Lehman Brothers collapsed. The potential of derivatives and a brittle financial sector to bankrupt the US was never demonstrated, but its possibility panicked the US Treasury and Federal Reserve which offered up trillions of dollars in bailouts.

Certainly there were structural contributors to the GFC such as the wall of money chasing ever more risky investments and the Federal Reserve's excessive liquidity which further promoted risky borrowing. There were also mechanical weaknesses such as the petit corruption of liar loans. But my favourite explanation for the GFC is given by *The Economist* (24 January and 30 May 2009), which says that 'swindles were not common. The crisis owed far more to incompetence than criminality' and – when explaining the causes – most observers 'plump for some mix of greed and incompetence'.

In short, people, not products, caused the GFC. The best evidence of the role of human weakness in the GFC comes from Andrew Gowers who had been head of corporate communications at Lehman Brothers in London during 2006–8 and wrote an insider's account of the firm's human failings in 'The Man Who Brought the World to Its Knees Exposed: Dick Fuld' (London's *Sunday Times*, 14 December 2008). Fuld was a towering character described by Gowers as intense and fostering a cult of personality which inspired equal parts of fear and loyalty. He was detail minded, and a ferocious man who promoted violent images such as a war between Lehman and the market. Gowers went on to finger the causes of Lehman's fall in a shaky corporate governance structure:

> … an over-mighty CEO, a top lieutenant eager to please and hungry for risk, an executive team not noted for healthy debate, and a power struggle between two key players. Furthermore, the board of directors was packed with non-executives of a certain age and woefully lacking in banking expertise.

It is actually very common to see human failings at the centre of financial collapses. For example, in *The Smartest Guys in the Room*, Bethany McLean and Peter Elkind (2004) look back at Enron's Icarus-like fall into bankruptcy and summarise it as

> a story of human weakness, of hubris and greed and rampant self-delusion; of ambition run amok; of a grand experiment in the deregulated world; of a business model that didn't work; and of smart people who believed their next gamble would cover their last disaster.

Regulators – who usually have the best view of what happened – also blame crises on the people involved. SEC Chairman Cox told Congress in late 2008[3] that it was 'abundantly clear … that if honest lending practices had been followed, much of this crisis quite simply would not have occurred … We have learned that voluntary regulation does not work.'

The centrality to financial crises of greed and incompetence is not, of course, a new observation. Well over a century ago, editor of *The Economist* Walter Bagehot (1873) synthesised reasons for the crises that had plagued Britain during the nineteenth century:

> The mercantile community will have been unusually fortunate if during the period of rising prices it has not made great mistakes. Such a period naturally

excites the sanguine and the ardent; they fancy that the prosperity they see will last always, that it is only the beginning of a greater prosperity ... The good times of too high price almost always engender much fraud. All people are most credulous when they are most happy; and when much money has just been made, when some people are really making it, when most people think they are making it, there is a happy opportunity for ingenious mendacity.

Following the GFC, many central bankers referred to Bagehot in mute testimony to how little they had retained of the institutional knowledge gained about their task through the previous century.

External directors face little risk, even in bankruptcy

If people are so clearly the cause of financial crises, it is interesting to ponder what induces them to take the risks associated with these heinous offences. Much of the answer seems to be that – whilst the actions are damaging to investors and the economy more broadly – they are usually not crimes in legal terms, and even when criminal actions are involved the perpetrators are rarely punished. In short, people who contribute to even the largest bankruptcy or financial crisis can expect to escape unscathed.

The most common reason for a corporate collapse is failure of self-regulation by the bank or firm involved: chosen strategies, processes and people are not appropriate for the task at hand. Validating such decisions is the responsibility of the board. Although the law in most jurisdictions has not traditionally distinguished between the responsibilities of internal and external directors, there is a general expectation that outside directors provide an independent oversight of management and will take particular care to protect the interests of smaller shareholders. Thus external non-executive directors could be expected to face scrutiny after a collapse, but the statistics on sanctions against them are sobering: the chance of an external director facing personal liability arising out of his or her firm's bankruptcy is close to zero.

The rare prosecution of directors of failed companies was shown by University of Texas Law Professor Bernard Black and colleagues (Black *et al.*, 2006) in their study of US bankruptcies between 1980 and 2006 which found that not a single outside director had been prosecuted for breach of their duties. That is, even though more than 270 companies with assets in excess of $1 billion went bankrupt during the period (plus far more numerous smaller firms) and outside directors were expected to protect shareholders' interests, not one *legally* failed to do so!

This makes it interesting to see that a significant number of directors of bankrupt firms are actually found to be criminals through convictions for other offences. For instance, 30 external directors in four of these companies suffered a criminal or financial penalty for insider trading or similar. Even those few sanctions required conditions equivalent to a perfect storm, specifically that the company is insolvent, damages exceed insurance cover, the company has lied in a prospectus or report (and the director had been negligent in failing to review it), and the culpable directors are wealthy.

A second deficiency in corporations regulation that protects directors is in its administration, particularly the fact that most sanctions for criminal offences are agreed by negotiation between the regulator and the affected firm. Through these negotiations it is normal for the firm to plead guilty to an offence and negotiate a deal where the company pays a fine and makes admissions and undertakings, but individuals suffer nothing more than minor penalties. Even then the offenders tend to be people in low positions who executed the transaction under instructions, rather than senior executives who established the defective framework.

The rationale for agreeing to a fine for the firm rather than prosecuting its executives seems to be that it benefits almost everyone involved. From the perspective of regulators, taking an action to trial brings delays, high costs and uncertainty in outcome. Ditto for the accused, with the added risk that senior executives could face criminal prosecutions. Negotiating a deal gives the regulator a successful outcome and headline-grabbing fine, and perhaps some restitution. For the criminals involved, costs are paid by the firm (and sometimes its insurer under Directors & Officers cover) and they avoid prosecution. The loser? Why investors, of course, who always pay for everything.

During recurring waves of bankruptcies, external directors have rarely been prosecuted, and they face minimal risk of personal financial liability. Certainly there is a reputational risk: being a director of a failed company would damage personal capital and limit future appointments. But penalties are rare. It is not unreasonable to suspect that the absence of sanctions for bankruptcy could encourage complacency amongst external directors especially for those in an ineffectively self-regulated environment such as finance.

In fact prosecutions are unlikely for any executives of large firms under the current philosophy of 'too big to jail'. It is common to say that no senior executive has been successfully prosecuted in the US for GFC-related crimes. An inkling of what is motivating authorities to be so benign is given by the testimony of US Attorney General Eric Holder to the Senate Judiciary Committee (6 March 2013):[4]

> I am concerned that the size of some of these [financial] institutions becomes so large that it does become difficult for us to prosecute them when we are hit with indications that if you do prosecute, if you do bring a criminal charge, it will have a negative impact on the national economy, perhaps even the world economy.

Such thoughts make a mockery of the claim that justice is blind, and of the sworn duty of law officers to ensure enforcement and retribution are equal for rich and poor, big and small.

Benign tolerance of insider trading

Insider trading involves use of information that is not public in order to guide yourself or others in buying or selling securities. I was sensitised to the existence and effects of insider trading at an early age when the father of a friend was appointed to the committee of management of a sporting ground in Melbourne whose wonderful city-edge venue raised money by hosting a greyhound race track. The three of us often went together, and on each occasion the father was given a racebook with his initials on the cover and the faintest pencil mark against one dog in each race. Blow me down, most of them won.

Since then, insider trading has always struck me as inequitable: it enables already-privileged investors to make money at the expense of those without connections. Thus in finance, it can bring harsh punishment. Amongst the counts that sent Enron COO Jeff Skilling to jail was insider trading.[5] Martha Stewart received a jail sentence for conspiracy and lying to investigators after selling her shares in a biopharmaceutical company when told by her broker that its CEO was dumping his stock.[6] In Australia, entertainer Steve Vizard, who had been appointed by the government to the board of telecoms giant Telstra, was fined and banned from being a director after he bought shares in a company that he learned was to be taken over by Telstra.[7]

Although insider trading is typically deplored as threatening to cause an investment strike, it has become illegal relatively recently. Amongst developed countries, only Canada, France, Singapore, Sweden and the United States had established insider trading laws before 1980; another 29 countries established them during the 1980s, with Germany not acting until as late as 1994 (Bhattacharya and Daouk, 2002).

Opportunities for insider trading appear legion because of the many events that have a possible impact on stock prices. In the United States alone, there are around 900 mergers and acquisitions (M&As) of listed companies announced each year.[8] Add to that exciting or disappointing results for mineral explorers, R&D firms, high tech entrepreneurs and other dealmakers, and literally every day sees numerous price-significant corporate events. Before each is publicly announced, the inside information inevitably becomes known to directors and senior executives, the company's financial, legal and public relations advisers, and – often – regulators and unions. Nor is the knowledge confined to senior executives, as secretaries, couriers, realtors and printers have been accused of trading knowledge gained in their duties. So dozens of people can be aware of the details: each has access to a phone, PC or internet brokerage account and can illegally trade in anticipation of the transaction. They can also tell friends, family and strangers in the street, each of which would also be illegal.

Investors' worst suspicions about the prevalence of insider trading are confirmed by the regular emergence of particularly shocking examples. In 2011, Donald Johnson pleaded guilty following charges that he had used information gained in his position as a managing director of NASDAQ on the exchange's market intelligence desk. He admitted to placing orders through his wife's brokerage account ahead of nine corporate events during 2006–9 that made him profits of over $700,000. Johnson was sentenced to 42 months' jail and forfeited the trading profits.[9]

These charges were part of Operation Perfect Hedge which began in New York after a surge in profits by hedge funds, and targeted insider trading within that sector.

The pace stepped up in the wake of the GFC, and more than 60 people have been charged.[10] One of the highest-profile victims is Raj Rajaratnam, founder of the Galleon Group hedge fund, who received an 11-year prison sentence in 2011. Another high-profile case involved seven employees of hedge funds who made $62 million in profits from trading in Dell stock using information about profit announcements obtained from an unnamed employee in Dell's investor relations department.[11]

Apart from corporate insiders, anecdotal evidence of anticipatory insider trading frequently emerges in the wake of major one-off events. For example, after the 11 September 2001 terrorist attacks, CBS Evening News reported an extreme imbalance in options trading with very high volumes of put options on American and United Airlines that it speculated may have been initiated by Osama bin Laden. A more detailed study by Allen Poteshman (2006) confirmed 'there is evidence of unusual option market activity in the days leading up to September 11 that is consistent with investors trading on advance knowledge of the attacks'.

Despite the occasional victory, it seems simple for even minimally sophisticated insiders to hide their trades amongst the 500 million transactions each day on global markets. So how common is insider trading? Judging from prosecutions, the answer is not very. For instance, during 2001–10 the US Securities and Exchange Commission (SEC) filed around 50 charges each year for insider trading.[12] Australia's Securities and Investments Commission (ASIC) reports bringing insider trading cases against 26 people between 2009 and 2012, and a third as many cases in the previous 15 years; it achieved just 14 convictions during 2001–10.[13]

However, studies conducted independent of regulators find insider trading is much more common. For instance, the *New York Times* commissioned a research firm to study share trading around 90 mergers valued at more than $1 billion in the year to July 2006 (Morgenson, 2006). It found that 'shares of 37 target companies exhibited abnormal trading in the days and weeks before the deals were disclosed ... [which] most likely involved insider trading'. The article reported that a similar UK study had found abnormal trading ahead of 29 per cent of mergers.

Academic analyses reach similar conclusions. A large-scale study of stock price changes around acquisition announcements by Bris (2005) concluded that insiders made positive returns in at least 30 per cent of transactions. Cornell and Sirri (1992) obtained detailed records of trading in a takeover firm during the month before its acquisition and found insiders bought 29 per cent of the stock sold. Meulbroek (1992) examined cases of insider trading detected by the SEC, and concluded that insiders were responsible for most of the abnormal trading volume prior to the announcement, and caused about half the pre-announcement price move.

Given the apparent high frequency of insider trading – involving around a third of M&As, for instance – it is not surprising that a number of analysts claim to be able to profit from them, including Dr Jon Najarian who writes an e-mail newsletter *Options Trader* (personal communication, 24 May 2008). He pointed out how well-placed insiders obtained early insights and some were induced by money to abuse their position. The clearest evidence can be seen in strong moves of stock and derivative prices ahead of announcements. He denies having access to inside information but anticipates where the smart money is going through his 'proprietary HeatSeeker technology [which] tracks unusual trading activity on the options exchange'. This means that illegal insider trading is economically significant, and so must impact investors.

Despite prosecutions by regulators, they seem to be barely scratching the surface of insider trading. Consistent evidence that a third of M&As are likely to be accompanied by insider trading means that the 900 M&As in the US each year would bring multiple instances of illegal insider trading each day. Add in other corporate activities, and thousands of transactions are involved, each with multiple likely insider traders. With only a few dozen prosecutions each year, illegal insider trading seems out of control.

Do investors have to worry about markets being manipulated?

As discussed above, investors are exposed to the possibility of insiders siphoning off their profits, banks ripping them off, bankruptcy of their investee companies, and collapse of mutual funds and hedge funds. But that is not the end of it because they also face risk from lack of integrity in markets where their securities are traded, particularly deliberate manipulation of prices.

From a theoretical perspective, economists generally reject the possibility of market manipulation in favour of their efficiency. But the existence of securities and corporations regulation is mute testimony to government fears of corruption. Again it is hard to compile statistics, but let's look at a couple of examples of market manipulation which should make investors wary.

One recent manipulation case involves energy trader Parnon Energy Inc, which was alleged by the Commodity Futures Trading Commission (CFTC) to have manipulated NYMEX crude oil futures prices.[14] The scheme was launched in January 2008 when Parnon bought five million barrels of West Texas Intermediate (WTI) crude oil, whose price is a global benchmark. The contract required delivery of the oil in Cushing, Oklahoma, in February, and the amount involved was close to expected inventory at the time. Parnon simultaneously bought futures contracts for 14 million barrels of oil. Prices then increased, at least in part because other traders were anticipating an attempt to corner the market (that is, where one trader holds a dominant or controlling position). Parnon sold its long futures position at a profit, and then established a short position of 12 million barrels. They completed the cycle of market manipulation by dumping the physical position on 25 January, which was the last day they could sell for cash and avoid physical delivery. This surprised the market and so prices fell, giving Parnon a profit on its short position. The traders repeated the scheme in February (and intended to do so again in March but were frightened off by a CFTC request for documents) and made at least $35 million profit.

Another case involved manipulation of the market for propane (which is a hydrocarbon gas) by oil giant BP. During January 2004 the company bought futures contracts for delivery of propane into the Texas Eastern Products Pipeline

Co. storage in Texas (or its associated pipeline) in February which is when inventories reach mid-winter lows. BP eventually established a position that at times exceeded the available inventory of propane and effectively cornered the market. Interestingly this was well known by other traders who jokingly gave their BP counterparts 'Hunt' surnames in reference to the Hunt brothers' attempt to corner the silver market in the 1970s. BP then withheld delivery of physical propane which meant that some traders could not fulfil their delivery obligations, and – to avoid shipping product in from elsewhere – they had to pay ever-higher prices. Ultimately, though, the strategy was not profitable because warm weather and imports lifted propane inventories and increased the costs for BP to maintain the corner. BP, though, was forced to pay a $US303 million fine to avoid criminal prosecution by the US Department of Justice.[15] The BP example shows that market manipulators are not just small traders operating in thin, or illiquid, markets.

It is interesting that many examples of market manipulation occur in the energy derivatives market. So, why energy? It is by far the largest commodity market worth trillions of dollars annually, offers numerous complex securities such as swaps, options and price spreads, and largely trades over the counter in opaque, unregulated markets. Add in geopolitical influences on oil availability and seasonal factors which can tighten supplies ahead of winter and summer demand peaks, and there are obviously lots of opportunities for mischief.

Other large targets of CFTC investigations include JP Morgan Chase and HSBC which are alleged to have used high-frequency computer trading software to distort silver prices.[16] This was discussed by former banker and investigative journalist William D. Cohen (*New York Times*, 2 March 2011, 'A Conspiracy with a Silver Lining') who outlined how the firms amassed over 85 per cent of the short positions in silver by flooding the market every time the price stopped falling.

Other markets have been squeezed, too. In September 2010 the Financial Industry Regulatory Authority fined Trillium Brokerage Services $1 million for equity market manipulation using high-speed computers and software algorithms to implement a technique called 'quote stuffing'.[17] The manipulation starts by Trillium entering a buy order at the best bid, or most attractive buy price; the Trillium trader then enters a series of sell orders at just above the best offer price which tricks other traders' computers into seeing a large volume of pending sales and so selling to Trillium in expectation of falling prices. Trillium then cancels the fake sell orders, and reverses the process by entering a sell order and numerous buy orders that indicate rising prices and then closes that position. Each trade effectively captures the bid-offer spread, and Trillium made 46,152 such trades for a profit of $575,765. Confirming that leopards do not change their spots, Trillium had been fined $225,000 in 2004 for violations of futures trading rules.

Not all market manipulators rely on state-of-the-art systems. Hedge fund manager Andy Kessler (2009) used an Op-Ed piece in the *Wall Street Journal* to describe bear raids or dump and pump schemes that he says were behind falls in share prices that brought several banks to the brink of collapse (or beyond) during the GFC. Because banks are financed through short-term funding which they invest for a much longer term, there is a mismatch in the duration of their debt (overnight or short-term funding) and assets (typically multi-year mortgages). After 2000, more of the banks' assets were made up of exotic OTC derivatives for which regulators required insurance, which took the form of credit default swaps (CDS). Under these, the buyer of the swap (that is, the bank) makes a series of insurance-type payments to the issuer of the swap (AIG dominated this market) and receives a payout if the counterparty on the bank's derivatives defaults. As the net value of CDS is usually a fraction of corporates' debt (Oehmke and Zawadowski, 2012), the bears were able to manipulate these links by buying the CDS which bid up their price, increased the apparent probability the counterparty would default, and raised their risk. This undercut the value of banks' derivatives, forced their write down and pulled down the banks' stock price. Bank of America, Bear Stearns, Citigroup and Lloyds Banking Group all lost over 90 per cent of their share price, apparently in the face of such raids (see also a research paper by Finnerty, 2005).

Market manipulation, like insider trading, seems rife.

Why do we tolerate short selling?

There is nothing wrong with selling a stock: markets require willing sellers, as well as willing buyers. Short selling, by contrast, involves sale of shares that you do not own in expectation of buying them back later at a lower price. Because this is illegal in most jurisdictions, short sellers need to borrow shares from an owner. This is typically arranged by stock brokers or trading banks who have agreements to rent the shares of mutual funds and custodians.

An investor who wants to short a stock (most trades involve hedge funds) places an order with the broker and puts sufficient funds into the margin account to cover any likely loss; the broker then borrows the shares and sells them. To close out the transaction, the investor places a buy order which the broker executes and returns these shares to the lender with a fee, usually less than 1 per cent on an annualised basis.

If you think this sounds crazy, you are on the right track. The owner of a share (who presumably hopes the price will rise) lends it to another investor whose sole purpose is to drive the price *down*. And the size of the market is huge, with at least 5 per cent of securities loaned out.

So what motivates securities lenders? Most is done by institutions such as mutual funds, exchange-traded funds and insurance firms, whose managers pass on only part of the benefits to the shares' owners (that is, investors in the fund). Thus a survey of European exchange-traded funds found that the managers of iShares and EasyETF take half of the gross revenue from securities lending.[18] For custodians there are benefits in lending out shares they hold in trust for investors: as the GFC unfolded in the first half of 2008, BNY Mellon and State Street earned over $500 million from lending $1.2 trillion of shares entrusted to their custody by clients.[19]

Custodians and managers of funds are keen to lend shares because they – rather than investors – receive a considerable portion of the benefit. This is yet another example of how investors' agents can destroy value for them.

Why do we tolerate the existence of derivatives?

Derivatives are invariably at the centre of market manipulation, financial crisis and bank failure. Derivatives prove consistently damaging because they can be bought on margin and provide opportunities for leverage; and because most of them are traded over-the-counter in opaque, weakly regulated markets. Despite the damage they do, derivative securities have few redeeming features, and do not serve to fund firms or governments. One would expect them to be treated in the same way as other high-risk products like explosives, narcotics and cigarettes.

Derivatives first sprang to prominence following a series of corporate disasters in the 1990s, and instantly entered the average investor's lexicon with a well-deserved evil image. A typical warning was sounded by *Time* magazine in a graphic 1994 article, 'The Devil's in the Derivatives',[20] that reported on an 86-year-old widow who lost her savings in a AAA-rated bond fund. Sound familiar?

The defining characteristic of derivatives is that they derive their price or value from an underlying security, usually something tangible like a share, bond, commodity or index. Thus the Share Price Index (SPI), which is a popular derivative in Australia, is priced at the value of the benchmark ASX 200 Index multiplied by $A25. Derivatives are often described as risk management products because investors can choose to either buy or sell them, which allows them to, respectively, profit from a rise or fall in the underlying security and so manage the risk of an adverse move in the price of other securities that they hold. Even though this justification is commonly advanced, it is disingenuous because most derivatives are used to take risks, not manage them.

Some derivatives are simple or vanilla, such as SPI futures which agree the price to buy or sell the SPI at a future date. Their final value is a function of the difference between the actual price of the security on the day the contract matures and the agreed price. Such simple derivatives are the staple of organised futures exchanges.

The most common form of derivative, though, is a swap where two parties agree to exchange the cash flows from two securities, perhaps the interest payments on 90-day bills and 10-year bonds. If bond yields go up relative to bills, then the party who committed to pay bond yields in the swap pays cash to the party who committed to pay bill yields. This obviously *could* protect a borrower who has a disproportionate amount of debt in bills or bonds and wants to swap it out. Naturally that is the finance industry's rationale for swaps.

Swaps are arranged not just on interest rates, but also currencies, shares and anything that has a regular set of cash flows. Most swaps are organised over-the-counter by a member of the International Securities Dealers Association, and are private contracts that – until recently – had been subject to minimal regulation. To arrange a swap, you go to a dealer (which is typically a financial institution), tell them the details (securities involved, principal, maturity date and so on) and they take care of everything.

The scale of global derivatives trading is reported by the Bank of International Settlements and is summarised in Table 7.1.

Table 7.1 Face value of outstanding derivatives contracts: global total in trillion US$ at December 2012[21]

Asset	Security	Futures exchange	Over-the-counter
Interest rate	Futures/FRAs	24	71
	Options	26	48
	Swaps		370
Foreign exchange	Futures/Forwards	0.2	32
	Options	0.1	10
	Swaps		24
Equity	Futures/Forwards	1	2
	Options	4	4
Credit default swaps			25
Other/unallocated			47
Total		55	633

To put these numbers in perspective, annual international trade at the end of 2012 was about $US30 trillion,[22] the total value of global debt was about $110 trillion ($84 trillion in domestic issues and $22 trillion in international issues[23]), and the capitalisation of global equity markets was around $54 trillion.[24] The table shows that the face value of interest rate derivatives is five times global debt, and foreign exchange derivatives is more than twice the value of annual international trade. Conversely, equity derivatives are only a fifth of the physical market. It is hard to resist the conclusion that derivatives in debt and FX markets are used primarily for speculation.

As discussed in Chapter 3, speculation involves purchase of a derivative when you do not have an exposure to the underlying security. A speculator does not use derivatives to hedge a position but to take on a position. So how does the table indicate speculation? Quite simply in the case of interest rates because the face value of derivatives is five times the value of all outstanding debt. Even if every debtor had hedged all their exposure, derivatives would only equal the face value of debt. So roughly 80 per cent of interest rate derivatives have no matching physical position and are a bet on interest rate movements. This situation contrasts dramatically with equity derivatives which are only a fraction of the market value of global equities.

The problem is compounded because less than a tenth of derivatives are sold through organised futures exchanges, with the rest sold over-the-counter as private contracts. The advantage of exchanges is that they are the counterparty to each transaction, and – by imposing margin requirements – make sure there are adequate funds on hand to cover any losses. It is not fool proof, but default risk is pretty low. Also the contracts are standardised and publicly traded, so there is usually a transparent market price; and futures markets are supervised by a government regulator.

The principal advantage of over-the-counter transactions is that contracts can be pliantly shaped to the needs of counterparties (whereas exchanges require uniform products in terms of size, maturity date and structure). Conversely, disadvantages of OTC derivatives are large, particularly the lack of liquidity which can make it hard to sell a complex derivative, and reliance on performance of a counterparty that may lack resources to settle any loss. Complex derivatives often prove impossible to value and there is no public trading so that margining is difficult and there is no regular independent valuation.

OTC derivatives have long been central to many financial crises and their risks are clearly apparent. So much so that since the 1990s insiders feared they could bring down the whole financial system because of their volume, limited capital backing and uncertain composition and counterparties, and because they had spread toxic tentacles across many banks. As McLean and Nocera (2010) describe in *All the Devils are Here*, there had been several proposals in the United States to regulate OTC derivatives and remove the opacity around them, but each was rebuffed by Congress and regulators.

OTC markets actually look like the classic bucket shop, which is an establishment that styles itself as a broking business, but does not actually trade in stocks and commodities and instead enables investors to bet on their rise or fall. It is illegal in many US states to operate a bucket shop, with the ban in North Carolina dating to 1905.[25] If OTC derivatives are used primarily for speculation, one wonders why nobody prosecutes their dealers for running nothing more sophisticated than a bucket shop.

Until recently the market for OTC derivatives had been self-regulated, and – in concert with a lack of market competition – offered rich pickings for big dealers and financial institutions. The lack of transparency, liquidity and reliable counterparties in OTC markets was why banks needed to be bailed out during the GFC. Many of the shortcomings of derivatives were neatly captured by one of the fund managers I spoke to who said that the GFC 'is best seen through the hot potato analogy where a lot of ill-understood assets were being traded around'.

Why are regulators so inefficient?

The decadal cycle of financial crisis and corporate collapse plotted at the start of this chapter and discussion of criminal and deceptive practices suggest that financial regulators lack either the ability or willingness to prevent crises. Testing this intuition is important because the current regulatory approach rests on two critical assumptions: legislators are able to anticipate actions by firms that will bring unwanted externalities and enact suitable controls; and regulators are able to observe firms' behaviour in real time and take action to prevent damage. Whilst these may reflect a naively touching faith in the power of government bodies, they are not the product of experience. Consider two of the most-cited US corporate failures: energy giant Enron and investment bank Lehman Brothers.

The collapse of Enron was perhaps the most significant corporate failure of all time for the sheer havoc it subsequently wreaked in board rooms around the globe. Like many collapses it seemed sudden: in mid-2000 *The Economist* magazine profiled Enron CEO Ken Lay under the headline 'The Energetic Messiah', but in December the following year the company filed for bankruptcy with debt of around $40 billion.

Although Enron had many shortcomings including appalling employee and customer relations, the reason it failed was because of aggressive manipulation of accounting earnings (Stewart, 2006). With full knowledge of the Securities and Exchange Commission and the company's auditors Arthur Anderson, Enron introduced a policy of mark-to-market accounting whereby it immediately booked the financial impact of every transaction: thus in the first year of an energy supply contract, Enron reported the expected profit over its whole term. This accelerated income whilst sales and markets were rising, but was reversed by write-downs when financial and energy markets turned down after early 2000.

The aggressive accounting practices that led to Enron's collapse were specifically approved by the SEC, despite recognition of their threat to the company. In evaluating the supervisory ability of regulators, it is important to realise that their detailed knowledge of Enron's fatal accounting practices did not prevent the firm's collapse.[26]

Lehman Brothers filed for Chapter 11 bankruptcy at the peak of the GFC firestorm, and became America's largest corporate failure. Although Lehman lost half its market value in 16 months to May 2008, this was similar to most banks' experience and it had capital in excess of statutory requirements. But then Lehman's share price halved again in little over a month and the company collapsed over a few days in September 2008.

The reason for Lehman's collapse is commonly traced to poor governance (e.g. Larcker and Tayan, 2010), which was widely apparent. Most obvious was the weak skill sets of Lehman's board whose 11 directors included an 82-year-old former actress, a 75-year-old Broadway producer, a retired Sotheby's CEO, and two other members aged over 75 years (Lehman, 2005). Hardly the right stuff to manage one of the world's great risk machines. Although the poor governance that contributed to Lehman's final collapse had been apparent for years, the end came swiftly and could not have been prevented by regulators.

Another striking feature of US securities regulation which is not a topic of polite conversation is the revolving door between Wall Street firms and those who regulate them. If you think about the four key groups of players in the finance industry – academia, corporates, banks and regulators – there is a lot of movement, but it occurs along narrow pathways. Few people from non-bank companies move into any of the other sectors, almost as if they find some hindrance in their background from making the transition. Although a few academics move into regulation, they tend to work (most often part time) for banks.

By far the heaviest traffic is the to-and-fro movement at senior levels between banks and regulators. There are so many transitions that suspicions inevitably arise that some people in finance look on public service with a regulator as the opportunity to create wealth for their colleagues. This leads to the allegation of crony capitalism where an industry has such strong relationships with government that it can secure self-serving policy.

Consider a few examples around the GFC when the US government set up the Troubled Asset Relief Program that committed $700 billion to buy the assets and equity of institutions at risk of bankruptcy. The main bank beneficiaries were Citigroup, Bank of America, American International Group, JP Morgan Chase, Wells Fargo, Goldman Sachs and Morgan Stanley.[27]

A central decision maker during the bailouts was Treasury Secretary Hank Paulson who was in office from 2006 until the early 2009 change in administration. Paulson had been CEO of Goldman Sachs for a decade before accepting the Treasury role, and this made it difficult to avoid the appearance of possible conflicts of interest. For instance, Newt Gingrich argued that the 'Goldman Sachs heavy crew of advisers' had misled policy makers during the GFC.[28] Other reports were more specific. As an example, Bloomberg reports that Paulson was in Moscow in 2008 at the time of a Goldman Sachs board meeting, and he met with the board. Suspicion about what went on was inevitable when Bloomberg reported that the event was omitted from Paulson's official calendar and Goldman had been asked to 'keep the [meeting] plans quiet'.[29] Another example reported by Bloomberg relates to a lunchtime meeting of hedge fund managers on 21 July 2008 that had been arranged by former Goldman Sachs partner Eric Mindich. In previous days, speculation had raged that Fannie Mae and Freddie Mac would require a bailout, but Paulson had told Congress and the media that they did not need one and should not receive it. This rallied the two firms' share prices. Bloomberg reported that Paulson told the hedge fund managers of plans to bail out the two firms.[30] One of the attendees contacted his lawyer who told him it was 'material non-public information' and he could not legally trade stock in either company. Paulson makes no mention of either meeting in his interesting memoir *On the Brink*.

Paulson steered US policy during the GFC, and it is interesting to see him quoted by the *Chicago Tribune* as saying after the bailouts:[31] 'It seemed like there was a good chance Morgan Stanley could go down, and if it did that could take Goldman down. It would have been all she wrote for the American economy.' He was one of many who apparently followed a tweaked version of the old saying to convince themselves that what was good for the banks was good for America.

Industries such as finance are so complicated that only people with extensive experience have any chance of success as a regulator. So gamekeepers should be recruited from the ranks of poachers. But the likelihood of embedding crony capitalism makes it a risky strategy to rely too much on them. However, the revolving door between regulators and regulated is not just a US or finance industry phenomenon. In Australia, for instance, when Graeme Samuel was appointed as Chairman of the Australian Consumer and Competition Commission in 2003, a radio interviewer put criticisms to him that he 'been labelled a hardline economic rationalist and too close to the big end of town, having been a merchant banker, a lawyer and the president of the Australian Chamber of Commerce and Industry'.[32] In 2004, Greg Bourne, who had recently retired as Regional President of BP Australasia, was appointed CEO of World Wildlife Fund Australia.[33] Just to show the traffic is not one way, Paul Gilding left Greenpeace International to establish his own firm that consulted to large companies on sustainability issues.[34]

A factor contributing to some banking regulators' inefficiency is limits on the capability of their staff. First, even the smartest regulator cannot be across every area of a company that could bring it down. It is simply not practical for outsiders to monitor a large company in the sense of being able to anticipate failure and enforce remedial actions in a timely manner. Regulation seems to be most successful when narrowly targeted with well-understood processes, such as approvals of pharmaceuticals and disease control (Hillinger, 2010). Corporations, by contrast, are broad with many processes that are not easily understood, and decades of experience have shown that government control simply does not work.

At best regulators can collate accounting and operational information and input it to a bankruptcy prediction model. But long experience shows that they lack sufficient scientific understanding of banks and other firms and are effectively blind to causes of failure that arise in real time such as poor strategic decisions, risky operations and questionable practices. As a result banks and other firms are left to regulate themselves in virtual secrecy, and some do so with little care for shareholders or the community.

Moreover, regulators can prove no match for corporate executives because the latter are so much better paid, and money attracts the best and brightest accountants, lawyers and other putative regulators to companies and their advisers. For instance, the 2010 salary of the chairman of the Federal Reserve Board was $199,700,[35] which was less than the salary of middle managers in banks that the chairman regulates. Similarly in Australia, the highest-paid employee of the regulator APRA received less than $445,000 at the time of the GFC, whereas a dozen employees at Australia's then largest bank, Westpac, earned more than twice as much. Certainly money is not the only inducement for talent, but the imbalance seems obvious. Because large companies attract the best and brightest, they are easily able to structure activities so that they stay within the law and run risks with potential losses so large that they must be met by taxpayers and the community (Wexler, 2010). The lack of regulatory expertise and resulting inefficiency in supervision is a well-recognised contributor to corporate failure (Moshirian, 2010).

Investment managers that I interviewed generally agreed with my analysis above. One made the obvious point that regulators are always behind the curve. He used the example of value-at-risk (VaR) that a decade ago everybody thought was the alpha and omega, but none understood that it doesn't work when there are large market movements. Similarly with the mortgage crisis, regulators should have been monitoring the banks' balance sheets to look at their investments and risk, but did not because they could not understand them.

Because regulators do not look at how to stop or limit risk, but address specific actions, they are always playing catch up, which leaves loopholes. According to one CIO: 'The market guys are smarter than regulators. They can find back doors in regulation, read the legislation differently and get it approved in court. The regulators need to be smarter than people in the market, but they cannot keep up. They are not able to take necessary precautions before a problem emerges.' The fund managers believe that irresponsible investors will always find a new way to make money. There will always be clever people who have access to capital who will take big risks to make more money. Fund managers fear that new regulation in the US and elsewhere will hurt the conventional approach of banking and finance, but do nothing to address avoiding future crises.

The last decade of financial regulation

Following the GFC, there has been no shortage of proposals for regulatory reform, most obviously through US legislation known as the Dodd–Frank Wall Street Reform and Consumer Protection Act (DFA).[36] It was described by President Obama as 'a sweeping overhaul of the financial regulatory system, a transformation on a scale not seen since the reforms that followed the Great Depression'.[37] The legislation establishes new watchdogs, strengthens the powers of regulators charged with supervising banks, toughens the regulations against fraud, and brings in requirements for greater market transparency.[38] Although it is beyond my scope to fully analyse the DFA, much of it appears to be just more of the same or unworkable.

A simple indication of shortcomings in the proposed reforms can be seen in their response to one of my major concerns – abuse of derivatives. The DFA requires specified OTC derivatives to be centrally cleared, which should eliminate the risk of counterparty default and so ensure that derivatives cannot cause systemic damage. Clearing will be conducted through Central Counterparties (CCPs) that will novate contracts made over-the-counter and impose margin requirements on the parties involved. Thus the credit risk associated with the derivatives is taken on by a CCP, and information is centrally collected and hence available for publication. The CCPs are intended to be established clearing houses such as the Chicago Mercantile Exchange (CME) and Intercontinental Exchange (ICE).

Because failure of a CCP could cause wide losses across the financial system they will become systemically important. But they seem to lack the resilience to do so as the face value of US OTC derivatives is over $200 trillion whereas the CME Group and ICE have shareholders equity of only $20 billion and $3 billion,[39] respectively. The effectiveness of central clearing depends totally on how well the CCPs margin the derivatives they clear, which means they must accurately price the derivatives and hold sufficient margins to cover losses. In an ideal world, the CCPs would impose high margins on complex, opaque derivatives and so push them towards standardised contracts similar to those traded on futures markets. But the volume of OTC derivative transactions (which make up 96 per cent of the derivatives contracts traded by the 25 largest US commercial banks[40]) will promote competition for the associated clearing fees that may encourage CCPs to be more lenient and tolerate under-collateralisation.

A second critical shortcoming from reliance on non-standardised OTC derivative contracts is that they do not have a public market, which means that they cannot be independently priced. In addition there is only limited sharing of information about the contracts, and their true risks cannot be known. Exactly this, of course, was the root cause of the GFC.

Obviously ineffective central clearing would offer little protection from counter-party default, and so the role of the CCP regulators – which will be the Commodity Futures Trading Commission (CFTC) and Securities and Exchange Commission (SEC) – is critical in establishing and monitoring prudential requirements.

In October 2012 the SEC adopted a new rule establishing minimum standards for the operations of central clearing agencies.[41] It required agencies to use risk-based models to set margin requirements, but did not specify their design and acknowledged that the procedures would vary between agencies (Proposal, pages 22 and 144). An unfortunate result is that much of the details of regulation will be left to the CCPs themselves, which will self-regulate their most critical function. Sound familiar?

The possibility of ineffective regulation of CCPs is not the only deficiency in the DFA approach to derivatives. An analysis by Citibank entitled *Ready or Not?* (Sleightholme and Singh, 2011) estimates that only 60 per cent of OTC derivatives will be centrally cleared, with parties to the rest taking advantage of the exemptions provided for foreign contracts, corporate end-users and small-market participants. Recall that spectacular derivatives disasters of the mid-1990s involved the corporate end-users Metallgesellschaft AG, Orange County and Proctor & Gamble. With about $100 trillion of derivatives not centrally cleared, there should be enough leeway for finance's crooks to wreak their havoc yet again.

Judging from the DFA's derivatives proposals, the legislative response to failure of Lehman Brothers and other banks mirrors that after Enron's collapse as it only fiddles with a totally ineffective strategy by slightly tightening regulations, and imposing a few extra curbs and perhaps some egregious penalties such as salary caps for executives. There is no reason, though, to believe the latest amendments will be any more successful in preventing future corporate disasters than previous tinkering.

Quite simply, the current approach to corporations legislation is not working. What is needed is to shine some light in the dark areas where excessive risks are being run so that all stakeholders can better understand them; outlaw practices that have proven disastrous; and penalise those who visit disaster upon us. That is the topic of the following chapter.

Conclusion

In summary, the collapse of large corporations is chronic, with a spectacular wave around the start of every recent decade. Post-audits show that most actions which contributed to failure were legal, and usually carried out in plain sight where they were observed by regulators and analysts. Although each crisis typically leads to a claimed strengthening of regulatory power, there is no variation in the totally ineffective core strategy of attempting to prevent unwanted externalities by real-time monitoring of firms' actions.

This chapter points to a consistent thread running through my analysis, which is that the finance industry is geared to profit institutional stakeholders – banks, company directors, mutual funds – and protect them at the expense of individual investors. The clearest evidence of this is that – apart from a few low-level credit staff – nobody has been prosecuted in the United States for offences related to losses in the GFC: given a five-year statute of limitations on fraud and other relevant offences, any prosecution is now unlikely.

Perhaps those who legislate, structure and regulate the finance industry see its institutional stakeholders as 'people like us': bankers and corporate executives went to the same schools as the judges, legislators and lawyers who make and oversee regulations; they all play golf or tennis at the same clubs, worship at the same church or temple, and have kids at the same school. Surely they deserve better treatment than common investors? And, when they do break the laws, surely they don't need to be treated like common thieves?

Even though financial and corporate failures and crises can usually be traced to individuals' actions, securities regulation is remarkably benign in dealing with them. For me, though, the social costs of the current corporations regulatory regime are simply too high to permit it to continue unchanged.

In this light, the most telling criticism of contemporary regulation is that it is accepted so passively by industry, presumably because they see it as benign.

Notes

1 CDO = collateralised debt obligation.
2 Data from www.bankruptcydata.com/reviewselections.asp
3 23 October 2008. www.sec.gov/news/testimony/2008/ts102308cc.htm
4 Market Watch, *Wall Street Journal*, 7 March 2013. http://blogs.marketwatch.com/thetell/2013/03/07/transcript-of-holders-admission-on-too-big-to-jail-banks
5 www.sec.gov/news/press/2004-18.htm
6 www.sec.gov/news/press/2003-69.htm
7 Ian Ramsay, 2005. 'Steve Vizard, Insider Trading and Directors' Duties'. www.law.unimelb.edu.au/cclsr/centre-activities/research/research-reports-and-research-papers
8 Merger Market League Tables. www.mergermarket.com
9 www.justice.gov/opa/pr/2011/August/11-crm-1040.html
10 www.fbi.gov/newyork/press-releases/2012/prepared-remarks-of-assistant-director-in-charge-janice-k.-fedarcyk-on-insider-trading-arrests
11 www.justice.gov/usao/nys/pressreleases/January12/newmantoddetalchargespr.pdf
12 www.sec.gov/news/testimony/2011/ts120111rsk.htm
13 ASIC deputy chairman Belinda Gibson on ABC Radio's *PM*, 25 February 2013. www.asic.gov.au/asic/asic.nsf/byheadline/Annual+reports?openDocument
14 www.cftc.gov/PressRoom/PressReleases/pr6041-11
15 www.cftc.gov/ucm/groups/public/@lrenforcementactions/documents/legalpleading/enfbpproductscomplaint.pdf
16 www.cftc.gov/ucm/groups/public/@swaps/documents/dfsubmission/dfsubmission26_051811-449.pdf
17 www.finra.org/web/groups/industry/@ip/@enf/@ad/documents/industry/p122044.pdf
18 www.indexuniverse.com/sections/features/4670-more-on-counterparty-risk-securities-lending.html?fullart=1&start=2
19 From the firms' second quarter 2008 10-Qs available at www.sec.gov/edgar/searchedgar/companysearch.html. BNY Mellon (BK) page 29; and State Street (STT) page 6.
20 John Greenwald and others 10 October 1994. www.time.com/time/magazine/article/0,9171,981587,00.html

21 Bank of International Settlements, 'Statistical Release: OTC Derivatives Securities'; and 'Derivative Financial Instruments Traded on Organised Exchanges'. www.bis.org
22 CIA, *World Fact Book*. www.cia.gov
23 BIS, 'Domestic Debt Securities' and 'International Debt Securities'. www.bis.org
24 World Federation of Exchanges, *2012 WFE Market Highlights*. www.world-exchanges.org
25 'An Act ... to Prevent the Dealing in Futures'. http://caselaw.lp.findlaw.com
26 In similar fashion Bernie Madoff was able to operate a destructive Ponzi scheme unhindered despite repeated warnings by whistleblowers to the SEC (Reuters, 28 February 2010).
27 See Congressional Research Service, 'Troubled Asset Relief Program'. www.fas.org/sgp/crs/misc/R41427.pdf
28 www.businessinsider.com/2008/9/newt-gingrich-calls-for-paulson-s-resignation
29 www.bloomberg.com/apps/news?pid=newsarchive&sid=atqAsBpkiQZE
30 'How Paulson Gave Hedge Funds Advance Word of Fannie Mae Rescue'. www.bloomberg.com/news/2011-11-29/how-henry-paulson-gave-hedge-funds-advance-word-of-2008-fannie-mae-rescue.html
31 http://newsblogs.chicagotribune.com/marksjarvis_on_money/2010/02/paulson-says-he-was-scared-and-clueless-during-lehman-collapse.html
32 www.abc.net.au/businessbreakfast/content/2003/s867031.htm
33 www.abc.net.au/am/content/2004/s1219762.htm
34 http://blogs.wsj.com/scene/2011/09/05/paul-gilding-optimist-environmentalist
35 The Federal Reserve Board, *Frequently Asked Questions*, available at www.federalreserve.gov/faqs/faq.htm
36 A brief summary of the legislation is available at http://banking.senate.gov/public/_files/070110_Dodd_Frank_Wall_Street_Reform_comprehensive_summary_Final.pdf. See updates by the Congressional Research Service at www.fas.org
37 Remarks by President Obama on twenty-first-century financial regulatory reform, 17 June 2009. Sourced from www.whitehouse.gov/the_press_office/Remarks-of-the-President-on-Regulatory-Reform
38 Senate Committee on Banking, Housing, and Urban Affairs, Summary: Restoring American Financial Stability. http://banking.senate.gov/public/_files/FinancialReformSummaryAsFiled.pdf
39 2010 10-Ks at http://investor.cmegroup.com/investor-relations/secfiling.cfm?filingID=1193125-11-50252; and http://files.shareholder.com/downloads/ICE/1698208099x0x456112/BF6F428C-F8B3-4835-B22C-3F350FF13B89/ICE_2010AR.pdf
40 Table 3, 'OCC's Quarterly Report on Bank Trading and Derivatives Activities'. www.occ.gov
41 SEC, 'Clearing Agency Standards', at www.sec.gov/rules/final/2012/34-68080.pdf. The Proposed Rule was set out at www.sec.gov/rules/proposed/2011/34-64017.pdf

8

IS THERE A BETTER BASIS FOR CORPORATIONS REGULATION?

> I sincerely believe, with you, that banking establishments are more dangerous than standing armies.
>
> Thomas Jefferson (1743–1826)

During my career, I was fortunate to live for four very enjoyable years inside the Beltway (which is the freeway that loops around Washington, DC), where Northern Virginia's gated communities display signs warning 'No solicitors' in cheerful disregard for the rest of the world's use of the word for lawyers. Talking to my neighbours who were Congressmen, their advisers and skilled observers of the political process (many of them trained as lawyers), it became perfectly clear that there is no point in even thinking about reforms to policy that are not simple, easy to explain, and intuitively likely to work.

This chapter, then, is determinedly cognisant of the need to be realistic when suggesting changes to finance regulation. Doctors may be confident that their prescriptions will be swallowed, but authors should not be. That is not to deny that my suggestions are radical; but each is simple, consistent with other legal controls, and clearly communicable. Moreover, they have proven successful in many settings and should help more effectively regulate finance.

The recommendations here also try to avoid the trap that has befallen much financial regulation which is to enact solutions to the most recent crisis. We need a system that is robust to future crises whose causes are unknowable. This means that it is fruitless to outlaw the causes of past crises (even assuming they can be agreed). To the contrary, my intuition is that legislation needs to target specific unwanted *outcomes* and ban them as criminal. This approach to investor protection is consistent with that which has proven successful in environmental protection, consumer legislation and workplace safety. It also matches best practice in finance regulation such as the International Financial Reporting Standards (IFRS) which is principles based rather than providing voluminous prescriptive guidance along the lines of the US Generally Accepted Accounting Principles (GAAP).

This chapter discusses the causes of failure of companies, especially banks, amplifies paradoxes in corporations regulation, compares different regulatory strategies, and proposes a new framework for corporations regulation.

To set the scene, let me summarise my proposed regulatory reform.

Reform of financial regulation: my proposal in a nutshell

The ultimate objective of corporations regulation is to prevent bankruptcy, which – by definition – means the firm is unable to meet its liabilities. Thus losses are incurred by counterparties, including employees, suppliers and holders of securities issued by the corporation. The evidence is clear that corporate bankruptcies are not just acts-of-god or good managers making honest mistakes, because – especially in finance as discussed several times above – so many failures can be traced directly to strategies, processes or products that have been allowed to fail. It seems important, then, to consider sanctions for corporate failure against individuals who commit finance crimes and permit their organisations to behave badly.

At a macro level, crime occurs in firms that are corrupt, or which permit corrupt individuals to thrive (Pinto *et al.*, 2008). The corrupt organisation emerges when senior managers use their authority to promote criminal actions that generally are intended to benefit the organisation. By contrast, corrupt individuals seek only to benefit themselves, and – because this is usually at the expense of the organisation – it requires senior managers to tolerate an environment that succours them.

Most companies and their managers are in continuous competition, so that they will mimic or exceed other firms' profit-making initiatives: the result is herding. In the case of high-risk behaviours, individuals' actions build synergistically and generate a wave of corporate collapses that hits developed economies roughly each decade. In its wake there is a lethargic update to regulations that try to eliminate the processes that are thought to have triggered failures of banks and other firms. Well-incentivised practitioners then spend the next few years moulding high-risk strategies to be regulation-compliant, and their commercialisation ushers in the next wave of collapses.

By comparison with regulation in general, that of corporations, including banks, is anomalous for three reasons. First, it pursues a qualitatively different strategy which controls *processes* that have previously led to corporate failure, whereas the approach in other sectors is to criminalise unwanted *outcomes*. Second, proving a breach of corporations legislation seems to require a much higher standard of proof in relation to individuals' intent to commit an offence than other legislation. Third, corporations regulation has proven powerless to stop the once-in-every-decade cycle of corporate collapse or financial crisis, whereas regulation elsewhere has brought sweeping improvements by cleaning up air sheds and waterways, and reducing crime and workplace injuries.

Inefficient, process-oriented financial regulation cannot prevent regular emergence of GFC-style financial crises and corporate collapses, and this chronic failure demands radical change in the strategy of corporations regulation. My objective is to leverage learnings from successful regulatory regimes, and to place a particular focus on firms that are 'too big to fail' and whose bail out by government imposes moral hazard that simply reinforces the collapse cycle.

The principal cause of collapse of large companies is a failure of self-regulation: their chosen strategies, processes and people are not appropriate for the task at hand. Eventually this leads to fatal errors that precipitate financial distress (Ooghe and De Prijcker, 2008). These arise either from inertia which prevents exploration of superior strategy, or from risk-seeking behaviour that is poorly judged. Generic causes of bankruptcy can be traced to a few key factors: poor internal processes, particularly the inability to produce accurate financial accounts; failure to understand the implications of financial strategies, particularly hedging and use of derivatives; poorly executed strategies, particularly acquisitions; and excessive debt. The inevitably bad consequences of those failings are often compounded by a disengaged CEO, aggressive CFO and inexperienced or docile board. The message of myriad studies and post-audits of corporate collapses is that they are not due to acts-of-god, but to venal management.

What, then, to do? For me the answer is to introduce a new regulatory regime directed solely towards large corporations, specifically those deemed too big to fail because of the scale of consequences that would be felt by creditors, employees, customers and society. As shown in the chart at the start of the previous chapter, we face increasingly serious waves of large company collapses. Perhaps we could tolerate these chronic disasters if large firms disproportionately added value. The evidence, though, is quite the opposite, and the relative benefits of large companies are minimal at best. Remember, small stocks provide the best returns to investors (Cooper et al., 2008). Boutique brewers, investment funds, manufacturers and tour operators perform at least as well as their large counterparts. Although there is a surprisingly limited literature on the relative benefits of large firms, the general conclusion is that big is rarely better (Blankenburg et al., 2010). When financial institutions have ever-larger scale and take on more risk, they increase the threat to the whole economy without any offsetting benefit.

It seems appropriate to differentially regulate large firms because the systemic consequences of collapse of even one are not offset by positive benefits from its surviving peers. Moreover, the threat of a large firm's collapse imposes an intractable dilemma for governments which feel pressure to avoid its political consequences and provide support, but fear the moral hazard this induces in surviving firms whose management might be emboldened to take additional risk expecting government bailout if it is misjudged. The social costs of the current corporations regulatory regime are simply too high to permit it to continue unchanged.

Although large firms constitute the majority of investor assets and – as the largest risks to the community and taxpayer – are too big to fail, they are few in number and so form a small group to control. In the United States, for instance, just 180 listed firms have assets above $50 billion and together they comprise 80 per cent of all assets. This small number of very large firms should face a uniquely tough regulatory regime with three planks.

First, large firms should be precluded from undertaking high-risk strategies. These include excessive leverage, use of OTC derivatives, and activities that cannot be observed such as off-balance-sheet investment. The second reform recognises that nobody outside a large firm can know anything but a portion of what is really going on inside the company and requires large firms to prepare an annual Risk Report that includes sustainability measures.

The final proposed change to the way that large companies are regulated is to hold their executives to higher performance standards by introducing a strict liability offence of managing a large company into bankruptcy. My intuition is that the best way to prevent bankruptcies is to move away from control of specific actions (because it has proven totally impractical) and punish those responsible for unwanted outcomes because this will be robust to changes in corporate criminals' strategies. Thus if a large company accepts government bailout monies or files for bankruptcy, company directors and officers at the date of the firm's most recent accounts would be guilty of an offence.

An obvious concern from these changes is their actual and opportunity costs. But confining changes to large firms means that inherently high-risk businesses such as mineral exploration or early stage R&D will not be affected. Superficially, too, the last suggestion may appear radical. To the contrary, its principles are already in wide use because criminal offences – homicide, speeding, theft – are proven by their outcomes, not breaches of any process. This approach works because it is the only one that is robust to changing products and processes that typify dynamic innovative businesses like finance. None of the recommendations here is radical in concept, only in its likely effect.

Implications from earlier chapters for regulatory reform

Readers will not be surprised that discussion in earlier parts of the book has been leading to this chapter. So, what are the points that have previously been made?

Number one is that financial crises – whether involving individual firms like Enron or whole markets like the GFC – are chronic. That is, they have proven a permanent feature of the developed world's financial landscape and occur like clockwork about every decade. It seems pretty obvious that the existing approach to securities regulation does not work.

Number two is that securities and corporations regulation in most countries typically consists of a long list of actions that are illegal such as insider trading, and of prohibited activities such as bucket shops. Most importantly, it requires proof of criminal intent to achieve conviction. Superficially this seems prudent as those in charge of running a company may not be party to the factors causing its bankruptcy. But it makes it very difficult to prosecute individuals. Moreover, people who run large companies are paid well: the CEO of Citibank, for instance, has a base salary of $1.75 million and stock and option awards that – in a good year like 2008 – could exceed $30 million; and the bank's directors each receive fees in excess of $200,000.[1]

Although these payments may not buy flawless execution, they should at least secure management that can avoid bankruptcy. Moreover, it seems inequitable that such well-paid executives can generally escape prosecution even when their unwise actions lead to bankruptcy and investor loss. It is true that firms are occasionally prosecuted, but this is typically after a deal is struck which avoids prosecution of senior executives. There is no acknowledgement of the obvious fact that some, albeit a small portion, of those working in the finance industry are criminals, frequently psychopaths who seek thrills from risk, despite the misery this causes to investors. Moreover, by fining the firm for its executives' behaviour, regulators punish shareholders who had little say in the company's management and not those who committed the offence.

Third, financial crises have originated – almost without exception – in markets involving over-the-counter derivatives. These are minimally regulated, with little data, and no independent valuations. In addition, they have no link to physical markets, do not contribute to the flow of funds between investors and entrepreneurs, and are not needed for traditional hedging. They are used for speculating and have risks that regularly prove toxic.

Finally, the threat of crippling economic and social costs from financial crises arises solely because the firms affected are large. This either brings systemic risk if they fail, or significant cost to taxpayers if they are deemed to be too big to fail and bailed out. Also, as noted earlier, there is no evidence that large firms *per se* bring any unique economic benefit.

To me, existing securities regulation suffers from three debilitating biases, as it: is based on a strategy of outlawing actions known to cause failure, and – being backward looking at the causes of the last crisis – is continually playing catch up; places a high bar on what constitutes criminal behaviour that effectively precludes prosecution of individuals who are responsible; and sees no disadvantage from emergence of firms that are too big to fail.

The need for a radical overhaul of regulation was confirmed during my interviews with fund managers, especially those outside the United States who had watched in shock as the GFC unfolded. An Istanbul CIO told me that US markets had lost the confidence of the rest of the world. He saw the US as a country of laws, but was convinced that its regulatory system must be fundamentally flawed to have enabled such corruption and poor decision making. He acknowledged that there have been attempts to improve regulation but felt they were cosmetic and do not really address the root causes of problems. For him, it would take another, much more serious crisis before Americans take the necessary actions.

The peculiar approach of corporations regulation

Without getting overly legal, it is worth recalling the key elements of a crime. Proof of a crime involves both a physical element through an act or omission which leads to the offence, and a fault element through intent, knowledge, recklessness or negligence, including wilful blindness. In most legal systems, successful prosecution requires proof that the offender knowingly intended to commit an offence and so it had both physical and fault elements. By exception, offences can be made subject to strict liability which has a lower bar for conviction because it is not necessary to prove fault, although there is a defence of mistake of fact in which the offender made appropriate enquiries and reasonably believed that an offence was not being incurred. An even lower bar for successful prosecution is set by absolute liability in which it is not necessary to prove fault and the mistake-of-fact defence does not apply.

The net is that offences that rely on strict or absolute liability can be proven without the need to establish intent or even indirect awareness of events involved in a crime. Minor examples include parking illegally or running a red light. Criminal offences that impose strict liability on individuals include statutory rape, while for corporates they include industrial manslaughter and pollution.

These distinctions are important in finance regulation. Take, for instance, Australia's Corporations Act. Offences of strict liability are limited to narrow, mostly procedural matters such as lodging of notices and reports, or publishing a misleading statement about the company's capital. More serious offences such as authorising or making a statement that is materially misleading require this to occur with the person's knowledge.[2] There are no offences of absolute liability. Like securities regulation in most countries, this provides almost total protection for directors even when their mismanagement and incompetence lead to bankruptcy because criminal convictions require proof that they wilfully and knowingly violated a rule or law and this is very hard to achieve.

Using such foundations, modern societies follow two approaches to regulate corporate and human citizens and restrict their externalities.

The first type of regulation is to impose sanctions on unwanted outcomes, leave it up to the individual corporation and citizen to avoid these outcomes, and then – with limited exceptions – impose penalties for breaches when offenders can be identified and their intent established. This type of regulation is most obvious with traditional criminal offences: theft and assault, for instance, are illegal; any occurrence triggers an investigation in anticipation of prosecution. But a similar approach also applies to modern regulation of the environment (fines for spills and the like), consumer affairs (product recalls and fines for defective products) and corporate offences such as industrial manslaughter. The same logic of preventing outcomes is applied through imposition of discriminatory taxes on unwanted behaviours such as cigarette smoking and consumption of fossil fuels.

This style of regulation that criminalises or penalises unwanted outcomes has been enormously successful in controlling crime, environmental damage, and anti-social behaviour. Importantly for my proposal, there is an emerging interest in implementing something similar in corporations regulation. For instance, Britain has proposed introduction of a new offence of 'reckless misconduct in the management of a bank' which would bring a seven-year jail term in the event of bank failure.[3]

The second type of regulation seeks to control damaging outcomes by restricting the processes that are thought to cause them. This is the basis of regulation of companies and financial markets that has been followed since the 1930s. It relies on the assumptions that criminals will repeat previous acts; and regulators will be able to anticipate unwanted outcomes and prevent their occurrence. Obviously, if criminals change their tactics and authorities cannot monitor corporate activities in real time, regulators cannot prosecute individuals or firms no matter how damaging their externalities.

This regulation of process which underpins corporations and securities regulation is unusual, and seems successful only with narrow objectives. A good example is early regulation of air pollution which required motor vehicle manufacturers to fit a catalytic converter to cars' exhaust systems and thus ensure full combustion of wastes. These end-of-pipe controls allow unwanted actions to occur (that is, production of vehicle pollutants) and then offset their effects. They are generally regarded now as primitive.

Despite the seeming deficiencies of process-based regulation, it is the preferred technique in most countries for regulation of markets and corporations. They make specific processes illegal, such as insider trading and use of leverage by retirement funds, or else prescribe how actions such as statutory reporting and acquisitions will be conducted. Although regulation's ultimate objective is to prevent corporate collapse, this is not an offence.

Compare this approach to that of criminal law where killing a person is an offence (except under the most limited of circumstances), whilst many of the contributing processes – owning a gun, knife or car, for instance – are quite legal. The significance of this distinction between the strategies used to regulate criminals and corporations is that, whereas crime rates have been declining in developed economies over recent decades (e.g. Zimring, 2007), during the same period most have experienced several waves of large company collapses.

Thinking of the desirability of changing corporations regulation to a basis of strict liability, it is instructive to note that its current pro-offender generosity is similar to that which once applied to owners of workplaces. During the nineteenth century, though, outrage grew at the appalling standards of workplace and factory safety and the fact that prosecutions were impractical because of the need to prove knowledge and intent on the part of managers and owners. More than a century ago legislation to ensure safe workplaces (and since the 1970s the environment) was amended to introduce strict liability offences along the lines proposed here for corporations regulation.

A second consideration promoting change in corporations regulation is the trend towards duty-of-care legislation in other arenas where firms are involved. Workplace safety legislation in many countries imposes a general duty of care on employers to ensure the safety of employees and others in the workplace. Typical legislation is the Wrongs and Other Acts (Law of Negligence) Act in Victoria where someone is negligent in not taking precautions against a risk that was foreseeable and significant, and where a reasonable person in their position would act.[4]

To illustrate the practical shortcomings of current corporations regulation, con-trast two recent disasters involving firms in the United States which resulted in that country's largest-ever, unwanted externalities. In April 2010 an explosion occurred aboard an oil rig in the Gulf of Mexico that had been leased by British Petroleum plc: it killed 11 workers, spilled about five million barrels of oil into the sea, and led to costs in excess of $50 billion.[5] The Federal Government immediately put BP on notice that it was responsible for solving the problem and threatened it with massive fines and criminal prosecution. BP was pilloried in the press and Congress.

My second example is the sub-prime crisis where the same Federal Government worked alongside banks during 2008 and set up the Troubled Asset Relief Program (TARP) that extended loans and other support of $10–100 billion to at least ten companies that had come to the brink of failure.

The contrast between legislators' reaction to these two unprecedented events could not be more stark. In the world's worst-ever environmental accident, pollut-ers are forced to meet massive costs without assistance, and existing environmental legislation seems adequate to cope. Threatened collapse of the banks and markets, however, brings immediate government aid, followed by what President Obama called a one-in-seventy-years overhaul of regulation.

Given the chronic failure of the finance sector's process-based regulation and clear evidence of the superiority of outcomes-based regulation, the conclusion seems irresistible that we need to try something radically different. The obvious solution is to thoroughly restructure its inefficient, unusual strategy.

I should point out that the need for radical change is not the mainstream view. Expert opinion sees flaws only in the detail of corporations regulation and not in its fundamental design (e.g. Moshirian, 2011). Despite the appalling record of regulators and their questionable motivation, SEC Chairman Cox insisted to Congress in 2008 that 'the vitally important function of securities regulation is best executed by specialists with decades of tradition and experience'.

There is little evidence, though, that the current regulatory strategy will ever contain corporate collapses. Even when it is instinctively strengthened after each episode of corporate failures, new legislation can be ponderously slow to emerge: almost five years after the start of the GFC, the rules governing the US financial system had not changed.

My proposal for regulatory reform

In developing a new strategy for financial regulation, my preference is to draw les-sons from approaches that have proven effective, such as those that improved pollution and workplace safety. In most major cities today, concentrations of air-borne pollutants are well below 1980s levels, despite doubling in vehicle numbers. Rivers running through urban areas such as the Potomac, Seine, Thames and Yarra resembled open sewers a generation or two ago, but now have fishermen on their lush banks. Workplaces, too, have become much safer. Bureau of Labor Statistics data, for instance, show that the annual frequency of lost-time injuries in US workplaces has slumped from four per 100 workers in the 1980s to 1.8 in 2009.[6] Suggesting that regulatory strategy in these areas is near optimum is that – even after the now only occasional very serious incident – little change is seen as necessary.

Certainly inspections and monitoring by regulators have played a role in these improvements. But the major contributor to better quality of the environment and safer workplaces has been legislation that set clear limits and backed them up with tough prosecution of breaches. If a workplace is dangerous or a firm spills chemicals, there is no examination of defects in the firm's processes, governance and intent. It is fined, usually substantially; and offenders are often forced to shame themselves by publishing details in the media. Thus the UK offence of corporate manslaughter, as an example, allows an organisation to be prosecuted when it is liable for a death. Industrial manslaughter is a similar offence when a senior manager causes the death of an employee. Although this approach is simple, bordering on the crude, it proves highly effective.

The success of environment and workplace regulation that punishes outcomes provides a striking contrast to ineffective financial regulation that targets hard-to-prove procedural breaches. The critical practical difference between financial regulation and that of the environment, workplaces and crime is in the allocation of risks, specifically the risk of prosecution. Criminals and polluters suffer penalties under the offender-pays principle, but even when a company collapses following obvious mismanagement, it is rare for directors or senior managers to face prosecution. As we saw in the previous chapter, in the quarter century to 2006 not one outside director of a failed US company was prosecuted for breach of their duties.

If large firms have little incremental benefit, but impose a growing need for bailouts, it is reasonable to limit their risks and hold them to higher performance standards. That is, the social licence that has been given to large firms that allows them to operate with minimal hindrance should be revised to restrict their risks and impose penalties in the event of failure.

Thus I propose three substantial changes to the way that large companies, including large banks, are regulated. Note clearly that these proposals relate only to large firms, which are those that are too big to fail. To give an indication of the changes' coverage, Table 8.1 shows data from Compustat on the assets of listed US firms.

A rough indicator of large companies might be firms with total assets in excess of $50 billion, which is a cut-off used in the Dodd–Frank legislation for intervention.

Table 8.1 Distribution of listed US companies by assets (end 2012)

Total assets: $ bill	No. companies	Combined assets ($ trillion)
≤ 1	2,406	0.7
2–9	1,561	5.3
10–50	458	10.1
50–100	67	4.6
≥100	115	58.4
Total	4,607	79.1

This would involve fewer than 200 companies in the United States (around half of them financial institutions, including insurers), and about 30 in a country like Australia. But they, of course, represent by far the largest risks to investors and the economy.

The first change to the way that large firms would be regulated is that they should be precluded from known high-risk strategies, such as excessive leverage and activities that cannot be observed such as investment that is not on the balance sheet nor through established markets. The most efficient way to achieve that is through the taxation system.

A useful concept in limiting leverage is that of thin capitalisation, which refers to the situation where a taxpayer who is over-reliant on debt does not receive a tax deduction for interest expense. In the case of corporations regulation, risks from excessive borrowing by large firms would be limited so they cannot claim a tax deduction for any interest expense on debt above a reasonable limit. A typical guide to leverage in finance is the debt:equity ratio which is the ratio of interest bearing debt to shareholders equity. In the case of the 94 listed US industrial companies with total assets above $50 billion, 62 have debt that is less than their equity, and only ten have debt more than twice the value of equity. The last could be a convenient cut-off. That is, total interest-bearing borrowings (including capitalised lease payments) should not exceed twice shareholders equity; if they do, then any interest expense on the excess debt is not allowable as a tax deduction. In the case of banks, 88 have more than $50 billion in assets, and a somewhat higher leverage level would apply, which might limit total borrowings to perhaps six times equity.

To improve transparency of large firms' strategies, they should report their share of the assets and liabilities of all subsidiaries where their ownership exceeds a nominal proportion (say 1 per cent). The current cut-off of 50 per cent means that firms can structure high-risk investments and not reveal details to stakeholders because only the net position needs to be reported.

Large firms quite properly use financial instruments to protect themselves against unwanted moves in markets, especially currencies, commodity prices and interest rates. Where they get into trouble, though, is when they bypass financial markets and trade financial instruments over the counter (OTC). OTC products do not provide any protection that cannot be obtained from market-based products, but have much higher risks because they are less closely reported and monitored, and can have limited liquidity and uncertain counterparties. Large firms should not be able to claim tax relief for costs and losses associated with OTC financial instruments (while paying tax on gains) and thus be encouraged to use more transparent market-based securities.

The second reform to corporations regulation recognises that nobody outside a large firm can hope to know anything but a portion of what is really going on inside the company. This opacity of large firms reduces scrutiny of their operations, which is compounded because the most important details of risks and strategies are not required to be reported. Although the subject of risk typically constitutes a quarter or more of company annual reports, few firms disclose anything beyond confusing tables of financial instruments and broad generic statements. None report an item as basic as their insurance cover. If badly judged risk is at the heart of many corporate collapses, taxpayers and shareholders deserve to know far more about the issue.

To strengthen disclosure of risky activities and allow independent scrutiny, large firms should be required to prepare an annual Risk Report (Emm *et al.*, 2007) that also includes sustainability measures from the Global Reporting Initiative. Useful risk measures include: historical statistics that give a picture of actual performance such as process failures; indicators of risk propensity – or choices the firm has made that reflect its willingness or not to take certain risks – and risk management such as insurance; details of known gaps that pose risks or require strategic initiatives such as competitive deficiencies; and evaluation of risks undertaken through post-audits of past decisions.

Another tool that can help investors and other stakeholders to better understand firm risks is readily available through firms' auditors. Despite their intimate exposure to firm risks, the reports of auditors are quite uninformative for shareholders, and their value has diminished as auditing standards have watered-down expectations. A typical US audit engagement letter, for instance, contains the following passage: 'Our audit is subject to the risk that material errors and irregularities, including fraud or defalcations, if they exist, will not be detected' (Carmichael *et al.*, 2007). The situation is similar wherever international audit standards apply, and Australia's model engagement letter contains the following (AASB, 2006):

> Because of the test nature and other inherent limitations of an audit, together with the inherent limitations of any accounting and internal control system, there is an unavoidable risk that even some material misstatements may remain undiscovered.

To me it is nothing short of outrageous that auditors can accept fees on such a basis. Audit reports should warrant there are no material mis-statements in the accounts nor fraud; the reports should be much more informative and shareholder-friendly; and any side letters to management should be made public.

The need for improved audit performance is obvious. Only recently, for instance, the chairman of Australia's Securities and Investment Commission released the results of an inspection report into audits which brought a scathing assessment that their quality had declined.[7]

In fact, a similar position is taken by clear-sighted members of the audit profession. KPMG, for instance, has produced a series of briefs built around the theme of 'Better Business Reporting' that argues for a 'shift [in business reporting] from our current compliance focus to an integrated and holistic business reporting approach'. Investors and companies, including banks, should welcome such changes as they would not just enhance communications but also contribute to better allocation of capital and improve investment decisions.

The final proposed change to the way that large companies are regulated is to hold their executives to higher performance standards. There should be a criminal offence, for instance, that applies to directors and executives of large companies which collapse or require government support. Strict liability would be imposed so that the offence is proven by acceptance of government bailout monies, filing for bankruptcy, or (in some jurisdictions) calling in a receiver. Those liable for the offence are company directors and officers at the date of the firm's most recent accounts. This simply recognises that those in charge of large firms should be held responsible in the event that the firm causes damage to its environment, broadly defined to include society and the economy.

This last change appears to be the most radical proposal as it introduces the strict liability offence of managing a firm into bankruptcy. However, such an approach mimics that of most criminal offences which relate to outcomes, not process breaches. Killing someone without just cause, for instance, is unlawful and is a serious crime (murder when intended, otherwise manslaughter or similar). How is killing a large corporation any different? Similarly environmental pollution by a firm is a crime. How is 'economic pollution' any different?

An obvious objection to making bankruptcy a criminal offence is made by the Cato Institute in a submission to Congress in light of Enron's collapse. It warned that it would be totally unfair if 'senior corporate managers may be held liable for an illegal action by some subordinate that the senior manager did not direct, condone, or even know about'.[8] In reality, though, most of the world's largest, most complex and dangerous organisations have in place systems which ensure that their staff – even when acting without the direction or knowledge of senior executives – do not breach the law. Examples include complex technologies such as nuclear-powered aircraft carriers, and global firms like BHP Billiton and ExxonMobil which operate legally and safely even though senior executives can oversee only a tiny part of their activities.

The best of these legal, safe organisations are described as having high reliability and have internal processes, operations, cultures and external relationships that establish a high probability of reliable, incident-free operations even when using the most complex and risky technologies (La Porte, 1996). These firms are characterised by clear objectives, appreciation of the risks and economic benefit of their activities, very high technical competence, stringent quality assurance, rewards for identifying error, and high levels of organisational slack or spare resources ready to swing into action if something goes wrong.

The important implication of high-reliability firms is that they show that failed firms – whether Enron or Lehman Brothers – are not uniquely hard for their executives to keep within the law. They simply had leaders that were not willing or able to ensure their reliability. Such leaders should be prosecuted for the damage they cause.

Let us discuss how these proposals would operate.

Serendipitously, the large-firm test that requires assets above $50 billion means that only a limited number of firms would be affected by my proposed changes in regulatory strategy and their large scale means that associated costs should be small. Big firms have quality systems in place that enable easy adjustment of accounting records, Treasuries that can restructure risk management, and good governance that can report on risks. Of course, any firms that are not easily able to accommodate the changes pose exactly the risks that we want to limit.

The second feature of the proposed regulation is that criminal charges only apply to executives of large firms that are unable to pay their creditors and file for bankruptcy or accept government financial support. People charged with the offence of managing a company that fails would include directors and officers of the firm (including the chief executive and chief financial officers) at the date of collapse, or – given that a characteristic of many failing firms is the hasty departure of directors and executives – incumbents at the time of recent annual reports. The latter option gives flexibility to charge culprits whose actions led to the firm's failure, but who resigned before the collapse.

The proposals obviously limit the preferences of large firms and impose greater disclosure requirements on them, which could bring actual and opportunity costs. The first limit on excessive debt hardly seems onerous given that disallowing tax relief for standard corporate expenses already applies to non-beneficial costs such as entertainment and fines. Nor does the second restriction on use of over-the-counter financial products appear onerous, as these have proven to have unacceptably high risk and organised futures markets provide a ready alternative.

Moreover, the US Federal Reserve and other central banks are already author-ised to limit the operations of financial institutions with assets above $50 billion that can be extended on a case-by-case basis to non-bank companies.[9] These powers include restricting or terminating the financial products that banks offer, and impos-ing stringent prudential standards in relation to their capital, liquidity and risk management. The Fed can also limit company size, so that a supervised bank or firm must notify it in advance of an acquisition of assets above $10 billion, which the Fed can then block (sections 121, 163 and 165 of the Dodd–Frank Act, DFA). The Basel Committee has also established more-complex requirements for banks that are sys-temically important in terms of their size, interconnectedness and complexity.[10]

The requirement to produce a risk report increases disclosure which is always a concern to firms. But a wide variety of sensitive company information is already divulged, including individual executives' salaries. It is hard to see how shareholders – for whom these companies are, after all, being run – and other interested parties such as employees and neighbours are hurt by a more informed understanding of companies' risks.

Finally, there is no doubt that these limitations are likely to see firms eschewing growth so they do not trigger the large company controls. And some firms may become less tolerant of excessive risk because their executives fear criminal sanc-tions. Again these are desirable outcomes. Large firms do not inherently add value, but are harder to operate safely, and bring excessive damage when their risks are badly judged. Limiting the number of big firms should reduce social costs. So, too, with excessive risk. There is no evidence that firms which take large strategic gam-bles add value; nor is there evidence that well-run firms with good performance records do not take well-judged risks. The changes proposed here will deter the cowboys, but have little effect on well-run firms. Their balance between discouraging collapses whilst not stopping desired corporate behaviour should complement good governance (Becher and Frye, 2011).

In summary, these proposals seek to eliminate the damaging consequences of large corporate collapses by discouraging high-risk strategies, illuminating the nature of firms' risks, and prosecuting those individuals who are responsible. This recognises that legislatures can never get ahead of strongly motivated expertise, and the destructive combination of greed and hubris displayed by some executives can only be tamed by imposing the real risk of significant personal sanction if the wrong outcome ensues. Everyone knows what could be done, but at-risk firms need explicit guidance on what *should* be done, or at least what outcome is unacceptable.

Investment managers' view on optimum regulation

I used fund manager interviews to validate my proposed regulatory framework. Most managers readily accepted limits on leverage and derivatives, and were enthusiastic about better disclosure. One commented that 'deregulation just went too far, and left incentives too open. Smart people were incentivised to create products that made money, not necessarily sense.' He favoured much tougher regulation.

A London private equity manager expressed concern that the interest rate and currency derivatives markets had grown to many times the size of the physical, which 'inverted the pyramid'. This should be contained, and he would also like limits on leverage ratios. In an interesting twist on the contribution of human failings to financial crises, he believes that computers should be moved into the background to make people more central in decisions, and weaken the disintermediation of loans and the tendency to rely on numbers.

In contrast to welcome acceptance of constraints on derivatives and debt, there was a much more mixed reaction to the proposed crime of managing a large company into bankruptcy.

One fund manager in Istanbul saw the benefits given that 'human nature caused the GFC'. He drew the interesting contrast between prosecution of the Iceland Prime Minister for mismanaging the economy, whilst the CEOs and senior management of banks who did an equally terrible job were free to claim their bonuses. The banks' culture forces a short-term view of how much money can be made today or tomorrow which has translated into excess risk to boost bonuses. This attracted him to the idea of prosecuting managers.

A few others more tentatively supported criminalising large company bankruptcy. One felt that managers who are paid high incentive bonuses tend to see anything that they did without being caught is legitimate, no matter the regulation. Another felt that investors would behave much more responsibly 'when they had their own skin on the line'.

On the other hand, several investment managers made the argument that modern banks have so many quite different sectors folded into one that it is impossible for any person to understand and monitor them all. Even though other large organisations exist safely, they argued that finance organisations are very complex by comparison.

Another view was that – although bankruptcy comes from bad decisions – they are not necessarily made with a bad intent like killing somebody. Even when the CEO is involved, it may have been beyond his skill or knowledge to correctly handle difficult, Black Swan-type conditions.

Conclusion: a better basis for regulation

In developed economies, corporations legislation is designed to protect stakeholders, particularly shareholders and creditors, and is based on free market principles and the rule of law. However, chronic financial crises have shown it is useless to rely on self-regulation or regulation that outlaws specific processes. Although a free market can properly devolve responsibility, this does not remove it. And excellent examples of efficient regulation can be seen in the success of the environment and workplace approach which suggests that more effective corporations regulation would make it an offence to run a company that fails.

Most countries have legislation that requires consumer products to be fit for service. Many expensive products such as cars and electronic goods come with explicit warranties of performance, and it is common to be able to exchange consumer products that prove defective even in the absence of a warranty. Not so in finance. Regulators charged with protecting the interests of investors, particularly the smaller or retail investor, are toothless and ineffective.

The core product of the finance industry – namely money – is the world's greatest motivator. Not surprisingly the amount of money we save and invest has proven a powerful stimulant for scam merchants whose fertile brains bring the Ponzi schemes, false accounts, doomed investments and myriad other rip-offs and thefts. Despite this, finance industry regulation concentrates on outlawing particular processes that are known to cause loss, not the loss itself. Thus running a firm into bankruptcy or losing all monies subscribed to an investment fund is not illegal, providing regulations have been followed. It is as if murder by shooting were legal providing the gun is registered and the shooter took the correct training courses!

Because of the systemic consequences of failure of a large firm, my proposal criminalises responsibility for their collapse so that being a director or officer of a large firm that fails would become *prima facie* evidence of an offence. The impact of higher personal risk for directors and executives will not be trivial. Most obviously, directors with a Lehman Brothers calibre will not dare to take on sinecures. The proposed approach can also be expected to bring about considerable improvement in the way that firms are governed, which – of course – is its objective. Directors will insist that fellow board members have relevant skills, particularly in finance and strategy, and are active in their role. Chief executives will be chosen for a proven ability to operate in the firm's industries and manage their risks, rather than for some generic skill set. Aggressive advisers promoting long-shot strategies will be shown the door. A particular impact will be on auditors, who will be forced to really audit, and not minimise their efforts by relying on management letters and hiding behind shortcuts such as samples or materiality tests.

Superficially punishing successful, growing firms may not appear sensible. But when the social costs of bigness become intolerable, then it should be constrained. My approach would take a governance-based perspective of bankruptcy. Firms fail because their managers pursue misguided or criminal strategies, not because of some systemic weaknesses or market failures. Perpetrating bankruptcy of a large firm should be treated as criminal. Importantly, too, my proposal does not affect the limited liability of shareholders, but will lift the personal risks of executives who mismanage a firm.

The beauty of the proposed approach is that there is no need for any additional regulatory bureaucracy because the people who are best placed to anticipate and avoid insolvency – that is, the directors and officers of large firms – are enlisted to avoid collapse. The few additional controls proposed can be readily administered through existing systems: tax for controls on debt and derivatives; and statutory accounts for risk reporting and limits on consolidation.

An important feature of the proposed regulatory changes is that it will force lower-risk behaviour by big firms and banks which – by definition – must adopt weak practices for systemic risks to emerge. The new regulatory approach would have minimal impact on well-managed firms, save to provide a much clearer depiction of their operational risks, winnow out less-effective directors, and tighten audit efforts. By contrast it would have a chilling effect on firms at risk of failure.

In closing I acknowledge an unanswered question: how can these sweeping reforms be enacted? Since derivatives scandals became chronic during the 1990s, there have been a number of stillborn proposals to regulate them, and controls remain limited even after the GFC. In this light, constraining the derivatives market and jailing failed CEOs seem hopelessly ambitious. My guess is that it will take another crisis-driven great recession before emergence of legislative independence of mind.

Notes

1 See Citigroup 2011 Proxy Statement at www.citigroup.com/citi/investor/quarterly/2011/ar11cp.pdf?ieNocache=441

2 Section 1308 (2) of the Corporations Act available at www.comlaw.gov.au/Details/C2013C00003/Download

3 'UK's Reckless Banking Charge to Carry Seven-Year Jail Term', Reuters, 1 October 2013. http://uk.reuters.com/article/2013/10/01/uk-britain-banking-reform-idUKBRE9900TA20131001

4 Available at www.legislation.vic.gov.au

5 After the Deepwater Horizon explosion, BP's share price fell from 650 pence just before the spill to stabilise around 400 pence in September 2010, which – with about 18 billion shares on issue – wiped £45 billion or $US75 billion off BP's market value. Direct costs include clean-up of at least $10 billion, compensation exceeding $20 billion, and fines of up to $20 billion.

6 '2009 Survey of Occupational Injuries and Illnesses' and prior years available at www.bls.gov/iif/oshwc/osh/os/osch0042.pdf

7 ASIC Press Release of 4 December 2012 following publication *of Audit Inspection Program Report for 2011–12.* Available at www.asic.gov.au

8 CATO Handbook for Congress, 2002, Section 2.2. www.cato.org/pubs/handbook/hb108/hb108-22.pdf

9 www.sec.gov/about/laws/wallstreetreform-cpa.pdf

10 www.bis.org/publ/bcbs207.pdf

9

CONCLUSION

Even if finance is unworldly, who cares?

> One can say this in general of men: they are ungrateful, disloyal, insincere and
> deceitful, timid of danger and avid of profit.
>
> Niccolò Machiavelli, *The Prince*

In writing this book, I am motivated to identify reasons why investors have seen poor returns through the last decade, and have traced its causes to a number of debilitating shortcomings in the modern finance industry. Let me briefly state the main findings.

1. Finance theory is a practical failure

Modern finance theory is elegant, but virtually every application requires use of data about the future that cannot be accurately estimated. This means that theory is not applicable in the real world. This is compounded by theory's strong mathematical base which pays limited heed to abundant qualitative data and so militates against detailed understanding of financial decisions. Our understanding of investment processes and markets remains primitive.

While the defects of theory are well known, they continue to be glossed over, and the regular occurrence of disasters on a GFC scale is never traced to deficiencies in theory. They should, however, prompt academics and practitioners to work on an industrial scale to build more reliable finance theory and develop practical investor guidance. This, though, is nowhere evident: flat earth and unworldly continue to stick label-like to any description of finance theory.

2. Finance has lost sight of its central purpose

The core mission of financial institutions (FIs) is to shepherd funding between entrepreneurs and investors at an equitable price. But, in the United States and other countries, FIs have adopted short-term profit objectives and target profits by trading on their own account using debt to squeeze more returns out of exotic products with thin margins, and take for themselves much of the economic rent that is provided by normal market operations.

The industry pays salaries to its employees and service providers that come at little personal risk. By contrast, firms which depend on finance's funding and investors who rely on returns are short-changed because they are not served efficiently.

3.   Market forecasting is a mug's game

Many observers have opined some variant on 'Prediction is very difficult, especially about the future' (including Niels Bohr, Mark Twain and Yogi Berra), but few in finance accept similar evidence across their industry. Some analysts have skill in market forecasting and stock picking, but it is rare, and those with skill usually skim off the profits so that little benefit flows on to investors. To cover this shortcoming, when dealing with customers finance concentrates on inputs such as cost of funds, research reports, investment strategies and the like. Investment success is largely accidental, and one of the few certainties about markets is that they regularly fall apart. Investors should act on the assumption that chaos is imminent.

4.   Investment through professionals has unfortunate consequences

Legislation in many countries provides incentives for saving with the excellent objective of promoting more financially independent retirees. Sadly this pushed savers into mutual funds that institutionalised the finance industry by concentrating investors' clout in the hands of professional money managers. The best of these are the major mutual funds, but even they have service arrangements that are complex and opaque, and are run in secret so that few investors receive an account of what happened to their money. The worst money managers have skewed compensation arrangements so they take excessive risks with funds for which they are responsible. This is a principal cause of the decadal cycle of market collapses.

5.   The finance industry is organised to benefit itself

There is no evidence of a conspiracy that runs the finance industry to benefit insiders, but it shows the expected hallmarks of one. Participating firms make profits out of all proportion to their economic contribution, despite delivering no net return to equities in over a decade. Low-level graft and corruption are endemic. Financial agents strip mine the wealth of productive clients and firms, but resist scrutiny of their own performance. Regulation is supine and even the most egregious failures are rarely punished. Salaries in financial institutions are such that the princes of finance earn millions and enjoy a lifestyle to rival the

Epicurians (whose motto was 'Dum vivimus, vivamus' – let us live while we live). This is funded by investors who write call options for their agents and bear all the losses of agents' poor or risky decisions. Industry professionals pay themselves first with fees from investor funds irrespective of performance, and put the remainder at risk for the chance of bonuses. Thus industry insiders secure most of the upside while investors and shareholders cover the downside when markets collapse every decade.

6. Financial entrepreneurs prefer the road less travelled

Incentives available in finance make the brains of some of the world's smartest people spin like hamsters in a wheel. Their creativity, however, is frequently misdirected to promoting new and exciting financial products where hype cannot be countered by evidence and experience. Finance is actually a shell game structured to draw investors' attention away from the overwhelming evidence of poor performance. For example, compensation packages that are robust to changes in market conditions are described as incentives to align manager and shareholder interests; and protection is assured by risk management tools that are forced to rely on historical data and so are backward looking. All this is designed to hide the obvious point that poor strategic decisions by funds and firms are investors' greatest exposure.

7. Academics have internalised the views of their rich patrons and media lapdogs are complicit

Finance academics relish part-time appointments as advisers and consultants to financial institutions. This encourages some to internalise the views of financial institutions and publish supportive research, with two unfortunate consequences. The first is that finance theory is trenchantly supported in the face of chronic shortcomings, at least in part because it supports the idea that professional investors have robust theoretical support. The second is that few academics point out the obvious fact that finance professionals lack expertise.

The media has also internalised the views of the finance barons and is compliant in the face of ineptitude. Bank talking heads get free rein to push their self-serving mantras on television and in other media; any politician who points to corruption in the finance industry is depicted as uninformed; and scandals are treated as isolated incidents rather than symptoms of a broken system.

8. The finance industry is devoid of trust, reliability and ethics

The quality of financial products determines the living standards of retirees. With such an important role to play, it is surprising that financial brands rate poorly, there is a high probability that mutual funds will not operate as advertised, and risks from agents and counterparties are high. Most graphically, finance is the only industry whose largest firms have received nine-figure fines for defrauding their customers.

9. Bankers never hesitate to blackmail their friends

Finance is a bastion of crony capitalism, most obviously in the revolving door between financial districts and government. Despite (or perhaps because of) this, whenever things get really tough for the finance industry, it never hesitates to warn that the sky will fall in unless government provides a bailout. It's blackmail, but few politicians call the bluff. Although none dare do a Bobbitt on finance, that's what the big swinging dicks need.

10. Regulation is worse than ineffectual

One of the biggest surprises about the finance industry is that the strategy behind its intrusive regulation is quite ineffectual: recurring crises over decades have shown that regulation is unable to control chronic insider trading and deceptive practices, nor can it prevent the regular collapse of banks and other firms. Even when someone is caught in a criminal act, regulators negotiate a deal so that the firm pays a fine and offenders go free. The mystery is why the finance industry is not made subject to a strict liability structure that has so effectively cleaned up other industries and sectors.

11. The finance industry is a pre-eminent example of market failure

Taking all these points together, finance epitomises an industry that avoids market discipline. It is characterised by a lack of transparency, protection from regulators, and support in crisis by government. Restrictions stymie competition, and the creative destruction inherent in capitalism. Looking ahead, finance theory needs a whole-of-industry effort to make it more practical, and legislation should remove destructive incentives that wreak such havoc.

The finance industry has a seamless web that links academics, financial planners, investment bankers and regulators who all rely on (and actively promote) several basic, intuitively appealing, but totally unsupportable premises: invest according to portfolio theory (diversification works), markets are efficient (security prices can be evaluated using information), return will be appropriate for the risk, and regulation is practicable. Teaching, marketing and investment advice incorporate these premises. Subterfuge, dishonesty and manipulation are used to gull the marks in what is little more than a rigged shell game, where investors are fleeced by charlatans acting as their financial agents.

The cautions of this book resonate for us all.

REFERENCES

AASB. (2006). *Auditing Standard ASA 210: Terms of Audit Engagements*. Auditing and Assurance Standards Board, Melbourne.

Adrian, T. and Shin, H. S. (2008). 'Liquidity, Monetary Policy and Financial Cycles'. *Current Issues in Economics and Finance*, 14, 1, 1–7.

Aggarwal, R., Erel, I., Ferreira, M. and Matos, P. (2011). 'Does Governance Travel Around the World? Evidence from Institutional Investors'. *Journal of Financial Economics*, 100, 1, 154–81.

Aggarwal, R. K. and Jorion, P. (2010). 'Hidden Survivorship in Hedge Fund Returns'. *Financial Analysts Journal*, 66, 2, 1–6.

Allen, F., Babus, A. and Carletti, E. (2009). 'Financial Crises: Theory and Evidence'. *Annual Review of Financial Economics*, 97–116.

Andersen, T. G., Bollerslev, T., Diebold, F. X. and Labys, P. (2003). 'Modeling and Forecasting Realized Volatility'. *Econometrica*, 71, 2, 579–625.

Anderson, E. W., Ghysels, E. and Juergens, J. L. (2009). 'The Impact of Risk and Uncertainty on Expected Returns'. *Journal of Financial Economics*, 94, 2, 233–63.

Andrade, G., Mitchell, M. and Stafford, E. (2001). 'New Evidence and Perspectives on Mergers'. *Journal of Economic Perspectives*, 15, 2, 103–12.

Arrow, K. J., Bernheim, B. D., Feldstein, M. S., McFadden, D. L., Poterba, J. M. and Solow, R. M. (2011). '100 Years of the American Economic Review: The Top 20 Articles'. *American Economic Review*, 101, 1, 1–8.

Baddy, C. R. (2011). 'The Corporate Psychopaths Theory of the Global Financial Crisis'. *Journal of Business Ethics*, 102, 255–9.

Bagehot, W. (1873). *Lombard Street*. Hyperion Press, Westport, CT, 1962.

Baghestania, H. (2010). 'Evaluating Blue Chip Forecasts of the Trade-Weighted Dollar Exchange Rate'. *Applied Financial Economics*, 20, 24, 1879–89.

Baker, M., Pan, X. and Wurgler, J. (2009). 'The Psychology of Pricing in Mergers and Acquisitions'. Available: http://ssrn.com/abstract=1364152 (Accessed: May 2009).

Baldwin, W. (1992). 'The Crazy Things People Say to Justify Stock Prices'. *Forbes*. Published 27 April 1992.

Bali, T. G. (2008). 'The Intertemporal Relation between Expected Returns and Risk'. *Journal of Financial Economics*, 87, 1, 101–31.

Barberis, N. and Thaler, R. (2003). 'A Survey of Behavioral Finance'. In: Constantinides, G. M., Harris, M. and Stulz, R. M. (eds.) *Handbook of the Economics of Finance*. Elsevier, North-Holland, Boston.

Barclay, M. J. and Smith, C. W. J. (1999). 'The Capital Structure Puzzle'. *Journal of Applied Corporate Finance*, 12, 1, 8–20.

Basel Committee on Banking Supervision. (2001). *Consultative Document: The New Basel Capital Accord*. Bank for International Settlements, Basel.

BCA. (2011). *Higher Education*. Business Council of Australia, Melbourne.

Beaty, J. and Gwynne, S. C. (1993). *The Outlaw Bank: A Wild Ride into the Secret Heart of BCCI*. Random House, New York.

Becher, D. A. and Frye, M. B. (2011). 'Does Regulation Substitute or Complement Governance?'. *Journal of Banking and Finance*, 35, 3, 736–51.

Beenen, G. and Pinto, J. (2009). 'Resisting Organizational-Level Corruption: An Interview with Sherron Watkins'. *Academy of Management Learning and Education*, 8, 275–89.

Berger, A. N., Demsetz, R. S. and Strahan, P. E. (1999). 'The Consolidation of the Financial Services Industry: Causes, Consequences, and Implications for the Future'. *Journal of Banking and Finance*, 23, 3–4, 135–94.

Berk, J. B. and Green, R. C. (2004). 'Mutual Fund Flows and Performance in Rational Markets'. *Journal of Political Economy*, 112, 6, 1269–95.

Besley, T. and Hennessy, P. (2009). 'The Global Financial Crisis – Why Didn't Anybody Notice?'. *British Academy Review*, 14, 8–11.

Bessis, J. (1998). *Risk Management in Banking*. John Wiley and Sons, Chichester.

Bhattacharya, U. and Daouk, H. (2002). 'The World Price of Insider Trading'. *The Journal of Finance*, 57, 1, 75–108.

BHP. (2000). 'BHP Portfolio Risk Management – A New Market Risk Management Strategy'. Mimeographed press release. (Archived copy available at www.sec.gov.)

Biais, B., Glosten, L. and Spatt, C. (2005). 'Market Microstructure: A Survey of Microfoundations, Empirical Results, and Policy Implications'. *Journal of Financial Markets*, 8, 2, 217–64.

BIS. (2012). *Semiannual OTC Derivatives Statistics*. Bank for International Settlements. Available: www.bis.org/statistics/derstats.htm (Accessed: January 2014).

Black, B., Cheffins, B. and Klausner, M. (2006). 'Outsider Director Liability'. *Stanford Law Review*, 58, 4, 1055–9.

Blankenburg, S., Plesch, D. and Wilkinson, F. (2010). 'Limited Liability and the Modern Corporation in Theory and in Practice'. *Cambridge Journal of Economics*, 34, 4, 821–36.

Bodie, Z., Kane, A. and Marcus, A. J. (2011, 9th edition). *Investments*. McGraw-Hill, New York.

Bouchaud, J.-P., Farmer, J. D. and Lillo, F. (2009). 'How Markets Slowly Digest Changes in Supply and Demand'. In: Hens, T. and Schenk-Hoppé, K. (eds.) *Handbook of Financial Markets: Dynamics and Evolution*. North-Holland, Amsterdam.

Boulding, K. E. (1935). 'The Theory of a Single Investment'. *Quarterly Journal of Economics*, 49, 3, 479–94.

Brealey, R. A., Myers, S. C. and Marcus, A. J. (2012). *Fundamentals of Corporate Finance*. McGraw-Hill Irwin, New York.

Bridgman, T. (2010). 'Empty Talk? University Voices on the Global Financial Crisis'. *Policy Quarterly*, 6, 4, 40–5.

Bris, A. (2005). 'Do Insider Trading Laws Work?'. *European Financial Management*, 11, 3, 267–312.

Brown, S. J. (2011). 'The Efficient Markets Hypothesis: The Demise of the Demon of Chance?'. *Accounting and Finance*, 5179–95.

Bu, Q. and Lacey, N. (2009). 'On Understanding Mutual Fund Terminations'. *Journal of Economics and Finance*, 33, 1, 80–99.

Busse, J. A., Goyal, A. and Wahal, S. (2010). 'Performance and Persistence in Institutional Investment Management'. *The Journal of Finance*, 65, 2, 765–90.

Carhart, M. M. (1997). 'On Persistence in Mutual Fund Performance'. *The Journal of Finance*, 52, 1, 57–82.

Carmichael, D. R., Whittington, R. and Graham, L. (2007). *Accountants' Handbook: Financial Accounting and General Topics*. John Wiley and Sons, Hoboken, NJ.

Cesarini, D., Johannesson, M., Lichtenstein, P., Sandewall, O. and Wallace, B. (2010). 'Genetic Variation in Financial Decision-Making'. *The Journal of Finance*, 65, 5, 1725–54.

Cifarelli, G. and Paladino, G. (2010). 'Oil Price Dynamics and Speculation: A Multivariate Financial Approach'. *Energy Economics*, 32, 2, 363–72.

Clarke, T. (2004). 'Cycles of Crisis and Regulation: The Enduring Agency and Stewardship Problems of Corporate Governance'. *Corporate Governance*, 12, 2, 153–61.

Cochrane, J. H. (1999). 'New Facts in Finance'. *Economic Perspectives*, 23, 3, 36–(.

Coleman, L. (2009). *Risk Strategies: Dialling up Optimum Firm Risk*. Gower, Surrey.

Coleman, L. (in press). 'Why Finance Theory Fails to Survive Contact with the Real World: A Fund Manager Perspective'. *Critical Perspectives on Accounting*.

Cooper, M. J., Gulen, H. and Schill, M. J. (2008). 'Asset Growth and the Cross-Section of Stock Returns'. *The Journal of Finance*, 63, 4, 1609–51.

Cornell, B. (2001). 'Is the Response of Analysts to Information Consistent with Fundamental Valuation? The Case of Intel'. *Financial Management*, 30, 1, 113–36.

Cornell, B. and Sirri, E. R. (1992). 'The Reaction of Investors and Stock Prices to Insider Trading'. *The Journal of Finance*, 47, 3, 1031–59.

Cowles, A. (1933). 'Can Stock Market Forecasters Forecast?'. *Econometrica*, 1309–24.

Cronqvist, H., Low, A. and Nilsson, M. (2009). 'Persistence in Firm Policies, Firm Origin, and Corporate Culture: Evidence from Corporate Spin-Offs'. Available: http://ssrn.com/abstract=954791 (Accessed: November 2013).

Dass, N., Massa, M. and Patgiri, R. (2008). 'Mutual Funds and Bubbles: The Surprising Role of Contractual Incentives'. *Review of Financial Studies*, 21, 1, 51–99.

DeYoung, R., Evanoff, D. D. and Molyneux, P. (2009). 'Mergers and Acquisitions of Financial Institutions: A Review of the Post-2000 Literature'. *Journal of Financial Services Research*, 36, 2–3, 87–110.

Dobbin, F. and Jung, J. (2010). 'The Misapplication of Mr. Michael Jensen: How Agency Theory Brought Down the Economy and Why it Might Again'. *Research in the Sociology of Organizations*, 30, 1, 29–64.

Drennan, L. T. (2004). 'Ethics, Governance and Risk Management: Lessons from Mirror Group Newspapers and Barings Bank'. *Journal of Business Ethics*, 52, 257–66.

Easton, S. A. and Lalor, P. A. (1995). 'The Accuracy and Timeliness of Survey Forecasts of Six-Month and Twelve-Month Ahead Exchange Rates'. *Applied Financial Economics*, 5, 6, 367–72.

Elton, E. J., Gruber, M. J. and Busse, J. A. (2004). 'Are Investors Rational? Choices among Index Funds'. *The Journal of Finance*, 59, 1, 261–88.

Emm, E. E., Gay, G. D. and Lin, C.-M. (2007). 'Choices and Best Practice in Corporate Risk Management Disclosure'. *Journal of Applied Corporate Finance*, 19, 4, 82–93.

Enders, W. and Hoover, G. A. (2004). 'Whose Line Is It? Plagiarism in Economics'. *Journal of Economic Literature*, 42, 2, 487–93.

Engle, R. F. and Granger, C. W. J. (1987). 'Co-Integration and Error Correction: Representation, Estimation, and Testing'. *Econometrica*, 55, 2, 251–76.

ExxonMobil. (1999). 'Joint Exxon and Mobil Proxy Statement'. Available: www.sec.gov/Archives/edgar/data/67182/0000950103-99-000262.txt (Accessed: January 2014).

Fair, R. C. (2002). 'Events that Shook the Market'. *Journal of Business*, 75, 4, 713–31.

Fama, E. F. (1970). 'Efficient Capital Markets: A Review of Theory and Empirical Work'. *The Journal of Finance*, 25, 2, 383–417.

Fama, E. F. (2010). 'My Life in Finance'. *Annual Review of Financial Economics*, 23, 4, 315–24.

Fama, E. F. and French, K. R. (1993). 'Common Risk Factors in the Returns of Stocks and Bonds'. *Journal of Financial Economics*, 33, 1, 3–56.

Fama, E. F. and French, K. R. (2003). *New Lists: Fundamentals and Survival Rates*. Amos Tuck School of Business at Dartmouth College, Hanover, NH.

Fama, E. F. and French, K. R. (2004). 'Capital Asset Pricing Model: Theory and Evidence'. *The Journal of Economic Perspectives*, 18, 3, 25–46.

Finnerty, J. D. (2005). 'Short Selling, Death Spiral Convertibles, and the Profitability of Stock Manipulation'. Available at SSRN: http://ssrn.com/abstract=687282 (Accessed: November 2013).

Fisher, I. (1906). *The Nature of Capital and Income*. Macmillan, New York.

Fox, J. (2009). *The Myth of the Rational Market*. HarperCollins, New York.

_____, M. (2007). 'Open Secrets'. *The New Yorker*. Published 8 January 2007.

Goyal, A. and Welch, I. (2003). 'Predicting the Equity Premium with Dividend Ratios'. *Management Science*, 49, 5, 639–54.

Graham, B. (1949). *The Intelligent Investor*. Harper and Brothers, New York.

Graham, B. and Dodd, D. (1934). *Security Analysis*. McGraw-Hill, New York.

Grecu, A., Malkiel, B. G. and Saha, A. (2007). 'Why Do Hedge Funds Stop Reporting Performance?'. *Journal of Portfolio Management*, 34, 1, 119–26.

Gropp, R., Hakenes, H. and Schnabel, I. (2010). 'Competition, Risk-Shifting, and Public Bail-out Policies'. *Review of Financial Studies*, 24, 6, 2084–120.

Gruber, M. J. (1996). 'Another Puzzle: The Growth in Actively Managed Mutual Funds'. *The Journal of Finance*, 51, 3, 783–810.

Haleblian, J., Devers, C. E., McNamara, G., Carpenter, M. A. and Davison, R. B. (2009). 'Taking Stock of What We Know about Mergers and Acquisitions'. *Journal of Management*, 35, 3, 469–502.

Hare, R. (1994). 'Predators'. *Psychology Today*, 27, 54–63.

Harford, J. and Kaul, A. (2005). 'Correlated Order Flow: Pervasiveness, Sources, and Pricing Effects'. *The Journal of Financial and Quantitative Analysis*, 40, 1, 29–55.

Heath, C., Huddart, S. and Lang, M. (1999). 'Psychological Factors and Stock Option Exercise'. *The Quarterly Journal of Economics*, 114, 2, 601–27.

Higgs, H. (ed.) (1926). *Palgrave's Dictionary of Political Economy*. Macmillan and Co, London.

Hillinger, C. (2010). 'The Crisis and Beyond: Thinking Outside the Box'. *Economics: The Open-Access, Open-Assessment E-Journal*, 4.

Hodgkinson, L. and Partington, G. H. (2008). 'The Motivation for Takeovers in the UK'. *Journal of Business Finance and Accounting*, 35, 1/2, 102–26.

Hodgson, G. M. (2009). 'The Great Crash of 2008 and the Reform of Economics'. *Cambridge Journal of Economics*, 33, 1205–21.

Hudson, R., Keasey, K. and Littler, K. (2002). 'Why Investors Should be Cautious of the Academic Approach to Testing for Stock Market Anomalies'. *Applied Financial Economics*, 12, 9, 681–6.

Hume, D. (1777). *An Enquiry Concerning the Human Understanding*. Clarendon Press, Oxford.

Hwang, S. and Satchell, S. E. (2010). 'How Loss Averse are Investors in Financial Markets?'. *Journal of Banking and Finance*, 34, 10, 2425–38.

IC. (2012). 'Investment Company Fact Book'. Available: www.icfactbook.org/ (Accessed: June 2012).

IMF. (2011). *World Financial Stability Report*. International Monetary Fund, Washington, DC.

International Federation of Accountants. (2003). *Enterprise Governance: Getting the Balance Right*. International Federation of Accountants, New York.

Jackofsky, E. F., Slocum Jr, J. W. and McQuaid, S. J. (1988). 'Cultural Values and the CEO: Alluring Companions?'. *Academy of Management Executive*, 2, 39–49.

Jefferson, T. (1816). *Letter to John Taylor, 28 May 1816*.

Jegadeesh, N., Kim, J., Krische, S. D. and Lee, C. M. C. (2004). 'Analyzing the Analysts: When Do Recommendations Add Value?'. *The Journal of Finance*, 59, 3, 1083–124.

Jensen, M. C. (1972). 'Capital Markets: Theory and Evidence'. *The Bell Journal of Economics and Management Science*, 3, 2, 357–98.

Jensen, M. C. (1978). 'Some Anomalous Evidence Regarding Market Efficiency'. *Journal of Financial Economics*, 6, 2, 95–101.

Jensen, M. C. (1993). 'The Modern Industrial Revolution, Exit, and the Failure of Internal Control Systems'. *The Journal of Finance*, 48, 831–80.

Jensen, M. C. and Meckling, W. H. (1976). 'Theory of the Firm: Managerial Behavior, Agency Costs, and Ownership Structure'. *Journal of Financial Economics*, 3, 4, 305–60.

Jensen, M. C. and Smith, C. W. J. (eds.) (1984). *The Modern Theory of Corporate Finance.* McGraw-Hill Inc, New York.

Jickling, M. (2009). 'Causes of the Financial Crisis'. Available: http://digitalcommons.ilr. cornell.edu/key_workplace/600 (Accessed: January 2014).

Jones, C. P. (2010). *Investment: Principles and Concepts.* John Wiley and Sons, Hoboken, NJ.

Jorion, P. and Goetzmann, W. N. (1999). 'Global Stock Markets in the Twentieth Century'. *The Journal of Finance*, 54, 3, 953–80.

Kahneman, D. (2003). 'Maps of Bounded Rationality: Psychology for Behavioral Economics'. *The American Economic Review*, 93, 5, 1449–75.

Kahneman, D. (2011). *Thinking, Fast and Slow.* Farrar, Straus and Giroux, New York.

Kaminski, V. and Martin, J. (2001). 'Transforming Enron: The Value of Active Management'. *Journal of Applied Corporate Finance*, 13, 4, 39–49.

Kamstra, M., Kramer, L. and Levi, M. (2000). 'Losing Sleep at the Market: The Daylight Saving Anomaly'. *American Economic Review*, 90, 4, 1005–11.

Kessler, A. (2009). 'Have We Seen the Last of the Bear Raids?'. *The Wall Street Journal*, 26 March 2009.

Keynes, J. M. (1936). *The General Theory of Employment, Interest and Money.* Macmillan Press Limited (1973 reprint), London.

Knight, F. (1921). *Risk, Uncertainty and Profit.* Houghton-Mifflin, Boston.

Kuhn, T. S. (1970, 2nd edition). *The Structure of Scientific Revolutions.* University of Chicago Press, Chicago.

La Porte, T. R. (1996). 'High Reliability Organizations: Unlikely, Demanding and at Risk'. *Journal of Contingencies and Crisis Management*, 4, 2, 60–71.

Lakonishok, J., Shleifer, A. and Vishny, R. W. (1994). 'Contrarian Investment, Extrapolation, and Risk'. *The Journal of Finance*, 49, 5, 1541–78.

Larcker, D. F. and Tayan, B. (2010). 'Lehman Brothers: Peeking Under the Board Facade'. Available: http://ssrn.com/abstract=1678044 (Accessed: 26 October 2010).

Lehman. (2005). *Proxy Statement (Schedule 14A) for LEH.* Lehman Brothers Holdings Inc.

Leontief, W. (1982). 'Academic Economics'. *Science*, 217, 104, 107.

Levin, C. and Coburn, T. (2009). *Excessive Speculation in the Wheat Market.* US Senate Permanent Subcommittee on Investigations, Washington, DC.

Lo, A. W. (2012). 'Reading About the Financial Crisis: A Twenty-One-Book Review'. *Journal of Economic Literature*, 50, 1, 151–78.

Loungani, P. (2001). 'How Accurate Are Private Sector Forecasts? Cross-Country Evidence from Consensus Forecasts of Output Growth'. *International Journal of Forecasting*, 17, July, 419–32.

Lucas, R. E. and Sargent, T. J. (eds.) (1981). *Rational Expectations and Econometric Practice.* The University of Minnesota, Minneapolis, MN.

Ma, C. (2010). *Advanced Asset Pricing Theory.* Imperial College Press, London.

Maddison, A. (2003). *The World Economy: Historical Statistics.* OECD, Paris.

Maher, J. J., Brown, R. M. and Kumar, R. (2008). 'Firm Valuation, Abnormal Earnings, and Mutual Funds Flow'. *Review of Quantitative Finance and Accounting*, 31, 2, 167–89.

Malkiel, B. G. (2003). 'The Efficient Market Hypothesis and Its Critics'. *The Journal of Economic Perspectives*, 17, 1, 59–82.

Margolis, J. D. and Walsh, J. (2003). 'Misery Loves Companies: Rethinking Social Initiatives by Business'. *Administrative Science Quarterly*, 48, 2, 268–305.

Markowitz, H. M. (1952). 'Portfolio Selection'. *The Journal of Finance*, 777–91.

Markowitz, H. M. (1959). *Portfolio Selection.* John Wiley and Sons, New York.

McGregor, D. (1960). *The Human Side of Enterprise.* McGraw-Hill, New York.

McLean, B. and Elkind, P. (2004). *The Smartest Guys in the Room: The Amazing Rise and Scandalous Fall of Enron.* Portfolio, New York.

McLean, B. and Nocera, J. (2010). *All the Devils are Here.* Portfolio Penguin, London.

Mencken, H. L. (1917). 'The Divine Afflatus'. *New York Evening Mail*, 16 November 1917.

Menkhoff, L. (2010). 'The Use of Technical Analysis by Fund Managers: International Evidence'. *Journal of Banking and Finance*, 34, 11, 2573–86.

Merton, R. C. (2003). 'Thoughts on the Future: Theory and Practice in Investment Management'. *Financial Analysts Journal*, 59, 1, 17–23.

Meulbroek, L. K. (1992). 'An Empirical Analysis of Illegal Insider Trading'. *The Journal of Finance*, 47, 5, 1661–99.

Miller, M., Weller, P. and Zhang, L. (2002). 'Moral Hazard and the US Stock Market: Analysing the "Greenspan Put"'. *The Economic Journal*, 112, 472, C171–86.

Miller, M. H. (1988). 'The Modigliani–Miller Propositions after Thirty Years'. *The Journal of Economic Perspectives*, 2, 4, 99–120.

Mitchell, J. (2001). 'Clustering and Psychological Barriers: The Importance of Numbers'. *The Journal of Futures Markets*, 21, 5, 395–428.

Morgenson, G. (2006). 'Whispers of Mergers Set Off Suspicious Trading'. *New York Times*, 27 August 2006.

Morningstar. (2012). 'Morningstar Direct Fund Flows Update'. Available: http://corporate.morningstar.com/decflows11/FundFlowsJan2012.pdf (Accessed: January 2013).

Moshirian, F. (2011). 'The Global Financial Crisis and the Evolution of Markets, Institutions and Regulation'. *Journal of Banking and Finance*, 35, 3, 502–11.

OCC. (2012). *OCC's Quarterly Report on Bank Trading and Derivatives Activities*. Comptroller of the Currency, Washington, DC.

OECD. (2012). *OECD.StatExtracts*. Paris. Available: http://stats.oecd.org/Index.aspx (Accessed: January 2014).

Oehmke, M. and Zawadowski, A. (2012). 'The Anatomy of the CDS Market'. Available at SSRN: http://ssrn.com/abstract=2023108 (Accessed: June 2013).

Oldfield, G. S. and Santomero, A. M. (1997). *The Place of Risk Management in Financial Institutions*. Wharton Financial Institutions Center, Philadelphia, PA.

Ones, D. S., Viswesvaran, C. and Dilchert, S. (2005). 'Cognitive Ability in Selection Decisions'. In: Wilhelm, O. and Engle, R. W. (eds.) *Handbook of Understanding and Measuring Intelligence*. Sage Publications, Thousand Oaks.

Önkal, D., Goodwin, P., Thomson, M., Gönül, S. and Pollock, A. (2009). 'The Relative Influence of Advice from Human Experts and Statistical Methods on Forecast Adjustments'. *Journal of Behavioral Decision Making*, 22, 4, 390–409.

Ooghe, H. and De Prijcker, S. (2008). 'Failure Processes and Causes of Company Bankruptcy: A Typology'. *Management Decision*, 46, 2, 223–42.

Orlitzky, M. (2008). 'Corporate Social Performance and Financial Performance: A Research Synthesis'. In: Crane, A., McWilliams, A., Matten, D., Moon, J. and Siegel, D. S. (eds.) *The Oxford Handbook of Corporate Social Responsibility*. Oxford University Press, Oxford, UK.

Partnoy, F. and Eisinger, J. (2013). 'What's Inside America's Banks?'. *The Atlantic*. Published January/February 2013.

Percival, J. (1993). 'Why Don't We Just Ask Them?'. *Financial Practice and Education*, 39.

Peters, T. J. and Waterman, R. H. (1982). *In Search of Excellence: Lessons from America's Best-Run Companies*. Harper and Row, New York.

Pinto, J., Leana, C. R. and Pil, F. K. (2008). 'Corrupt Organizations or Organizations of Corrupt Individuals? Two Types of Organizational-level Corruption'. *Academy of Management Review*, 33, 3, 685–709.

Popper, K. R. (1959). *The Logic of Scientific Discovery*. Hutchinson, London.

Poteshman, A. M. (2006). 'Unusual Option Market Activity and the Terrorist Attacks of September 11 2001'. *Journal of Business*, 79, 4, 1703–26.

Quigley, C. (1966). *Tragedy and Hope*. Macmillan, New York.

Reuters. (2009). 'Three Top Economists Agree 2009 Worst Financial Crisis Since Great Depression'. *Reuters*. Available: www.reuters.com/article/2009/02/27/idUS193520+27-Feb-2009+BW20090227 (Accessed: January 2014).

Ritter, J. R. (2005). 'Economic Growth and Equity Returns'. *Pacific Basin Finance Journal*, 13, 5, 489–503.

Rose, C. (2011). 'The Flash Crash of May 2010: Accident or Market Manipulation?'. *Journal of Business and Economics Research*, 9, 1, 85–90.

Russell, B. (1919). *Proposed Roads to Freedom*. H. Holt and Company, New York.

Schwartz, D. J. (1977). 'Penn Central: A Case Study of Outside Director Responsibility under the Federal Securities Laws'. *UMKC Law Review*, 45, 3, 394–421.

Scruggs, J. T. (1998). 'Resolving the Puzzling Intertemporal Relation Between the Market Risk Premium and Conditional Market Variance: A Two-Factor Approach'. *The Journal of Finance*, 53, 2, 575–603.

SEC. (2010). 'Findings Regarding the Market Events of May 6, 2010'. Available: www.sec. gov/news/studies/2010/marketevents-report.pdf (Accessed: June 2012).

Sharpe, W. F. (1964). 'Capital Asset Prices: A Theory of Market Equilibrium under Conditions of Risk'. *The Journal of Finance*, 19, 3, 424–42.

Shefrin, H. (ed.) (2001). *Behavioral Finance*. Edward Elgar Publishing, Cheltenham, UK.

Shojai, S. and Preece, R. (2001). 'The Future of the U.S. Asset Management Industry'. *Journal of Financial Transformation*, 172–9.

Sleightholme, M. and Singh, B. (2011). 'Ready or Not? Here it Comes'. Available: www. transactionservices.citigroup.com/transactionservices/home/securities_svcs/fund/docs/ otc_white_paper.pdf (Accessed: June 2012).

Smith, A. (1776, reprinted 1937). *The Wealth of Nations*. The Modern Library, New York.

Soros, G. (1994). 'The Theory of Reflexivity'. Available: www.soros.org/textfiles/ speeches/042694_Theory_of_Reflexivity.txt (Accessed: November 2003).

Stewart, B. (2006). 'The Real Reasons Enron Failed'. *Journal of Applied Corporate Finance*, 18, 2, 116–19.

Sullivan, A. (1999). 'London Fog'. *The New Republic*. Published 14 June 1999.

Sutter, D. (2009). 'The Market, the Firm and the Economics Profession'. *The American Journal of Economics and Sociology*, 68, 5, 1041–61.

Taleb, N. N. (2007). *The Black Swan: The Impact of the Highly Improbable*. Random House, New York.

Thurow, L. C. (1981). *The Zero-Sum Society*. Penguin Books, New York.

Tosi, H. L., Brownlee, A. L., Silva, P. and Katz, J. P. (2003). 'An Empirical Exploration of Decision-Making under Agency Controls and Stewardship Structure'. *Journal of Management Studies*, 40, 8, 2053–71.

Treynor, J. L. and Black, F. (1976). 'Corporate Investment Decisions'. In: Myers, S. C. (ed.) *Modern Developments in Financial Management*. Praeger Publishers, New York.

Tuchman, B. W. (1962). *The Guns of August (also August 1914)*. Constable, London.

Turner, A., Haldane, A., Woolley, P., Wadhwani, S. and Goodhart, C. (2010). *The Future of Finance: The LSE Report*. London School of Economics and Political Science, London.

Twain, M. (1894, reprinted 1996). *The Tragedy of Pudd'nhead Wilson*. Oxford University Press, New York.

van Meerhaeghe, M. A. G. (1971). *Economics: A Critical Approach*. Weidenfeld and Nicolson, London.

Wermers, R. (2000). 'Mutual Fund Performance'. *The Journal of Finance*, 55, 4, 1655–95.

Wexler, M. N. (2010). 'Financial Edgework and the Persistence of Rogue Traders'. *Business and Society Review*, 115, 1, 1–25.

WFE. (2011). 'WFE Market Highlights' Available at: www.world exchanges.org (Accessed: June 2012).

Wray, L. R. (2009). 'The Rise and Fall of Money Manager Capitalism: A Minskian Approach'. *Cambridge Journal of Economics*, 33, 4, 807–28.

Yuan, K., Zheng, L. and Zhu, Q. (2006). 'Are Investors Moonstruck? Lunar Phases and Stock Returns'. *Journal of Empirical Finance*, 13, 1, 1–23.

Zimring, F. E. (2007). *The Great American Crime Decline*. Oxford University Press, Oxford, UK.

INDEX

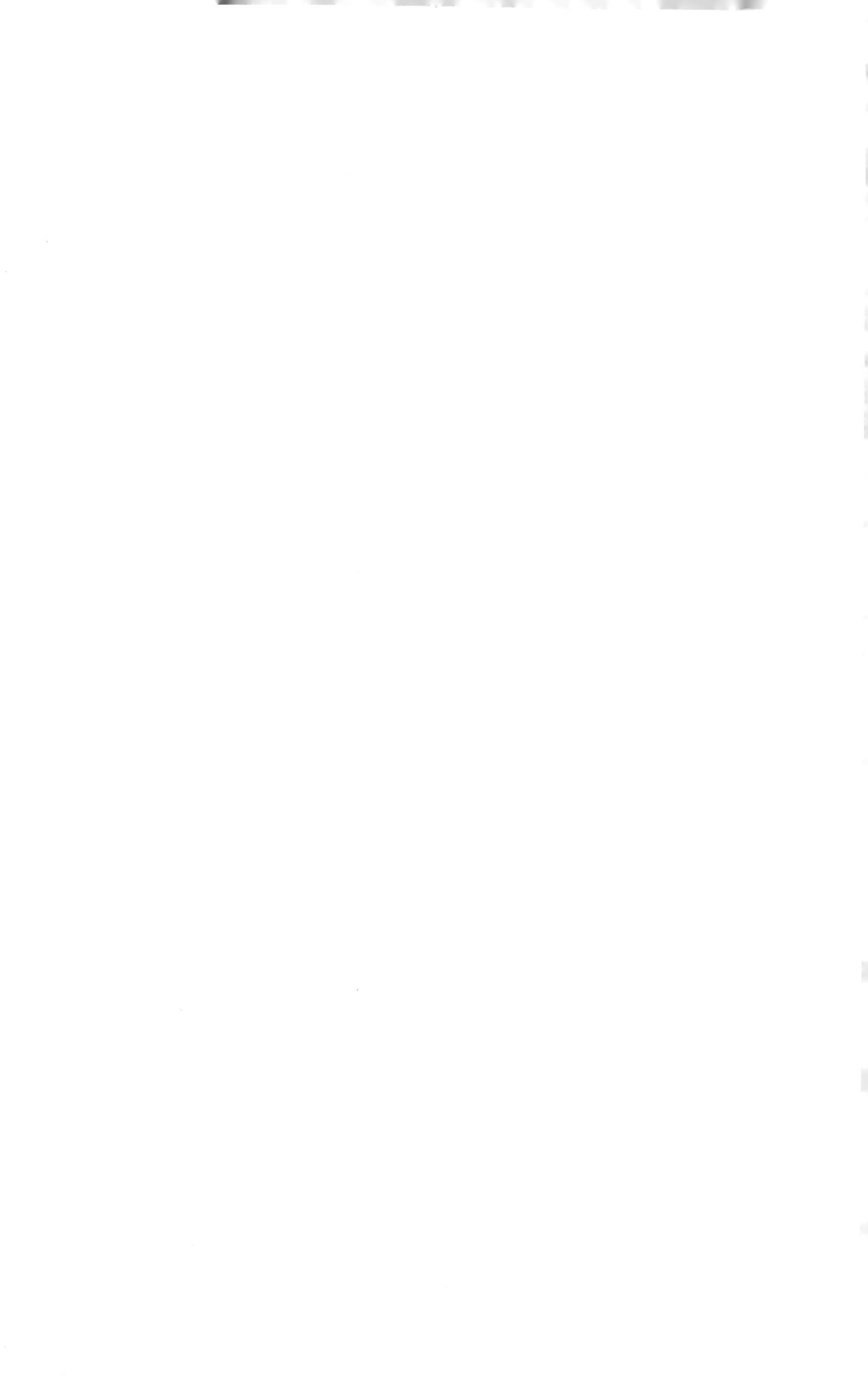